ROUTLEDGE LIBRARY EDITIONS: COMMUNICATION STUDIES

Volume 13

COMMUNICATIONS POLICY FOR NATIONAL DEVELOPMENT

COMMUNICATIONS POLICY FOR NATIONAL DEVELOPMENT
A Comparative Perspective

Edited by
MAJID TEHERANIAN, FARHAD HAKIMZADEH
AND MARCELLO L. VIDALE

LONDON AND NEW YORK

First published in 1977 by Routledge & Kegan Paul Ltd

This edition first published in 2016
by Routledge
2 Park Square, Milton Park, Abingdon, Oxon OX14 4RN

and by Routledge
711 Third Avenue, New York, NY 10017

Routledge is an imprint of the Taylor & Francis Group, an informa business

© 1977 Iran Communications and Development Institute

All rights reserved. No part of this book may be reprinted or reproduced or utilised in any form or by any electronic, mechanical, or other means, now known or hereafter invented, including photocopying and recording, or in any information storage or retrieval system, without permission in writing from the publishers.

Trademark notice: Product or corporate names may be trademarks or registered trademarks, and are used only for identification and explanation without intent to infringe.

British Library Cataloguing in Publication Data
A catalogue record for this book is available from the British Library

ISBN: 978-1-138-93903-5 (Set)
ISBN: 978-1-315-67052-2 (Set) (ebk)
ISBN: 978-1-138-94154-0 (Volume 13) (hbk)
ISBN: 978-1-138-95963-7 (Volume 13) (pbk)
ISBN: 978-1-315-67043-0 (Volume 13) (ebk)

Publisher's Note
The publisher has gone to great lengths to ensure the quality of this reprint but points out that some imperfections in the original copies may be apparent.

Disclaimer
The publisher has made every effort to trace copyright holders and would welcome correspondence from those they have been unable to trace.

Communications Policy for National Development
A Comparative Perspective

EDITED BY
Majid Teheranian
Farhad Hakimzadeh
Marcello L. Vidale

ROUTLEDGE & KEGAN PAUL
London, Henley and Boston
in association with
the Iran Communications and Development Institute and
the International Institute of Communications

First published in 1977
by Routledge & Kegan Paul Ltd
39 Store Street,
London WC1E 7DD,
Broadway House,
Newtown Road,
Henley-on-Thames,
Oxon RG9 1EN and
9 Park Street,
Boston, Mass. 02108, USA
Photoset in Times by
Weatherby Woolnough, Wellingborough, Northants
and printed in Great Britain by
Lowe & Brydone Printers Limited, Thetford, Norfolk

© Iran Communications and Development Institute 1977

No part of this book may be reproduced in
any form without permission from the
publisher, except for the quotation of brief
passages in criticism

British Library Cataloguing in Publication Data

Communications policy for national development.

   1. Mass Media – Political aspects   2. Underveloped
areas – Mass Media
   I. Teheranian, Majid   II. Hakimzadeh, Farhad
   III. Vidale, Marcello L.   IV. Iran Communications
and Development Institute   V. International
Institute of Communications
380.3'09172'4   P92.2

ISBN 0-7100-8597-4

To Reza Ghotbi

For his vision of the future,
Inspired by his patriotism,
Tempered by his humanity.

Contents

Contributors *ix*
Preface and Acknowledgments *1*

I Communications and Development: The Parameters of Theory and Policy
1. Communications and National Development ... *Majid Teheranian* 17
2. Communications Policy and Planning ... *Edward W. Ploman* 51
3. The Cultural Compass and the Transmission of Values ... *Abraham Moles* 78
4. An International Survey of the Future of Broadcasting ... *Farhad Hakimzadeh and Donald Meals* 92

II The Role of Mass Communication in National Development: Facets of Innovation
5. Cultural Continuity and Change ... *Elihu Katz* 109
6. The Governance of Mass Communication ... *Ithiel de Sola Pool* 130
7. Multi-Media Education ... *Ivor K. Davies* 149
8. National Development Support Communication ... *Edwin B. Parker and Ali Mohammadi* 167

III National Experiences in Communications Policy
9. Integrated Development Support Communication in Dahomey ... *Armand Defever* 205
10. Communications Policy in Brazil ... *Dov Shinar and Marco Antonio Rodrigues Dias* 225

11 Communications Developments in India ... *Robert T. Filep and Syed M. S. Haque* 242
12 The Role of Broadcasting in Iran: Report of a National Survey ... *Majid Teheranian* 257
13 Towards a National Communications Policy for Iran ... *Amin Banani* 279

Contributors

Amin Banani
Professor of History, Center of Middle Eastern Studies,
University of California at Los Angeles

Ivor K. Davies
Professor of Education, Assistant Executive Director Audio-Visual Center,
Indiana University,
Bloomington

Armand Defever
Chief, Multimedia Field Operations Section,
Food and Agricultural Organization of the United Nations,
Rome

Marco Antonio Rodrigues Dias
Vice-Rector,
University of Brasilia

Robert T. Filep
Professor of Communications and Education,
Director, University-Wide Learning Systems Center,
University of Southern California, Los Angeles

Farhad Hakimzadeh
Research Fellow, Iran Communications and Development Institute,
Tehran

Syed M. S. Haque
Research Associate, College of Human Medicine,
Michigan State University,
East Lansing

Elihu Katz
Director and Professor, Communications Institute,
The Hebrew University,
Jerusalem

Donald Meals
Senior Consultant,
Arthur D. Little, Inc.,
Cambridge, Mass.

Ali Mohammadi
Assistant Professor of Educational Technology,
Iran Communications and Development Institute,
Tehran

Abraham Moles
Professor of Communications,
University of Strasbourg

Edwin B. Parker
Professor of Communications,
Stanford University

Edward W. Ploman
Executive Director,
International Institute of Communications,
London

Dov Shinar
Professor, Communications Institute,
The Hebrew University
Jerusalem

Ithiel de Sola Pool
Professor of Political Science,
Massachusetts Institute of Technology,
Cambridge, Mass.

Majid Teheranian
Iran Communications and Development Institute,
Tehran

Marcello L. Vidale
Research Fellow,
Iran Communications and Development Institute,
Tehran

The innovator makes enemies of all those who prospered under the old order, and only lukewarm support is forthcoming from those who would prosper under the new ... because men are generally incredulous, never really trusting new things unless they have tested them by experience—Niccolò Machiavelli (1469-1527), *The Prince*

I am certain that in 300 years historians will say that in our times we were attempting to accommodate democracies as they have evolved with the old direct democracy of Athens. Pericles could speak directly to the people of Athens: a phenomenon that disappeared for over 2,000 years is finally coming back—André Malraux, *Newsweek* interview, 1974

Preface and Acknowledgments

The leisurely tempo that characterized traditional societies in the past made it inevitable as well as appropriate that the diffusion of new ideas and technologies proceed at a comparable leisurely pace. Innovation and change tended to come about through evolutionary means, and hence were gradual enough to be assimilated and accepted by the people involved.

In rapidly developing countries this time scale has had to be greatly accelerated. The rate of change has been such as to strain people's capacity to cope with the process of change inherent in the concept of national development. Various resources are being brought into play by governments concerned about smoothing the difficult yet requisite transitions; among these, the mass communication media loom large.

In the west it took several centuries before the first industrial revolution turned into a second one characterized by the application of information technology to all aspects of life. In developing countries, both revolutions are occurring in a single historical period. The role played by mass communication media in this context is of critical importance. In socio-cultural development mass communication media are affecting beliefs, behaviours and skills. In the field of economic development they serve to mobilize human resources by raising expectations and propagating knowledge. In political development they provide those subtle ties of common national identity and interest that are essential for the formation of a nation-state and for the promotion of participatory democracy. In educational development they are becoming an increasingly indispensable

Preface

tool for improving both the quality and reach of formal educational opportunities. In technology and management they are setting a fast pace in technological transfer and managerial innovations. Finally, in the field of international relations they help to break down national boundaries and establish a community of world interests and world culture.

Broadcasting in developing countries cannot afford to play a neutral or passive role. Nor can that role be narrowly defined or confined to broadcasting alone. National Iranian Radio and Television is a case in point. It has had to enter into a myriad of activities in order to provide the necessary support for the performance of its own broadcasting responsibilities as well as to fill some existing vacuums in national life. Formal and informal education, development support communication, sponsorship of cultural and artistic activities are examples of extra-broadcasting functions which NIRT is currently undertaking. By conceiving their mission in this broad and activist fashion the mass media of Iran have already become catalysts for change and stimuli to national development.

It is within this framework and in order to assist communication policy makers formulate general guidelines that NIRT initiated in June 1974 a Prospective Planning Project with the specific objective of exploring what future role mass communications could and should play in Iranian society.

The purposes of this Project were fourfold:
(a) to provide a survey of the state of the art in the mass communication field including future technological developments;
(b) to assess the views of international and Iranian mass communication professionals on future trends in their fields of specialization;
(c) to formulate a perspective for NIRT's national mission, roles and functions in the context of Iran's development; and
(d) to pave the way for a research institute that will focus on a continuing study of the role of mass communication in Iran's national development, including the role that media should play in educational, political, economic, socio-

Preface

cultural, technological, organizational and international developments.

As part of the Project's initial activities, four investigations were undertaken: a study of NIRT's organizational requirements; an assessment of anticipated developments in broadcast technology; an international survey of worldwide trends in broadcasting; and a national survey of the reactions of Iranian opinion leaders and communications professionals to NIRT's programming policies.

To have its own work evaluated and also to elaborate further the relevant policy issues, the Project organized two symposia during 1975. The first, held in Shiraz from 18 to 24 May, was attended by senior members of the NIRT management and other Iranian communication experts. The second one, held in Mashad from 25 June to 1 July, brought together a group of international and Iranian communication specialists.

These two gatherings served as a kind of collective planning panel. The reports of working committees were presented and discussed in plenary sessions, out of which emerged a consensus as to the principal goals and missions of NIRT. These may be summarized as follows:

— To strengthen the bases of national unity and participatory democracy through a steady improvement in the quality of the dialogue between government and public.
— To assist in the revitalization of the Iranian national culture consistent with contemporary needs but rooted in the traditions of its millennial history.
— To sponsor artistic and cultural activities at the local, regional and national levels.
— To provide recreational programmes tailored to the taste and preferences of every major sector of Iranian society.
— To expand national support communication services in fields such as medicine, literacy, agriculture, family planning, consumer information.
— To contribute to the creation of multi-media educational facilities.
— To foster the development of a socially aware and patriotic youth.

Preface

— To raise the cultural level and social status of the more sensitive or less privileged groups such as children, women, peasants and labourers.
— To promote a greater understanding of Iranian culture and civilization abroad and of foreign cultures and civilizations among Iranians.
— To promote research and development in the technical as well as the socio-cultural aspects of mass communication.

Lessons of the Planning Project

The Prospective Planning Project generated a number of tangible results, several of which are currently being implemented by NIRT. Others, either broader in scope or less specific, are recognized by NIRT management as valuable guidelines for setting long-term policy and goals.

Among the recommendations now being put into effect are: (a) plans for the reorganization of NIRT, (b) a network expansion programme, and (c) the establishment of an institute for the study of problems of mass communication and national development.

NIRT organizational structure

The basic principles which underlie the proposed organizational structure are accountability and decentralization. With three constituencies to be satisfied (namely, the government, the audience and the broadcasters themselves who seek to uphold their own standards of professional conduct), certain tensions and conflicts are inevitable which no structural reorganization can wholly eliminate. There do exist, however, organizational patterns which tend to minimize rather than exacerbate conflicts. Accountability combined with decentralization and delegation of responsibility, it is felt, lessens areas of friction and permits the co-existence of seemingly irreconcilable points

There are additional compelling reasons for subscribing to the principle of decentralization such as the projected continued growth of NIRT both in size and complexity; the need for more communication channels (transmitters, communication satel-

Preface

lites, microwave links); the demand for new or expanded services (telemedicine, educational television); and the concomitant necessity to develop an adequate number of capable middle management specialists.

The proposed organizational structure attempts to meet the complex needs of NIRT at this critical stage in its history. The key element is the introduction of internal competition within this public broadcasting monopoly through the establishment of two autonomous 'red' and 'green' networks, while at the same time preserving the requisite degree of central control to allow for the co-ordination and execution of national plans.

The principal operating divisions of NIRT as proposed in the organizational structure are the two national networks, the regional and international stations and the News Division. They rely on broadcasting and engineering services for support. The Instructional Communications Division (currently in a dynamic state of development) and the Research and Development Division (a relatively new concept within NIRT) would operate as semi-independent units in accord with general management guidelines.

A transition to this new organizational framework is now in progress. It is evolving gradually, however, so as not to interfere with the vast expansion programme at present under way.

Network expansion programme

In line with the recommendations of the Project, four radio broadcasting systems are planned to be operational by the end of the Sixth Development Plan (1977-82). First, the Voice of Iran, which will broadcast nationwide on medium wave, and beyond Iranian borders by short wave. Second, the Voice of the Province, which will emanate from each of Iran's eleven provinces and will emphasize regional needs and interests. Some of its programmes will be in local dialects. Third, a national network which will broadcast primarily cultural programmes on AM and FM bands. Finally, a network of FM stations (one per city of 50,000 or more) devoted exclusively to musical programming. Additional services will be provided for specific audiences—students, tourists, etc.

Preface

As for television, four channels are being planned. One will provide national programming; the second will offer a mix of national and regional programmes; the third will be exclusively educational and the fourth one will broadcast in English, French and German and will serve primarily Iran's foreign community. Cable radio and television will be added within the coming decade.

Iran Communications and Development Institute

A further tangible outcome of the Project, worthy of note particularly in the context of the present volume, is the formation of a communications and development institute devoted to responding to NIRT's policy concerns and research requirements. The Iran Communications and Development Institute will pursue the following objectives:
— Conduct theoretical research in the fields of communications and development sciences in order to forge interdisciplinary tools for empirical investigations.
— Undertake studies in those aspects of Iranian national culture which can contribute to harmonious national development.
— Assist in the revitalization and translation of traditional cultural elements into modern media forms.
— Participate in the development of multi-media educational programmes in order to improve quality of instruction and expand educational opportunities.
— Promote an understanding of the role of development support communications in fostering national integration and reducing imbalances between different regions and sectors of the population.
— Contribute to the planning of development support communications in literacy campaigns, agricultural extension services, public health, family planning, etc.
— Engage in studies of the international aspects of communication and development and contribute to mutual understanding and co-operation between Iran and other countries.

Preface

Policy Guidelines of the Planning Project

In addition to the foregoing, the Project developed certain policy orientations which are meant to assist NIRT in formulating long-range plans. Far from being applicable only to Iran, their relevance extends to the broadcasting systems of any society undergoing rapid development.

The need for two-way interactive communication

In a single leap, developing countries have jumped from oral communication to electronic media, skipping the intermediate stages of literacy and the printed word. One of the consequences of this phenomenon is that broadcasting agencies, knowing relatively little about their audiences, tend to treat them as undifferentiated. This approach, combined with the cultural-levelling effects of mass media, threatens the traditional and autonomous forms of self-expression and may impoverish rather than enrich the cultural life of the people. The fact a large portion of all programmes is imported may be an additional source of alienation. To use a well-worn metaphor, they may project a shadow of the shadow of the truth, an image of foreign life-styles as conveyed by American Westerns and sentimental serials.

The most serious obstacles to the production of indigenous programmes are shortage of local talent and the costs involved. Only time and the accumulation of knowledge and experience will correct the imbalance. Meanwhile broadcasters can improve the situation by exploring every possible means of two-way interactive communication with their 'silent' audiences. Several essays in this volume deal with experiments in this field. Among such experiments should be mentioned the organization of radio and television clubs, the synchronization of programmes dealing with a single issue by different media (radio, television, newspapers, magazines, radio and TV clubs) with immediate feedback on their effectiveness; and direct broadcasting of local and regional festivals and other social activities so that people may hear and see as well as be heard and seen.

Besides such activities, broadcasters can also promote cre-

Preface

ative opportunities for cultural self-expression such as art festivals, theatre and music workshops or symphony orchestras. The responsibility for the development of other media forms may also be thrust upon them in order to prevent newspapers, books, magazines from being overwhelmed by the electronic media. These are all areas into which NIRT has increasingly moved in recent years.

The need for an integrated national communications policy

The rapid development of communications technology has opened up a wide range of opportunities in multi-media education, telemedicine, socio-economic evolution and cultural revitalization. For most developing countries, however, the cost of a comprehensive and fully integrated communication system (including postal service, telegraph, telephone, telex, computer facilities, as well as electronic media) is so high that careful planning, a co-ordinated approach and a judicious phasing of new investments become mandatory.

Inter-agency rivalries, sometimes fed by the conflicting interests of a heterogeneous population and of powerful pressure groups, may prevent such co-ordination. Where a single ministry has been assigned the task of overseeing every aspect of the communication spectrum, results have proved less than satisfactory because of the large and cumbersome bureaucracy such centralization inevitably entails. On the other hand, a national communications council with an overall policy-making role is not sufficiently involved in the practical realities of decision-making to be really effective. A third alternative might be a 'Development Support Communication Agency' which reports to the highest level of government. Its function would be to initiate, coordinate and monitor the many and diverse communications support activities administered by the appropriate government agencies.

The need for decentralization and accountability

In developing countries broadcasting frequently plays an extremely sensitive role in the political process and is often called upon to foster a sense of nationhood among a fairly heterogeneous population which is traditionally segmented along ethnic, religious or regional lines. The tendency is to lean toward excessive centralization and the consequence is banal and unpopular programmes. The need for decentralization is keenly felt. But decentralization has to be disciplined by the mechanism of accountability—to the government, to the audience and to the professional standards of broadcasting. Accountability can be achieved by relying on modular rather than functional organizations, by responsiveness to audience preferences and tastes as determined through audience research, by introducing some measure of competition within the broadcasting organization through the purchase of programmes and services from outside the public monopoly.

The need for political credibility and cultural authenticity

In developing countries broadcasting organizations face two serious dangers: (1) to function exclusively as the propaganda arm of the government and thereby lose credibility with their audience and (2) to become primarily channels of diffusion of an alien culture and thus a foreign and irrelevant spokesmen.

These dangers are both aspects of the same process of political and cultural transition to a modern society. The media are the nerve centres of an evolving body politic in search of new forms of expression and participation. In cultural terms they mediate between traditional cultural forms and the demands of modern communication. The essence of the challenge is the development of new forms, skills and institutions.

The need for openness to the world

The most significant aspect of the communication revolution in developing countries is probably what Daniel Lerner calls 'the multiplier effect' of the media on psychic mobility. Exposure to the media discloses new worlds and may result in a manifold increase in one's capacity for role-playing, empathy and adaptive ability.

In developing countries, individual loyalties are rapidly

Preface

expanding outward from the primary kinship group to the village, the town, the province, the nation and supra-national groupings. This may lead at one extreme to parochial nationalism or at the other to a cosmopolitan prismatic culture.

Broadcasters, for their part, may concentrate on nationalistic themes in their news and documentaries to enhance a spirit of national identity while at the same time relying heavily on foreign programmes for entertainment. This dualism tends to widen the cleavage between political outlook and mass culture.

The depoliticization of cultural life may induce broadcasters to favour bland and banal programmes over more provocative and controversial ones. Under such circumstances it takes professional courage to keep the broadcasting channels open to the diversities of the world as well as to a world of diversities.

Prospectus

The present volume is a compendium of essays covering the major issues bearing on the subject of communications policy and national planning. Most of the contributors were participants at the Mashad symposium of the Prospective Planning Project. Their views express in large measure what emerged from organized and informal group discussions.

The first four papers, which comprise section I—Communications and Development: Parameters of Theory and Policy—deal with broad theoretical and policy questions; the next four examine the role of mass media in selected fields; the last five comment on experiences in a few specific countries.

In 'Communications and National Development', Majid Teheranian provides a broad historical perspective on the role of communication in economic development and in the modernization process. He reviews major communications and development theories, comments on their relevance to contemporary realities and concludes with an interpretation of the dialectical process of social change.

'Communications Policy and Planning' by E. W. Ploman provides an overview of communications practices in developed and developing countries. Until recently, planning efforts were

Preface

hampered by the absence of comprehensive, clearly articulated policies but lately there has emerged a recognition of the need to study, formulate and find agreement on basic issues taking into account the interactions between communication and other major sectors of society. Ploman's paper reviews institutional structures, the role of policy-making and advisory bodies, the activities of international organizations and concludes with a discussion of major issues in the field of communication.

Abraham Moles examines the role of mass media in a sociological context. In 'The Cultural Compass and the Transmission of Values' he argues for the need of a 'cultural compass' which will monitor 'what currently is' and 'what is going to be' in a society concerned simultaneously with promoting its development and upholding or developing the specific characters which belong to its tradition. By comparing the culture of today with emerging changes, 'signals' will be generated which can be injected as a regulating element of cultural activity.

'An International Survey of the Future of Broadcasting' by Farhad Hakimzadeh and Donald Meals summarizes the findings of an international survey aimed at obtaining a worldwide perspective on the future role of broadcasting institutions. Opinions and comments were solicited from a panel of specialists with specific reference to conditions in their country regarding several critical policy issues: (a) integrated versus segmented approach to audiences, (b) controlled versus autonomous broadcasting institutions, (c) treatment of values —single value versus active encouragement of multiple values, and (d) centralized versus decentralized organizational structures.

It is well recognized, points out Elihu Katz in the first paper in section II—the Role of Mass Communications in National Development: Facets of Innovation—'Cultural Continuity and Change', that broadcasting should contribute to the process of national integration and to socio-economic development. And indeed, mass media have had a measure of success in these areas. But today a further demand is made of broadcasting— that it promote the continuity of traditional culture. The desire

Preface

for more indigenous self-expression in broadcasting poses difficult dilemmas: how to reconcile tradition with modernity, regionalism with nationalism, nationalism with internationalism.

'The Governance of Mass Communication' by Ithiel de Sola Pool expresses alternative ways in which a national broadcasting system might be financed, governed and organized in the light of social requirements, developmental goals, technical and financial resources. It stresses the extent to which policy decisions in the field of broadcasting are inevitably influenced or dictated by considerations which, in the last analysis, can be discussed only in terms of fundamental political theory.

In 'Multi-Media Education', Ivor K. Davies is concerned with the effective (as distinct from efficient) utilization of modern media technology for educational purposes. He recognizes that all too often media technology simply consists in providing classrooms with sophisticated hardware. What is needed is the design of a total learning environment so that hardware, software and traditional teaching methods complement one another. He points out the advantages of 'piecemeal' planning whereby neither ends nor means are picked at the outset. Planning should be viewed as a process of successive approximations with ends and means interacting to give rise to an adequate and feasible plan.

Edwin B. Parker and Ali Mohammadi in their paper 'National Development Support Communication' review the goals of national development, the factors and constraints influencing development and the strategy options available. The specifics of communication in support of development are discussed including communications technology, institutional structure and information content as well as overall policy and planning issues.

Section III—National Experiences in Communications Policy—starts with 'Integrated Development Support Communication in Dahomey', in which Armand Defever reports on an FAO rural broadcasting project designed to break the farmers' isolation, inform and motivate rural committees, contribute to their education and seek their participation in the national economic plans. The study reviews the problems which had to be overcome as well as the impressive results achieved through the formation of radio forums and the opening of a dialogue between communicators and audience.

'Communications Policy in Brazil' by Dov Shinar and Marco Antonio Rodrigues Dias focuses on the role of mass communication in development planning. Brazil is a country of enormous size and extreme diversity which is experiencing dramatic economic growth but also facing severe problems of national integration. The authors review past and present legislation and offer a comprehensive set of recommendations based on their understanding of existing social and political constraints.

'Communications Developments in India' by Robert T. Filep and Syed M. S. Haque discusses the relationship between communication, technology and development in India, reviews past and present communication strategies aimed at resolving problems of illiteracy, health, overpopulation and low agricultural productivity and analyses the Satellite Instructional Television Experiment.

Majid Teheranian's 'The Role of Broadcasting in Iran' deals with a national survey of the views of government officials, communication specialists, opinion leaders and several critical segments of the audience. It solicited their views on the contribution of broadcasting to national development and their opinions as to the performance of NIRT both in terms of what it attempts to accomplish and of their individual expectations. Included is a brief history of broadcasting in Iran from 1940. the year when the first radio station was inaugurated in Tehran.

In his paper 'Towards a National Communications Policy in Iran', Amin Banani argues for the need of fostering unity within a framework of cultural diversity. It is essential, that in this period of rapid transition Iranians preserve a sense of identity with the traditions of their country. It is NIRT's responsibility to strike a balance between individual interests and collective welfare and to help narrow the gap between the people and the elite which in the past has hampered social, political and economic development.

Preface

The publication of this volume has been a co-operative effort to which many have contributed. The editors owe a profound debt of gratitude to Mr Reza Ghotbi, Managing Director of National Iranian Radio and Television, for his unfailing support of the Project out of which this collection of studies emerged. Whatever insights they provide will require a wisdom such as his to be translated into action. To him this volume is dedicated and through him to socially responsible broadcasters the world over.

We also wish to express our appreciation to the participants of the Prospective Planning Project. Their lively and stimulating discussions made the preparation of this volume an exciting and rewarding enterprise. We also wish to thank Mrs Robab Mani for her patient typing of the manuscript through successive drafts.

Finally, our heartfelt thanks to Mr Edward Ploman and Mrs Judith Acton of the International Institute of Communications for their generous assistance in nursing the manuscript through to publication.

Tehran
June 1976

Majid Teheranian
Farhad Hakimzadeh
Marcello L. Vidale

I
Communications and Development: The Parameters of Theory and Policy

1
Communications and National Development
Reflections on Theories and Policies

Majid Teheranian

The purpose of this paper is first, to provide a historical perspective on the role of communication in the process of rapid development and modernization; second, to review the major communications and development theories; and third, to suggest the rudiments of a taxonomy of communications policy in the context of national development.

The general perspective here will be to consider development as a holistic and dialectical process in which sequences, lags and contradictions vary from society to society. It will be argued that orthodox development and communications theory has sought too many uniformities that either do not exist or have not the same meaning in different historical and cultural contexts. It will be further argued that inadequate attention has been paid to one of the most unique qualities of social systems, i.e., their ability to confound theorists by creating new structures of meaning, technologies and interactions that have few or no historical precedents.

The Historical Context

National development for countries that have made the historical transition from an agrarian to an industrial society has involved three fundamental revolutions, which may be identified as 'economic', 'political' and 'communications'. In the advanced industrial world we are possibly going through a fourth revolutionary process that has not yet taken a distinct shape but can be felt in most aspects of life.

Perhaps the most readily understandable way of looking at these four revolutionary processes is to consider them as fulfilling the hierarchy of human needs proposed by Maslow (1954):

Physiological needs (food, air, water, behavioural space, etc.);
safety needs (protection from weather, other species and other humans);
belongingness and love needs (family and social groups membership);
esteem needs (having the respect of oneself and one's peers in society);
self-actualization needs (fulfilling one's potentials in one's private and public capacities);
cognitive needs (understanding one's relation to society and comprehending order in nature and the cosmos);
aesthetic needs (perceiving beauty and order in experience).

If the need for self-transcendence (transcending the barriers of time and space to experience infinitude) is added to this hierarchy, the list reveals that the first orders of priority are economic in nature, while socio-political, communication, artistic and religious needs follow. While the most advanced industrial societies may have provided for the fulfilment of the lower orders of needs, the search is still going on for ways to fulfil the higher orders. Furthermore, each society has its own special priorities and there is no single index (such as *per capita* income) with which we can rank them on the degree of fulfilment of the above categories of needs. In fact, one may reasonably argue that the hierarchy should not be thought of as a hierarchy in strict terms, but rather as groupings of needs before each individual and social group that have to be fulfilled all at the same time. Given its resource constraints, each individual and social group tries to optimize among these sometimes competing and sometimes complementary needs.

In terms of the history of development, however, we may discern a sequence that starts with an economic revolution and then turns into political and communications revolutions. This sequence is best observed in the historical experiences of the western European countries, where it finds also its most eloquent theoretical exponents. However, in the experience of the rest of the world, and particularly that of the colonialized world, the sequences do not necessarily follow the same order.

In fact, the three revolutionary processes have virtually coincided in the less developed countries. This compression effect (compressing several centuries of development into a few decades) has created some contradictions, problems and unique opportunities, and may be considered both the curse and the blessing of 'backwardness'.

The economic revolution entails a transition from self-sufficiency to commodity production. Depending on the resource endowments of each country, the requirements of this transition vary immensely from society to society as do the implied consequences. Such fundamental attitude changes towards time, work and human relations seem to be universal in scope. In its most radical form, this new worldview can be studied in the work of classical economists who conceive man as selfish, rational, and given to a natural 'propensity to truck, barter, and exchange one thing for another' (Smith, 1776). While this may be an idealized picture of an eighteenth-century English bourgeois generalized into *'homo economicus'*, there is reason to believe that the nature of this economic transformation changes men universally into greater time-consciousness, higher achievement motivation, and more functional rather than affective human relations.

The political revolution, by contrast, requires that men re-establish the human bonds which the 'cash nexus' has impaired. It leads them into new forms of association which involve a transition from various forms of political subjugation (serfdom, colonialism, all forms of political disenfranchisement) to modern citizenship and participation. It is interesting to note that the two contemporary European theorists of this process, De Tocqueville and Marx, starting from more or less similar distastes for bourgeois democracy arrive at different predictions. While Marx argues for the politicization of the working class along class interests so that their political interests (socialism) would take precedence over economic interests (trade unionism). De Tocqueville looks with suspicion upon the masses and believes them ready to give up their newly-won freedoms in favour of maintenance of social equality. Marx is optimistic about the future of political democracy; De Tocqueville, instead, warns against its corruption into a 'tyranny of the majority' that foretells much about the totalitarian systems of the twentieth century. In his own words, 'among the laws that rule human societies there is one which seems to be more precise and clear than others. If men are to remain civilized or to become so, the art of associating together must grow and improve in the same ratio in which the equality of conditions is increased' (1835, II, 118).

Political mobilization is happening faster than political institutionalization of participation. Particularly in the context of the developing world where this phenomenon holds, the consequence is either political upheaval, or political decay, or both (Huntington, 1965). The politicization of the masses and the emergence of a *homo politicus* in contrast to a *homo economicus* is a process that started with the great bourgeois revolutions of the eighteenth and nineteenth centuries and has reached its culmination with the Russian and Chinese revolutions in the twentieth century. It was the inability of the traditional societies in Russia and China to realize the economic revolution that hastened the processes of a radical political revolution in these countries.

In the less developed world of Africa, Asia and Latin America, the economic and political revolutions have run into a third kind of revolutionary process—a revolution in communications. While colonialism and imperialism may have delayed the economic and political revolutions in these countries (Baran, 1957), they inadvertently hastened the process of a communications revolution by the construction of transport facilities, introduction of a *lingua franca* (French, English, Portuguese, Spanish) wherever one did not exist, and the establishment of a modern educational (sometimes missionary) system. Independence has accelerated this process by increasing the spread of literacy, newspaper, radio and television. The communications revolution has been a double-edged sword, however. It has mobilized the population, increased the level of national consciousness and created the conditions for possible national integration; but it has also generated demands for more 'modernity' than can be delivered and has resulted in a 'revolution of rising frustrations' (Lerner and Schramm, 1967). Increased communication may also generate reactions against modernity by activating traditionalist groups (Huntington, 1965), especially since in developing countries the political arena is often dominated by the more modernist groups. The alliance between such incompatible ideologies as Marxism and religious ideologies is one possible outcome of this phenomenon. Increased communication may also moblize minority ethnic groups who were once relatively indifferent to politics but who have now acquired national consciousness and demand a hearing on a par with the dominant national group.

The worldwide revolution in communications has gone, however, far beyond these considerations. It has made possible a transition from oral traditions to multi-media interactive systems of communication; it has cut continental distances into mere hop-overs; it has generated a new educational technology that systematizes the process of learning and makes its fruits available to vast numbers of people; by introducing automation into the production process it has activated what has come to be known as the 'Second Industrial Revolution'; it has created a whole new mass culture with its own ideologues and prophets; and, finally, it has invented a new image of man and society that employs information and communications metaphors rather than economic and political ones, an image which may be summed up as *'homo communicus'*.

For the developing countries, this multi-revolutionary process (economic, political and communications) has created historic challenges and opportunities. The resulting sequences, lags, and contradictions in this process have opened up a complex variety of possible strategies of modernization. At the risk of an over-simplification, we may identify at least three possible strategies: (1) An economic strategy which gives economic objectives and methods first priority over political and communications aims and methods. Countries that have resorted to a market economy which primarily employs the profit motive in generating the productive forces pursue such a strategy of modernization. (2) A political strategy which gives political objectives and methods first priority. Countries that experienced a social and political revolution (China, North Korea, Cuba, North Vietnam) have had to subordinate economic and communications objectives to the primacy of politics. (3) A communications strategy, largely adopted by default, which has given priority to the spread of literacy and media communications as well as the construction of transport facilities. Countries which could neither mobilize an economic revolution nor have experienced a political revolution have been subjected, often inadvertantly, to this strategy.

National development is a multi-dimensional process; the economic, political and communications infrastructures are needed to provide the opportunity for each individual to realize his fullest potential. To reduce man to one dimension only (be it economic, political or communicative) leads to an impoverishment of his spirit. Although the technology of mass communications provides unparalleled opportunities for economic, political, educational and cultural development, its potential for national development will remain unrealized unless it goes well beyond one-way mass communications towards two-way interactive systems. Indeed, the term 'mass communications' itself may be considered self contradictory (Elliot and Golding, 1974). To reach a better understanding of the role of communications in national development we need a better grasp of the process of development itself.

The Dialectics of National Development

Orthodox theories of modernization fall into one or a combination of the following four categories: (1) *Stage theories*, the best-known examples of which are those of Marx, Weber and Rostow. (2) *Index theories*, which have been largely advanced by economists but tacitly accepted by others who correlate the sociocultural indices of development with those of economic indices (Higgins, 1968). (3) *Differentiation theories*, largely advanced by sociologists and political scientists who seek understanding of the process of development in the increasing differentiation of structures and functions (Parsons, 1960, 1962; Almond and Powell, 1968; Almond and Coleman, 1960). (4) *Diffusion theories*, advanced primarily by social psychologists, suggesting that the development process starts with the diffusion of certain ideas, motivations, attitudes, or behaviours (Hagen, 1962, 1968; McClelland, 1953; Lerner, 1958).

Since the perspective on national development that will be offered here differs markedly from some orthodox views, it may be useful to start by viewing them critically.

Observations on the orthodox views of development[1]

Although it is difficult to lump together a great diversity of development theories, it is fair to say that economists have so far led the way in setting the pace and the conceptual range in this field.

In recent years, historians, anthropologists, sociologists and political scientists have added impressive contributions to the empirical and theoretical fields, but the process of integration of these new insights with the older findings is just beginning.

Aside from problems of disciplinary fragmentation in development theory, the traditional theories are also characterized by problems of *ethnocentrism and unidimensionality*, as well as *deterministic* and *ahistorical* perspectives. Most development theories are of a typological kind that conceal built-in ethnocentric biases. The models which most development scientists, economists and non-economists, have generally set forth as the ideal type of a developed society either implicitly or explicitly bear unmistakable signs of the western historical experience. Economists have largely defined development as a steady rise in *per capita* income. Other indices such as welfare, literacy and life expectancy are presumed to be dependent functions of income. While this view may reflect Western historical evidence, there are indications to suggest that the process is reversed for latecomers to industrialization. In other words, factors such as nationalism and solidarity against foreign domination, revolutionary movements against traditional society and authority, large-scale transfer of modern science and technology have preceded and provided the engines of industrialization.

The ethnocentric bias reveals itself in a different guise in the sociological and political sciences, though the typologies tend to be subtler. The Weberian typology of traditional, charismatic and rational-legal structures of authority has been almost universally adopted to suggest a mode of development from traditional, to transitional and to modern societies. Theories of entrepreneurship have been infected by the Weberian notions of the 'Protestant ethic'—the notion of a professional calling, frugality, calculation, and of achievement and profit motivations (Weber, 1904-5; McClelland, 1953; Hagen, 1962). While it is difficult to fault these theories on their own grounds, successful attempts at modernization in Japan and China, for instance, suggest that economic growth may take place within a wholly different set of cultural and motivational patterns.

More recent theories of political development shy away from traditional ethnocentric notions which view Western democratic institutions as the *sine qua non* of political maturity. Nevertheless, some rudiments of ethnocentrism persist. Almond and Powell (1966), for instance, have suggested structural differentiation, cultural secularization and subsystem autonomy as the major determinants of political development. While there is merit to their view, their formulation of variables and typology is strongly western-oriented. Structural differentiation without a corresponding measure of integration at the structural and cultural levels would have disintegrating social consequences. While it is probably true that modernization demands the adoption of a rational and scientific world-view, the result need not be secularization and abandonment of religion altogether. The function of religion will surely change but the total denial of man's spiritual needs would lead to psychological alienation and social disintegration.

A fundamental difficulty with most typological theories of development derives from the fact that they posit ideal models of a developed society toward which history is moving or ought to move. Since it is extremely difficult for theorists to free themselves from ethnocentic biases, it would be best to so redefine development as to allow each social system to determine its own images of the future at any given point in time and space.

The second problem with most development theories lies in their unidimensionality. We have already touched on this problem by suggesting that the fragmentation of development theory into competing disciplinary perspectives has given us a fragmented view of development. Other problems are a consequence of the preoccupation of economists with material quantities, of political scientists with power, and of sociologists with social functions. Each view tends to exclude the other variables from its own unique domain of analysis. But the development of social systems is, by its very essence, an exchange of values, energy and information. The interconnections which are the most significant features of the system tend to be disdained by the disciplinary theorists.

The third problem derives from their deterministic perspectives which often exhibit certain ethnocentric overtones based on preconceived models of developed societies. Rostow's (1960) theory of economic growth from traditional societies to the age of high mass consumption is presented as a metaphor which compares a traditional and stagnant economy to a jet aircraft prepared for take-off into self-sustaining growth, maturity and high mass consumption.

Rostow's optimism and determinism contrasts with the pessimism of Nurkse (1953) and the vicious-circle-of-poverty theorists who view foreign investment as a major instrument for development. The fact that countries such as Japan and China have made the breakthrough without the benefits of much foreign investment seriously undermines the validity of these notions.

The fourth and possibly the most serious problem with orthodox theories lies in their ahistoricity which may take several different forms. The vicious-circle-of-poverty theorists argue that poor countries are poor because they are poor, as if this were an immutable law of history which has nothing to do with international division of labour. The fact is, as oil exporting countries amply demonstrate, that international terms of trade can change drastically if the less developed countries learn to use their bargaining power more effectively. Theorists who couch their views in socio-psychological terms suggest that a 'culture of poverty' (Lewis, 1961) deters development, as if culture were immutable and unaffected by environmental factors. Both ahistorical and ethnocentric is the notion that the future of the less developed countries is but a pale version of the western historical experience. While it is true that the challenges of modernization are very much alike, the responses of a traditional but seasoned society tend to be unique and peculiar to its own cultural *Weltanschauung*. Japan, China, India, Egypt and Iran are examples of older centres of human civilization whose responses to the challenges of the modern world can not be comprehended except in terms of a deep understanding of the historical images and memories embedded in their heritage. These are societies that present a perplexing melange of development and underdevelopment, cultural sophistication and technological backwardness.

Strategic determinants and deterrents of national development

The following theoretical formulation of development assumes that societies, and particularly those that are subject to feelings of 'backwardness' or 'underdevelopment', go through a multitude of experiences that may be summed up in terms of the following five effects: (a) *Demonstration effects*, whereby the 'less developed' world tries to 'catch up' with the 'more developed' by adoption of their methods. (b) *Fusion effects*, whereby the 'less developed' world tries to combine the 'best features' from several different social systems that may be characterized as developed. (c) *Compression effects*, whereby the less developed world attempts to accomplish the task of development in less time than it took the more industrialized countries. (d) *Preventive effects*, whereby the less developed world tries to do all of this at less human, material, and environmental cost than was paid by the presently industrialized countries. (e) *Stylization effects*, whereby the uniqueness of national identity and culture are maintained and enhanced as development proceeds.

Traditional development theory tends to view as dim the possibility that all or any of these contradictory approaches will bear fruit. It measures development along universal value scales that account for the homogeneities rather than the heterogeneities of the development experience. As complex adaptive systems, however, human societies develop along unexpected, probablistic, non-linear paths, reaching not only the same destination via different routes (equifinality) but also defining and redefining their destinations and routes as they go along (multifinality). The process of development should be defined therefore in such a way as to avoid ethnocentric biases and to account for each social system setting its own image of the future in terms of its own perceived needs.

Second, one should avoid the problem of unidimensionality in order to show as fully as possible the interdependence of the parts within the whole of an evolving social system. The insights of various development sciences can be integrated to achieve this goal.

Third, and finally, the process of development should be defined so as to demonstrate its ever-changing and ever-contradictory nature. In fact, the process is better understood in terms of points and counterpoints than in terms of a set of fixed value continua along which society can move indefinitely.

A dialectical view of development serves all three of these purposes. A set of five complementary-contradictory variables are proposed to suggest the deterrents of the developmental process. These are variables which cut across disciplinary lines, though they incorporate the insights of all social science disciplines on development. Each variable is negated by a counter-variable, while the conflict between them produces a unity of opposites in a synthesis of the two that sets the stage for the next and higher state of development. From this perspective, no value is viewed as an absolute end in itself: it is the harmonious realization of all these values which defines integrated and optimal national development.

27

Majid Teheranian

Our dialectical correlates of the developmental process are as follows (and see Figure 1).

1. *Increasing production, pollution and welfare.* Economists mostly define development in terms of increases in real output *per capita*. They acknowledge, however, that increasing production results in the pollution of the environment and depletion of resources. In the process of economic growth, productivity or output per man-hour of labour increases over time. Increasing productivity is itself a function of capital accumulation, discovery of new natural resources, improvement of human skills, extent of the market, existence of effective demand, technological progress, positive human motivation, efficient social organization and presence of entrepreneurial or managerial talents. Some of these factors are heavily dependent on the level of welfare. In the long run, therefore, increases in production, pollution depletion and welfare correlate positively. But in the short run, increases in pollution may work against productivity.

2. *Increasing mobilization, dislocation and participation.* The process of national development is characterized by the increasing mobilization or politicization of the populace. As more people reach political consciousness, unfulfilled expectations turn into social and psychological dislocations which express themselves in rising frustrations, anomie, crime, and sometimes violence. These conflicting demands may lead to the emergence of new structures of national participation that provide channels for compromise and conflict resolution. Failures to develop such structures of aggregation and participation may lead to political decay rather than development (Huntington, 1965; Pye, 1966).

Mobilization can be measured in many different ways (Deutsch, 1966). Here, we suggest three different indices: physical, social and psychic mobility. Physical mobility measures the extent to which people and material resources can be moved across space. Mobility, in this sense, is obviously a function of the development of the transportation and communication networks as well as the extent to which the fetters of traditional institutions have been overcome.

Social mobility measures the extent to which horizontal and vertical movements are possible for an individual in a given society. Horizontal social mobility measures the extent to which an individual can change occupations, while vertical mobility measures the extent to which an individual can move up (or down) the social hierarchy. Both indices are a function of the social structure of opportunity—the extent to which a society is open or closed.

Psychic mobility is a still more complex index. It may be defined as the extent to which an individual can empathize or put himself in other people's shoes. It measures an individual's capacity to relate to the rest of the world and to adapt to new circumstances. Although difficult to quantify, this index may be measured through culturally-sensitive psychological tests. As literacy grows and communications media expand, psychic mobility may be expected to increase. In this sense the multimedia communication systems act as a 'mobility multiplier' (Lerner, 1958).

Increased mobility will mobilize people and resources, will generate new aggregations of interests and greater demands for participation—economic, political, and psychic.

Mobilization, dislocation and participation are thus correlated in essentially the same way as production, pollution and welfare; over the long run, there is a tendency towards a positive correlation between the three variables. In the short run, however, the deterrent factor may retard political development. In developing countries mobilization has often outdistanced aggregation and participation and has resulted in political decay and violence.

3. *Increasing differentiation, bureaucratization and integration.* At the level of social structures and functions, development involves a process of increasing differentiation and specialization of labour. This process is to some extent counterbalanced by a process of bureaucratization that results from the emergence of a mass industrial society (Weber, 1904-5). In order to transcend this conflict, social and cultural integration is needed to unify increasingly diverse social groups around common goals and values.

Majid Teheranian

The three variables are thus correlated in that at each higher level of differentiation we may anticipate greater tendencies toward bureaucratization which demand a higher level of integration. Nevertheless, at times, high levels of integration (as in very traditional societies) may correlate negatively with differentiation.

4. *Increasing communication, cognitive dissonance and plurality.* Communication is a ubiquitous feature of all social systems; so much so that it is tempting to explain the whole phenomenon of development in terms of communication metaphors. But this would be reducing a complex phenomenon into a unidimensional model. And yet, development does always involve an increasing level of physical, social and psychological communication. However, increases in communcation (particularly when it is one-way mass communication) do not necessarily lead to mutual understanding; they may lead to greater cognitive dissonance which is a deterrent to communications development. By cognitive dissonance we mean the presence of masking noise in the communication system, cross-purposes in communication, the use of conflicting symbols. As the communication system overcomes these problems a plurality of epistemic communities emerge each with its own set of symbols recognizable only by its own members but co-existing side by side with a high level of integration and tolerance. The development of different scientific disciplines or religious and political ideologies, each with its own particular language, which use a meta-language to communicate across disciplines and ideologies is a clear example of this process.

5. *Increasing individuation, conformity and adaptation.* At the level of the individual, development involves an unfolding of unique potentialities. But the emergence of a mass industrial society imposes considerable social conformity (Riesman and Glazer, 1950). The dialectical conflict between these two forces gets resolved in time as the capacity of the social system for internal and external adaptation grows and permits increasing diversity and autonomy.

Conformity may act as a deterrent against higher orders of social adaptation. A group of autonomous individuals co-operates better than a group of dependent and conformist individuals. But individuation and autonomy beyond a certain point may become dysfunctional for timely responses to a changing environment. The different performance of dictatorships and democracies in times of national stress seems to illustrate the point. Dictatorial regimes can often mobilize resources more rapidly than democracies; democracies, on the other hand, seem to outperform dictatorships over the long haul.

6. *Increasing rationalization, alienation and innovation.* As a society moves from traditional to modern structures, its culture shifts from sacred to secular world-views, from the unseen to tangible designs, from absolute dogmas to relativistic legislation, from belief to reason and experimentation. But reason, practical reason in the Hegelian sense, alienates one from one's own sources of emotional energy and from the social system that has imposed rational calculations on life. We try to overcome this alienation through innovation and creativity. To the extent that work in an industrial society is unimaginative, routine and removed from one's inner world, alienation acts as a deterrent to innovation.

Historically, national development has involved an increasing tempo of cultural and technological innovation. It has also increased rationalization of culture and social organization on the basis of science and its application. Cultural rationalization, in part, means secularization. But the shift from a religious to a secular and scientific culture does not mean that religion loses its function altogether in a modern society; it suggests that the place and function of religion undergoes some fundamental changes. Whereas traditional religious world-views begin with the assumption of an unseen world to whose design the real world must conform in order to be saved, modern religions often confine themselves to the strictly spiritual and personal spheres of life. Some traditional religions, such as Judaism and Islam, have worked out the Divine Law in considerable detail to apply to all spheres of life. By contrast, modern belief systems are less positivistic and tend to work on the basis of general principles that may be altered or reinterpreted as reason and experience dictate.

Cultural rationalization does not mean the banishment of the religious function from society. In the words of the Sermon on the Mount, it means giving to Caesar (the secular world) that which is Caesar's and to God (the sacred world) that which is His. A secular world-view allows for religious worship, but it does not allow for religious dogmas to command science, technology and social legislation.

On the whole the rationalization of culture appears to correlate positively with technological innovations. It took a cultural Renaissance and a reassertion of human reason against the dogma of the Church to launch the scientific, technological and industrial revolutions. Nevertheless, exclusive reliance on the scientific method may prove counterproductive to the processes of cultural innovation which depend so vitally on imagination and intuitive leaps.

Rationalization and innovation mean an increasing social capacity to learn, i.e., to map the environmental changes and to adapt accordingly. But, as history has shown time and again, total reliance on reason without those delicate ties of faith and affection that bind humans together could destroy a civilization's capacity to learn, innovate and adapt.

A rational and innovative culture does not maximize reason or faith but optimizes both. In terms of the personality structures of its individual members, this means the growth of capacity to empathize or an ability to see the world from another man's perspective, as well as growing capacity for self-doubt, self-examination, and self-correction—in short, the growth of an open personality.

Figure 1 suggests, through positive and negative signs, the positive and negative feedback loops which seem to operate in this model of national development. Aside from the inter-loop feedback systems, the intra-loop feedbacks also assume certain positive correlations between economic welfare and social and political mobilization, political participation and the development of new forms of social aggregation *and* differentiation, increasing social integration *and* higher levels of communication, the emergence of a plurality of epistemic communities *and*

Communications and National Development

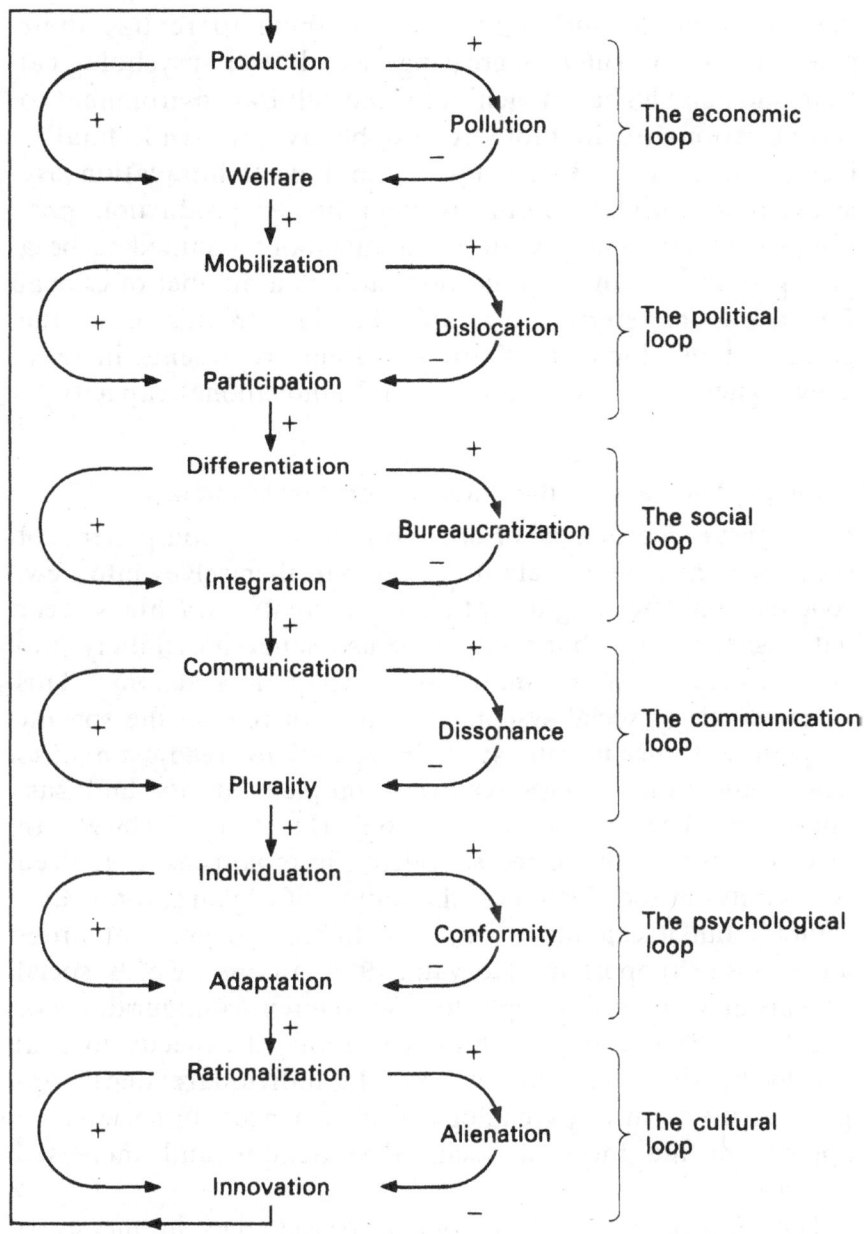

Figure 1 Strategic generators, deterrents and determinants of development (adapted from Teheranian (1974)

the ability of the individuals within them to realize their potentials more fully, increasing social and psychological adaptation *and* higher capacities for the cultural environment to accept rationality in thought and behaviour. And, finally, increasing levels of social and technological innovation are assumed to correlate positively with higher production possibilities. Development is thus fundamentally assumed to be a process of innovation amplification through a number of critical feedback loops referred to in this diagram. In this sense, the process of development of social systems represents increasingly higher orders of complexity and innovational capacity.

Ideology, Utopia, and the dialectics of development

In contrast to mechanical or organic systems, the components of social systems have the ability to regroup themselves into new, coherent and meaningful patterns of activity. Machines wear out, organisms age, but social systems change indefinitely into new structures of meaning and group interactions. This characteristic of social systems may in turn rest on the specific properties of their members: 'their capacity for readjustment to new configurations, with renewed complementarity and sustained or renewed communication' (Deutsch, 1948-9). In machines, we see organized simplicity; in organisms, organized complexity; in social systems, the nature of organization is also complex but it can range between different degrees of order and chaos (Rapoport and Horvath, 1959). In other words, social systems may either develop into new coherent configurations or decay into chaotic relationships with reduced capacity to deal effectively with their environment. In individuals, decay appears in the form of psychological disturbances. In societies, it appears in the form of social dysfunctions and increased violence.

The essence of the development process lies in the ever-increasing ability of social systems to map faithfully their environment. This is not always a harmonious process. It takes place primarily by trial and error as the variety in the environment is matched against the cognitive structures within the system. Development means an ever-increasing encoding of the environmental variety within society's structures of meaning (culture) and structures of action and interaction (functions and social groups). Cognitive dissonance results whenever there is a mismatch between these structures and the existing and emerging varieties in the environment.

Deviation is at the core of the developmental process. The dialectics of development may be considered as the dialectics of deviation. The social system as a whole reacts in three distinctly different ways to the phenomenon of deviance. It tries to reduce, preserve, or amplify deviation. Deviation-reduction mechanisms work to maintain stability within the existing structures. Deviation-preservation mechanisms work towards social experimentation with new ideas and technologies. Deviation-amplification mechanisms work towards the growth of new structures of meaning, action and interaction. All of these processes take place under conditions of tension, conflict and at times violence. The process of social selection of deviant behaviours to establish new social norms is characterized by social, political and ideological conflicts. Decisions and non-decisions, i.e., decisions that are made by default, may be considered the foci of these conflicts. A systems theory of development views the process in terms of individuals interacting socially in a matrix of dynamic assessments and inter-communication of meanings, evaluating, emoting, deciding and choosing.

The process of social selection takes place under the prevailing environmental conditions of which time and space are the two most important dimensions. The interaction of time and space, in turn, provides the breeding grounds for certain ideological and utopian configurations that have proved important in determining the direction and strategies of social change in different social systems. While ideologies perform system preservation functions, Utopian thoughts operate towards systems transformation (Mannheim, 1929; Berger and Luckmann, 1966).

Our conception of the strategic determinants of development suggests a general direction of requisite change. This is in part based on Ashby's 'law of requisite variety', which states that variety within a self-regulating system must be at least as great as the environmental variety against which it is attempting to regulate itself. The emphasis is shifted from conformity and control of deviation to its creative regulation. Our conception of development reveals the social significance of such concepts as socialization for self-reliance and relative autonomy, education for creativity, ideational flexibility and the open mind, communicating by presenting the full spectrum of viewpoints, and decision-making by a process of discussion (Buckley, 1968). In other words, instead of smuggling democratic concepts unsystematically as if they were only residual considerations or ill-concealed value-judgments, we have built them into the concept of development. By contrast, conditions of decay suggest a declining measure of internal variety relative to variety in the environment. Pathological deviance often results under conditions of decay when environmental pressures have outweighed the capacity of the system to provide for mechanisms of innovation.

The requisites of democratic innovation may be summed up as follows: the broad and deep dissemination of its codified findings; the absence of significant long-lasting subcultural cleavages, power centres and vested interests, whether on a class or ethnic basis, to break or hinder the flow of information or feedback concerning the internal states of the system; and the promotion of a large variety pool by maintaining freedom in the relations of the component parts—for example, providing a number of real choices of behaviours and goals.

There is no necessary or pre-determined road to these goals. We have emphasized their universal significance by setting the following seven as environmental expectations placed before the modern nation-state: national security, individual freedom, political participation, social equality, economic growth, world peace and ecological balance. These values are not always harmonious; there may be also a trade-off among them. Moreover, some states may have internalized them more than others. The principles of equifinality as well as multifinality are at work in all open social systems. The same objectives may be reached via different paths, and we may arrive at different destinations from the same starting-point.

The choice of a strategy of development centres on (a) defining the system objectives, (b) establishing priorities among these objectives, and (c) providing a strategy of reaching those objectives within a defined time horizon. Barrington Moore, Jr. (1966) has identified at least three distinctly different paths to modernization: parliamentary democracy in the west, communism in the Soviet Union and China, and fascism in Germany and Japan. They all have achieved successfully the goals of an industrial society. The difference lies in their strategies of development: each strategy presents a different constellation of priorities among the competing goals of the state system. The capitalist democracies seem to have emphasized individual freedom (including rights of property), political participation and economic growth somewhat at the expense of social equality, world peace and ecological balance. The communists seem to have emphasized social equality, political participation and economic growth at the expense of individual freedom and some other values. The fascists seem to have emphasized economic growth, national power (security) and political participation at the expense of social equality and world peace. This is only a rough estimate of each system's strategic priorities: it could be considerably refined and elaborated. Other constellations of priorities are also possible and are being experimented upon by the less developed countries on their paths to modernization.

In the search for alternative strategies of modernization, the important lesson to learn is that (a) there is no one path to the same objectives, (b) the choice of any strategy has an opportunity cost in terms of other strategies and goals, and (c) there are 'advantages to backwardness' in that we may learn from the experiences of others.

There is no substitute for understanding the dynamics of each system in its own terms. Social systems, as we have tried to show, are not mechanical or organic systems; they are open, negentropic, morphogenic, self-regulating, self-directing systems. At the centre of these systems stands the human individual with all of his complexity, ambiguity and manifold potentialities. All we know about this central element of the social system is that he behaves not only in terms of certain instinctual impulses but also in terms of certain images, roles, Utopias that are the constructs of his cultural conditions and his own unique processes of creativity. Man creates his culture and his culture creates him.

No matter how refined our scientific tools may be, there is thus no escape from having to know, as best as we can, toward what image of the future and of man we are striving. The present model of the national system and its development may be a useful tool for making the nature of our possible strategic choices more explicit, but it will not make the choices for us. Such choices shall have to be made by man ultimately in the process of making his own history.

Normative theory and Utopian thinking may be considered as much a part of the social scientific enterprise as empirical and policy-orientated research. Man lives not by bread alone; he lives also by the stuff dreams are made of. The dream of a society in which the harmonious development of each is the condition for the harmonious development of all lies at the bottom of what we might call 'the modern democratic culture'. There is no single route for reaching this goal. Nevertheless, choices on strategy must be made by each nation if they are not to be made by default.

National Development and Communication Policy: Rudiments of a Taxonomy

Having defined development as a process leading to increasing orders of complexity and innovational capacity (Buckley, 1968; Teheranian, 1974), we will attempt to identify the role of mass media in terms of a recording metaphor. Each new groove on the record disc shown in Figure 2 represents a new order of complexity and innovation. At the centre of the disc stands a core of primitive and complex historical images and memories inherited from the past. The older a civilization is, the richer and the more concentrated is its historical memory bank. The

Communications and National Development

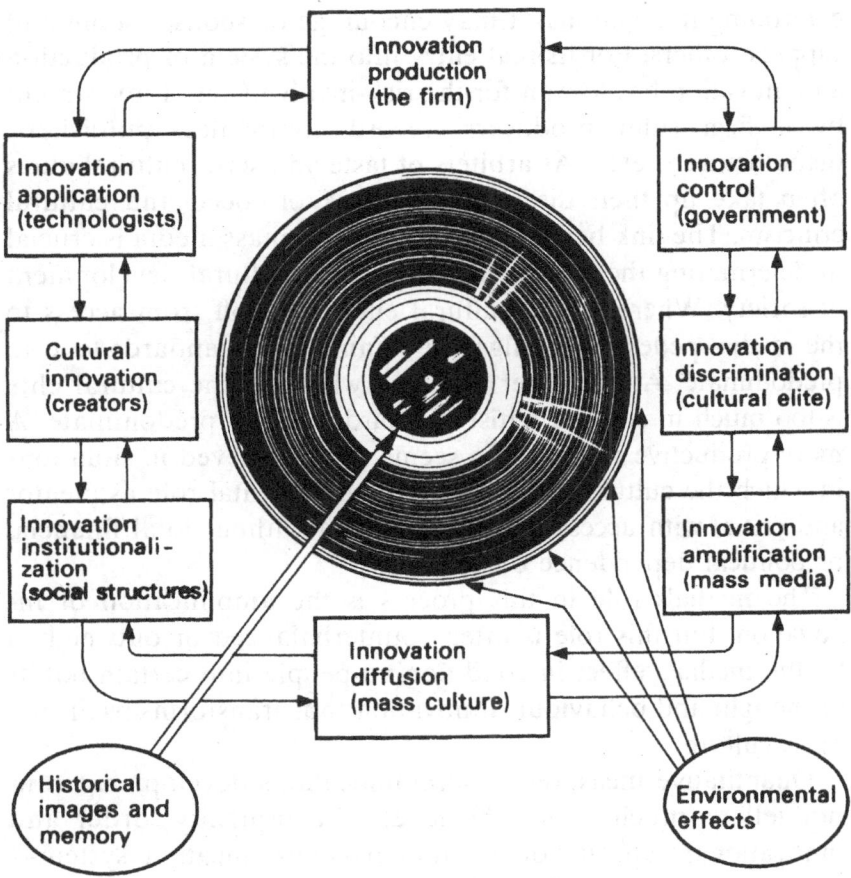

Figure 2 The process of cultural innovation

latest innovations are recorded towards the outer edges and are therefore less dense, i.e., less institutionalized. The boxes around the disc represent the crucial points, or the key notes, at which innovations are recorded on the face of the disc. The order of these innovational interventions varies from society to society, but most intervention points shown here are universal.

Innovation begins with the cultural creators (artists, scientists, philosophers, entrepreneurs). The technologists (engineers, production managers) then take up the task of technological applications. Through the patenting system and other means, the government or the socio-political system plays its role in controlling innovations; it may encourage or sponsor some and suppress others. For its real entry into the system of production an innovation has to wait for the risk-involved act of investment by a firm (film producers, record companies, publishers, manufacturers, etc.). As arbiters of taste and style, cultural elites often take up their discriminating task of social and cultural criticism. The link between this group and mass media is crucial in determining the role media play in the cultural development of society. Wherever the cultural elite is cut off from access to the media, pedestrian (vulgar or commercial) standards tend to predominate. At the other extreme, wherever the cultural elite is too much in control, elitist standards tend to predominate. A more productive relationship seems to be achieved in situations in which the cultural elite plays a dual and vital role as creator and critic, with access to the media but without total financial or political dependence on it.

The media's role in this process is the amplification of innovation, but this role is often counterbalanced or outweighed by the media's effect in conditioning people into certain habits of thought and behaviour. Innovation thus transforms itself into mass culture.

Quantitative measures of communications development cannot tell us much about the level of complexity, order and innovational capacity of a national communication system—measures that are essentially qualitative in nature. Figure 3 attempts to portray the basic components of a taxonomic model of a national communication system. The model uses a basic input-output concept to show how the communication inputs of the system (here defined as objectives, resources and technologies) are transformed into policy outputs (here defined as decisions on communication policy). Two chains of feedback loops, here labelled as positive and negative, may be identified in this model to represent those which lead to system transformation and those responsible for system maintenance. The following are the components of the system.

The monitor. This is a hypothetical leading component which, by interacting with the changing environmental conditions, sets the system's strategy of adaptation and self-transformation.

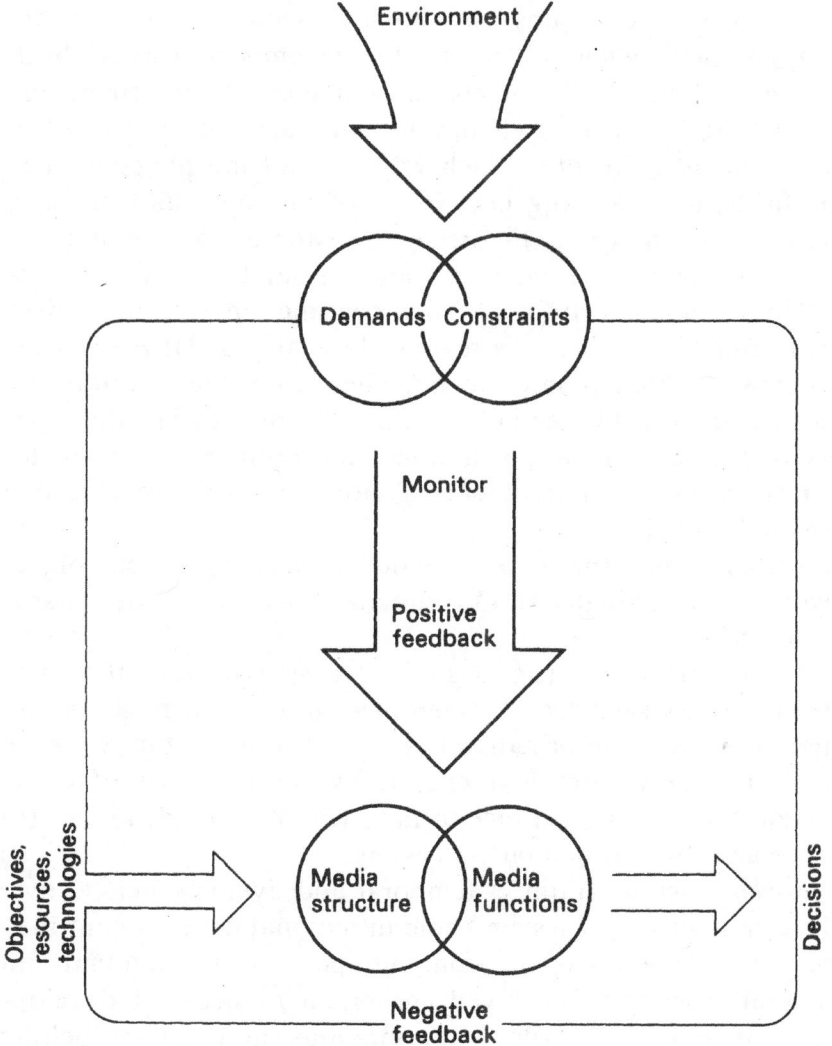

Figure 3 A systemic view of the communication system

The monitor's central function is the allocation of the system's limited resources to its unlimited needs and demands (Easton, 1953, 1965 a, b). This allocation must be authoritative, i.e., must be generally accepted, but need not be optimal: it may be sub-optimal or emergent. In a communications system the central issues to which the monitor has to address itself consist of such questions as 'who says what to whom, when, how and with what effect'. If the system's messages (both content and media of delivery) do not serve its objectives, the monitor would have to change its aims or strategy sooner or later. This is a function which we may call morphogenic, i.e., the function of creating new forms of messages and message delivery. As shown in Figure 3, the Monitor acts under the impact of environmental needs and demands as well as possibilities and constraints. The conjunction of the three interacting factors defines a region which may be labelled as the system's feasible region of action. The greater their overlap the larger is the feasible region of action. In other words, the more needs/demands fit the possibilities/constraints and the greater our awareness of environmental factors, the larger our feasible region of action.

System inputs. Inputs are defined to include system objectives, resources (material and human) and technologies (hardware and software).

Media structures. From a static and spatial view, the communications system may be identified in terms of media structures or modes of information transfer. In terms of the sequence of their historical development the five basic modes of information transfer are: (1) face-to-face, (2) graphic, (3) audio, (4) video and (5) information processing.

Media functions. From a temporal and dynamic perspective, the communications system's role in national development may be viewed in terms of its economic, political, educational and cultural aspects. As observed earlier, the process of development is not necessarily a harmonious and self-propelling process; on the contrary, it often generates a great deal of conflict and self-contradiction. Progress is often the fruit of the resolution of seemingly insoluble inconsistencies.

In socio-economic development, the role of mass media may be interpreted in terms of its productive-supportive, consumptive, and linkage effects. The produtive-supportive effects consist of those support activities in which the media directly or indirectly take part, ranging from telemedicine, agricultural extension services, library services, market and marketing information (e.g., stock market news, advertisements), to such intangibles as imparting of need-for-achievement motivation (McClelland, 1953) through its programmes—in other words, activities which contribute to the mobility and improvement of factors of production (land, labour, capital, technology and management) can be considered as supportive of the process of socio-economic development.

Acting as possible deterrents are those socio-economic effects of the media which directly or indirectly encourage consumption through demonstration effects or conscious policy choices or advertisers' efforts, all of which may be labelled 'consumptive effects'.

Ultimately, the media's most direct role in socio-economic development consists of its linkage effects, i.e., its role in creating and sustaining certain linked industries such as the electronics industry, film production, printing presses, paper industries, publishing.

With respect to the role of the media in socio-political development, it might be useful to view it in terms of its legitimative, mobilitive and participative effects. Insofar as most broadcasting systems as well as newspapers operate either directly under the auspices of the government or at its pleasure, the legitimative role of the media is one towards which most media people harbour a deep ambivalence. Broadcasting organizations are often caught between the conflicting demands of their sponsors and their audiences. Autonomy from both of these sources of pressure is what most media systems seek for themselves, but even the most autonomous of them has to take a position with respect to whether or how it wishes to legitimize the existing political system and practices. This role is related to the process of political socialization which starts at childhood in the family but goes on in the later stages of life. Generally the credibility of a media system is determined by the extent to which it reflects the truth, and this depends in part on its autonomy.

The mobilitative effects of the media are closely linked with the extent and intensity of geographic, social, and psychological mobility of the population. When the rate of social mobilization (i.e., level of expectations) exceeds the rate of upward social mobility (real improvements in income and status), we may anticipate a growing level of discontent. An appropriate role for the media to play in such a context may be to 'sail against the prevailing winds'. That is to say, for the sake of maintaining some level of social progress as well as social harmony, a responsible medium should try to raise expectations when the rate of social mobilization is less or equal to the rate of social mobility and lower them when the conditions are the reverse.

The fundamental political function of the media is to act as responsible channels of communication between government and audience, i.e., to maximize its feedback-participative effects. Aside from its traditional roles in this respect, the new interactive communications technology allows the media to play a greater role in arranging town meetings, teleconferences and international gatherings on scientific and political matters.

The media's role in educational and scientific development is a complex one intimately connected with institutions outside of the broadcasting system. To what extent the media can by itself engender general behavioural changes is yet unclear (Rogers and Shoemaker, 1970). But there is evidence to show that under suitable environmental conditions it can be a powerful factor in accelerating change in attitudes and beliefs.

On the instructive effects of the media, it would appear that with the media fully integrated into the instructional system the results are far more effective than with conventional methods of instruction alone. Multi-media instruction cannot replace face-to-face methods of education; it can only complement it. A useful way of looking at the complementarity of these two types of educational experience is to think of various educational systems as stretching along a continuum. At one end we find the educational systems that concentrate on 'Learning to Be' while at the other end those that concentrate on 'Learning to Do'. While the primary goal of the former process is the gaining of *insight,* the goal of the latter is the acquisition of *skills.* The processes used by the two systems to achieve their objectives are, respectively, *education* and *instruction*—a distinction best observed in the terminal behaviour of the learner. While the former process builds up certain character traits in the learner, the latter teaches him only to behave in a certain way under certain conditions. The total educational process is always an admixture of both processes, but our distinction does suggest how multi-media methods can free the educational system of many of its repetitive and time-consuming tasks (by relegating them to broadcasting as well as computer-assisted instruction and evaluation) in order to leave time for the teacher and the learner to enter into a more creative face-to-face educational experience.

Finally, the media's most pervasive role in educational development consists of what might be called its 'scientific fall-out' effects. To the extent that programmes directly or indirectly convey scientific messages, some scientific knowledge and attitude is imparted to the audience. To expect, however, that these random effects will provide the mechanism for transforming a traditional culture into a scientific one is to expect more than the media can accomplish.

Viewed as a dialectical process, the role of the media in cultural and artistic development may be interpreted as consisting of three major effects: *recuperative, stupefying* and *integrative*. The recuperative effects of the cultural programmes provide inexpensive and accessible entertainment for large numbers of people.

The stupefying effects of the media call for some explanation. One of the most compelling powers of the media is their ability to manipulate. This power can take several harmful forms: (a) media may distort reality by selective and biased presentations; (b) may treat an audience as a means to an end rather than as an end in itself; (c) may provide audiences with programmes that aim at satisfying antisocial drives (sex, violence, racial prejudices and hatreds, etc.); and, finally (d) may lull audiences with dreams and illusions (soap operas, sentimental serials, etc.).

The longer-run cultural effects of the media might be called integrative. At the national level, particularly in countries with a heterogeneous population, the media may be employed to create a national identity and culture. The diffusion of a dominant language and belief system together with the spread of common artistic expressions contributes to national integration. Within broader geographic boundaries such as western Europe, the media may strengthen the bonds of regional consciousness and co-operation. Internationally, unfortunately, the media has created a media-culture of light and vapid entertainment programmes. The world may not have become what Marshall McLuhan has termed 'a global village' but is well on its way to becoming 'a global circus'. The media's role in creating the bonds of a world community may be subject to arguments, but its role in creating instant awareness of a dozen events and cultural symbols in the minds of millions throughout the world is beyond doubt.

Summary and Conclusions

The role of mass media in the national development of less developed countries has been a subject of considerable debate (Schramm, 1964; Pool, 1963; Lerner, 1963; McQuail, 1972; Pool et al., 1973; Elliott and Golding, 1974; Golding, 1974; Lerner and Schramm, 1967). Those who have suggested an autonomous role for the mass media as a generator of social change are opposed by those who consider communications as a dependent variable. The two sides are not irreconcilable if we consider development as a dialectical process of social change in which, to have an effect, every idea or experience transmitted by mass media must have its counterpart in social reality. In the absence of such linkages between media and other social institutions, a dialectical process of change begins in which the role of opinion leaders (in the terminology of this paper, the communications monitors) is of crucial importance. The effect of the media in the process of national development depends vitally on how closely the media work with or against opinion leaders who are safeguarding traditional ideas and institutions or pioneering new ones. In other words, a multi-step flow model of social communication that recognizes the existence of many different epistemic communities is more relevant to communication policy than a one-step or two-step flow.

Communications and National Development

Without assuming an ethnocentric view of social change, one may still identify the key generators, deterrents and determinants of national development as suggested in this essay. The media may pursue either of the following three strategies: (a) It may assume an unaware or unconcerned posture vis-a-vis the historical conflicts which the developmental process generates. Some commercial systems committed to the profit principle and some public systems committed to formalist principles, often follow this line of policy. (b) It may, with a strongly partisan view on the issues at hand, try to induce social change. Unless and until the media receives the support of genuine opinion leaders in the society at large this strategy is doomed to failure and may in fact create more social discord and alienation than was probable otherwise. (c) It may try to understand as best as it can the complex process of social change in its environment and attempt to soften and sometimes to resolve the ensuing contradictions. This strategy is perhaps the most intelligent and most difficult to assume since it hinges upon the good will and understanding of the media's sponsors. The adoption of this strategy is made even more difficult by the fact that the media's sponsors are themselves party to the social conflicts at issue and are, therefore, tempted to manipulate the media for their own ends.

The role of communication in rapidly developing societies is further complicated by the fact that a huge historical transition is being condensed within a few decades. This transition involves a revolutionary process of change in economic, political and communications structures. The transition from self-sufficiency to commodity production for the markets, from political subjugation to citizenship and participation, from oral to multi-media communication systems is not a simple or harmonious process. The sequences, lags, advances and contradictions of this process have already given rise to some problems unique to the conditions of these countries. The availability of relatively cheap technologies of medical care and maeeoedia has already produced a population explosion and a state of what might be called 'communications shock'. The latter phenomenon may be characterized by a 'prismatic mass culture' that has few roots in the people's past cultural heritage, small links with their present life situation and fewer links with their future aspirations. The media's contribution to this 'dualistic culture of underdevelopment' is that it broadcasts news, entertainments and even cultural programmes that suit other times and other places.

From the foregoing comments we conclude that the fundamental function of a responsible media system in the process of national development should be the following: (a) to recognize the needs/demands as well as the constraints and possibilities of the socio-cultural environment; (b) to tailor policies and programmes closely to respond to concrete social, economic and cultural needs; (c) to work closely with opinion leaders and institutions in a position to co-operate in the performance of the media's duties; and, finally, (d) to maintain a high level of awareness, autonomy and responsibility so as to safeguard its credibility and effectiveness vis-à-vis opinion leaders and the general audience.

Note

1 The following sections are a revised version of an earlier publication of Tehranian (1974, 50-67).

References

Almond, Gabriel A. and Coleman, James S., eds (1960), *The Politics of the Developing Areas*, Princeton University Press.

Almond, Gabriel A. and Powell, G. Bingham, Jr. (1966), *Comparative Politics: A Development Approach*, Boston: Little, Brown.

Baran, Paul M. (1957), *The Political Economy of Growth*, New York: Monthly Review Press.

Berger, Peter and Luckmann, Thomas (1966), *The Social Construction of Reality*, Penguin Books.

Buckley, Walter (1968), 'Society as a complex adaptive system', in *Modern Systems Research for the Behavioral Scientist: A Sourcebook*, ed. Walter Buckley, Chicago: Aldine.

Deutsch, Karl W. (1948-9), 'Some notes on research on the role of models in natural and social science', *Synthese*, 532.

Deutsch, Karl W. (1966), *Nationalism and Social Communication: an Inquiry into the Foundations of Nationality*, Cambridge, Mass.: MIT Press.

Easton, David (1953), *The Political System: An Inquiry into the State of Political Science*, New York: Knopf.
Easton, David (1965a), *A Framework for Political Analysis*, Englewood Cliffs: Prentice-Hall.
Easton, David (1965b), *A Systems Analysis of Political Life*, New York: Wiley.
Elliot, Philip and Golding, Peter (1974), 'Mass communication and social change: the imagery of development and the development of imagery', in *Sociology and Development*, ed. Emanuel de Kadt and Gavin Williams, London: Tavistock.
Golding, Peter (1974), 'Media role in national development: critique of a theoretical orthodoxy', *Journal of Communication*, 24 (3), Summer.
Hagen, Everett E. (1962), *On the Theory of Social Change*, Homewood, Ill.: Dorsey Press.
Hagen, Everett E. (1968), *The Economics of Development*, Homewood: Richard D. Irwin.
Higgins, Benjamin (1968), *Economic Development: Problems, Principles and Policies*, New York: Norton.
Huntington, Samuel P. (1965), 'Political development and political decay', *World Politics*, 17 (3), pp. 386-411.
Lerner, Daniel (1958), *The Passing of Traditional Society*, Chicago: Free Press.
Lerner, Daniel (1963), 'Toward a communication theory of modernization', in *Communications and Political Development*, ed. L. W. Pye, Princeton University Press.
Lerner, Daniel and Schramm, Wilbur, eds (1967), *Communication and Change in the Developing Countries*, Honolulu: East-West Center Press.
Lewis, Oscar (1961), *The Children of Sanchez*, New York: Random House.
McClelland, David (1953), *The Achieving Society*, Princeton: Van Nostrand.
McQuail, Denis, ed. (1972), *Sociology of Mass Communication*, Penguin Books.
Mannheim, Karl (1929), *Ideology and Utopia: an Introduction to the Sociology of Knowledge*, London: Routledge & Kegan Paul.
Maslow, Abraham Harold (1954), *Motivation and Personality*, New York: Harper & Row.
Moore, Barrington, Jr. (1966), *Social Origins of Dictatorship and Democracy: Lord and Peasant in the Making of the Modern World*, Boston: Beacon Press.
Nurkse, Ragner (1953), *Problems of Capital Formation in Underdeveloped Countries*, Oxford: Blackwell.
Parsons, Talcott (1960), *Structure and Process in Modern Societies*, Chicago: Free Press.

Parsons, Talcott and Shils, Edward A. eds (1962), *Toward A General Theory of Action*, Cambridge, Mass.: Harvard University Press.

Pool, Ithiel de Sola (1963), 'The role of communication in the process of modernization and technological change',: *Industrialization and Society*, ed. Bert Hoselitz and Wilbert E. Moore, The Hague: Mouton, pp. 279-95.

Pool, Ithiel de Sola, et al. (1973), *Handbook of Communication*, Chicago: Rand McNally.

Pye, Lucian W. (1966), *Aspects of Political Development*, Boston: Little, Brown.

Rapoport, Anatol and Horvath, William J. (1959), 'Thoughts on organization theory', *General Systems*, 4, 87-91.

Riesman, David and Glazer, Sidney (1950), *The Lonely Crowd*, New York: Doubleday Anchor.

Rogers, Everett M. and Shoemaker, F. Floyd (1970), *Communication of Innovations*, New York: Free Press.

Rostow, Walt W. (1960), *The Stages of Economic Growth*, Cambridge University Press.

Schramm, Wilbur (1964), *Mass Media and National Development: the Role of Information in Developing Countries*, Stanford University Press.

Smith, Adam (1776), *An Inquiry into the Nature and Causes of the Wealth of Nations*, New York: Modern Library.

Teheranian, Majid (1974), *Toward A Systemic Theory of National Development*, Tehran: Industrial Management Institute.

Tocqueville, Alexis De (1835), *Democracy in America*, 2 vols, New York: *Phillips Bradley*, 1945, Knopf.

Weber, Max (1904-5), *The Protestant Ethic and the Spirit of Capitalism*, trans. Talcott Parsons (1930), London: Allen & Unwin.

2
Communications Policy and Planning
A Comparative Perspective with
Particular Emphasis on Broadcasting
Edward W. Ploman

Introduction

Broadcasting has aptly been described as an activity in a state of continuous crisis. The wider field of communications may similarly be characterized in one word: confusion.

The reasons for this state of affairs are as manifold as its expressions. An immediately striking feature is the general lack of coherent planning except in isolated sectors or for limited aspects. This should not surprise. The planning effort has been hampered by the absence of comprehensive, clearly articulated communication policies. Recently, however, there has been an emerging recognition of the need to study, formulate and find agreement on basic policies integrated in a wider social context.

The current difficulties in defining such policies seem explicable enough. Traditional approaches and frameworks have proved inadequate. Slightly more advanced theoretical insights, changes in social values and economic conditions, and a rapidly evolving technology are forcing us to take a new look at the entire communications/information complex.

Already initial reappraisals have shown that, at this stage, we are not well equipped to deal with communications in a comprehensive enough manner to cover the whole gamut of involved phenomena, from electronics to copyright. We also seem to find it difficult to relate the communications sector in a meaningful way to other sectors and activities in society.

In so far as they are articulated, much is made of policies adopted for various media or for certain aspects of telecommunications. However, these policies are often formulated and implemented by different bodies in pursuit of limited, unco-ordinated and sometimes contradictory objectives. The lack of co-ordination becomes particularly serious when media and telecommunication policies, whether implicit or explicit, are not linked to general development policies.

Confusion, then, becomes the rule rather than the exception. At the international level, it is not unusual to see governments, on the same or similar issues, maintain one attitude in the United Nations, another in the International Telecommunications Union (ITU) a third in UNESCO and if required, a fourth in the World Intellectual Property Organization (WIPO).[1]

It is therefore not surprising that attitudes towards new communications technology are contradictory. Euphoric, technology-based forecasts provide as little guidance as equally exaggerated anxieties. The evaluation of the social consequences of new communications systems is no less confused: some fear an electronic Big Brother or the Global Village at the same time as others, with equal fear, foresee a lack of social cohesion through utter fragmentation of audiences and producer entities.

However, in many respects it is the advance of technology which itself is a major cause for a changing perspective in communications. The speed and scope of technical innovation has forced us to focus on the social implications of introducing new technology. We have come to realize that engineers and technicians have related their work to one branch, one mode of communication only, without any overall view. The most obvious feature in present communication services is in fact the paraphernalia of technical devices, each serving a single purpose: telephones, radio sets, record players, teleprinters, photocopiers, television receivers, videotape recorders... Each piece of equipment is generally linked to only one communication service which in turn is associated with a specific transmission or distribution system, each often with its own legal and institutional framework and mode of financing. Our technology-based approach in communication has been amply revealed: technology, and not policy nor social requirements, has, to a large extent, determined developments.

One major factor in the new attitude to communications is

Communications Policy and Planning

thus an interest in the organization of the communication systems themselves. Such considerations have led to a different approach in dealing with the possibilities and implications of new technology. Instead of trying once again to evaluate a list of devices and gadgets already available or on the drawing-board, attempts should be made to discern the trends in these developments and to judge how they coincide—or can be made to coincide—with social and cultural priorities.

There is, however, emerging a new field of research, study and discussion which so far goes under the name of 'telecommunications policy research' or 'communications policy research'.

Whatever the agreed-upon definitions are in terms of policy and planning, telecommunications can no longer be considered in a vacuum, apart from other systems used for the transport of ideas—or for that matter for the transport of people carrying the ideas. Electronic communication patterns must therefore be studied in conjunction with the mail service, the circulation of printed material and also, in a wider perspective, in relation to transport and to urban and regional planning. If nothing else, the paper crisis should have taught us that the kind of basic question to be asked is whether we can or should or must use electronics instead of paper for certain kinds of information transfer.

If, at one end of the scale, telecommunications has a close connection with transport and physical planning, at the other end of the scale it merges with 'mass communication' and 'mass media' in classical and new guises. Here one finds that the strict distinction between traditional categories of communication services tends to blur; the concept of 'mass media' is being questioned and extended to a degree which makes clear the need for new concepts and policies.

Recent legislation in a number of countries has tried to grapple with some of these issues together with the consequences of changing social attitudes. Since there is no generally accepted theoretical framework, current policy debate is to a large extent concerned with basic concepts and definitions. Much effort is also lavished on the creation of institutions which can serve as tools for the formulation of policy and planning. The few traditional institutional models do not seem to be adequate; some of the new forms are interesting but too recent to allow any conclusive evidence.

These issues seem particularly acute in 'developing' societies. The more rapid the rate of development, the more crucial the need for study and clear definition of objectives and policies. Also, the communications sector will have to take on greater responsibilities in rapidly developing societies, since response to the speed of change in such sectors as education and culture will be inadequate or too slow.

There is evolving a new awareness of certain factors that so far have almost totally been left out of policy considerations on the future of communications. A relatively new approach studies the relationship between communication systems and man as an organic information system, man as a receiver-transformer-transmitter of information. It implies a focus on the biological aspects of communication: the functioning and basic structure of the central nervous system, the frequency of its malfunctioning and the capacity of the individual to deal with information transmitted over different communication systems.

In this perspective, major issues are information under-nourishment and information overstimulation or overload; the distinction to be made is between 'real information' resulting from an active participation in the information process and 'pseudo-information' or 'noise' in the sense of a constant flow of passively received, fragmented, unstructured information acting as a kind of visual and acoustic pollution.

Following this line of thought, communication policies and planning must be formulated in terms of the information flows between the individual and the total environment, physical as well as social.

Such an approach would be similar to the one now emerging in education exemplified by such expressions as the 'learning environment' or the 'educational function of the environment'. In communications, an 'ecological' approach has so far not been pursued. Little attention has been paid to the total information environment of individuals and groups; instead we

Communications Policy and Planning

are handed the abstractions of the 'newspaper reader', 'radio listener' or 'television viewer' who in real life are individuals using all or some of the available media or communication systems as part of their total information environment.

It would be useful to complement this concept of the information environment of individuals—or groups of individuals—with the concept of the communication ecology of societies. Both concepts are needed for an overall approach which can include all factors relevant for the discussion and formulation of policy as a basis for planning. Admittedly, the framework is large. However, without such a wide approach it seems impossible even to formulate the right questions.

There is a need to put communications in a proper global perspective. In a situation characterized by a series of new and unprecedented challenges—of energy and raw materials, of population and environment, of new economic and social relations, of changes in the pace and objectives of development—we need to consider what kind of communications systems and information flows are required nationally and internationally. This is the background proposed for an evaluation of present attempts at communications policy formulation and planning. It will be seen that only in rare cases has a wide perspective characterized this work but it is the standard against which current efforts must be judged.

Institutional Structures and Framework

General

A major problem in the formulation of communications policy is the present lack of an adequate framework, conceptual and institutional.

Broadcasting provides a practical example of these problems. In one sense, broadcasting is a radio communications service to be regulated in terms of telecommunications generally. If broadcasting is to be carried out via satellites, a new field must be added which includes the evolving concepts in space law. In another sense, radio and television are mass media to be dealt with in relation to measures adopted for other media and, ideally, in relation to information, educational and cultural policies.

The situation becomes even more complicated when broadcasting techniques are used in new ways, such as the distribution of text information (CEEFAX, ORACLE and similar systems). And how is the combination of telefacsimile and broadcasting to be handled?

One of the main difficulties is that each of the areas involved has developed separately, with its own traditions, its own legal, structural and policy framework. Further problems arise when broadcasting is considered in terms of economic and social development, when the relation between communications media and development policy and planning becomes a crucial factor.

Obviously, the structures and institutions set up to deal with communications vary from country to country, even more from region to region. However, looking at the operation of modern communication systems, only a limited number of models are actually applied:

— telecommunications are run according to some few basic models which roughly can be described as lying along a scale ranging from state undertakings via public corporations to private, commercial enterprises; in all cases, however, certain telecommunications matters are regarded as a national task to be regulated by a central government (e.g., frequency allocations);

— similarly, broadcasting services may be classified in some few groups: they are run mainly as local, national or federal services; they are financed through advertising, licence fees or government grants; they are operated as commercial, public or government services.

The same seems to be true about the policy-making machinery. Roughly speaking, only three models appear to be applied in the world:

— communications policy is left to already existing institutions and carried out on a sectoral basis;

Communications Policy and Planning

— special bodies are set up on a permanent basis to deal with overall policy and regulatory issues in more or less specified areas;

— special *ad hoc* temporary committees, commissions, inquiries, etc., are set up to study specific aspects, with the objective of proposing policy and legislation.

Communications policy formulated on a sectoral basis

In those cases where the formulation of communications policy is left to already existing bodies, the responsibility is divided among a number of entities—usually, traditionally defined ministries.

The overall responsibility for telecommunications is—often together with the postal services—handled by a Ministry of Communications (or Post and Telecommunications) to which operating agencies are responsible. Broadcasting is often placed under a Ministry of Information, which in many cases also acts as the official public information body of the government. In countries without this type of information structure, broadcasting can be found under various ministries such as Education, Culture, Interior or even Public Works. Other relevant aspects are dealt with by the ministries responsible for legal questions, foreign affairs, education, etc.

This model has been extensively applied, in industrialized and developing countries alike. How well it has worked is open to question. It is characterized by fragmentation and by an often narrow concept of communications which encompasses no more than the classical telecommunications services defined according to technical criteria. In the perspective of a new and more comprehensively defined communications concept, this model does not seem adequate. A stimulating exception is the work undertaken by the National Telecommunications Planning Branch of the Australian Telecommunications Commission, in looking to the future of telecommunications in Australia over the next twenty-five years (for further information see p. 72).

The situation of broadcasting, uneasily perched between telecommunications and the press, is one example of the difficulties inherent in this model. It is interesting to note that in many countries broadcasting started as an adjunct to existing telecommunication services and emerged as an activity in its own right only after long and often protracted struggles for autonomy in relation to telecommunication authorities. It seems ironic that the trend to provide for broadcasting a status similar to that of the press occurs at a moment when the print media themselves are moving towards electronics.

Another more general and serious issue of this sectoral approach concerns the co-ordination of policies in the communications sector and overall development policy and planning. A classical example is the difficulty in planning and co-ordinating the telecommunication, broadcasting and education sectors with regard to the introduction of new educational technology such as ETV. However, this problem is no more than a specific instance in the wider context of general economic and social development. The effective use of communications for development purposes presupposes co-ordination between all sectors requiring the delivery of social and cultural services through available and planned channels of communication: thus, not only the traditionally defined education sector but also health, agriculture, vocational training, community development, etc. are concerned. If communications are to serve such varied purposes, the need for high-level and comprehensive co-ordination for policy and planning becomes obvious as does the need for an adequate policy-making structure.

Permanent special policy-making bodies

North America

The classical examples of permanent bodies specifically created to deal with communications policy and regulation are to be found in North America.

In the United States, the responsibility for communications policy and regulation is divided between the States and the Federal government. The federal agencies are the most

Communications Policy and Planning

interesting in this context. Jurisdiction over wire and radio communications was at various times handled by the Department of Commerce, Post Office Department, Inter-state Commission and the Federal Radio Commission. In 1934 all the regulatory functions were handed to a single agency set up by the Communications Act: the Federal Communications Commission (FCC).

The FCC is enjoined primarily to provide for orderly development and operation of radio services, to make available a rapid, efficient, nation-wide and world-wide telegraph and telephone service at reasonable cost. Its major activities include allocation of frequency bands to all non-government communication services and assigning frequencies to individual stations; licensing and regulating broadcasting stations and operators and common carriers engaged in inter-state and foreign communication.

Judgments on the value and performance of the FCC have varied considerably. Seen from the outside, this system has appeared to many observers to be an advance over the sectoral approach. In the internal American discussion, a number of shortcomings and risks have been pointed out. According to some, the Commission has become an instrument for those interests it was supposed to regulate; according to others, it has not formulated policy as required.

In many respects Canada seems to be the country which has gone further than any other in its attempts to formulate comprehensive national communications policies. It is significant that the Broadcasting Act of 1968 is described as 'an Act to implement a broadcasting policy for Canada'. By means of this Act a special body was created, the Canadian Radio-Television Commission (CRTC), to 'regulate and supervise all aspects of the Canadian broadcasting system' with a view to implementing the broadcasting policy enunciated in the Act. The CRTC is responsible not only for over-air broadcasting but also for cable television. This follows from the fact that broadcasting is defined in the Act so as to include cable installations and that cable television has been declared an integral part of the Canadian broadcasting system.

Edward W. Ploman

Developing countries
Variations of this model have been adopted in a number of developing countries, mainly in Latin America.

In Argentina, the National Telecommunications Law of 1972 established a National Telecommunications Council (Consejo Nacional de Telecommunicaciones, CONATEL). According to the law, CONATEL shall 'orient, co-ordinate, promote and encourage the development, intervene with regard to the authorizations and taxation of telecommunications activities'. It is particularly mentioned that the Council shall participate in the formulation of the national telecommunications policy and intervene in the co-ordination of the telecommunications plans in order to serve the national policy and strategy. Apart from giving detailed information concerning the tasks of the Council, the law also prescribes its composition: a president who shall be the Secretary of Communications and one representative each from the Ministries of Foreign Affairs, Interior, Defence, Public Works and Communication, Culture and Education, Joint Chiefs of Staff, and the Planning Secretariat. Broadcasting matters are handled by a Federal Broadcasting Committee in the President's Office. It consists of one president and eight members nominated by the executive in accordance with proposals from the concerned ministries. The Committee has the regulatory powers in broadcasting matters including the issue of licences to radio and television stations.

The Brazilian government has given a high priority to telecommunications. According to the present four-year development plan, investment in telecommunications is to be more than 50 per cent higher than investment in electric power. The organization of the telecommunications sector has been subject to a number of far-reaching changes during recent years. Until the early 1960s, telecommunications development was carried out 'unsystematically' by a number of private companies. In 1962 a 'Brazilian Telecommunications Code' was adopted which generated a number of additional measures, such as a national plan of telecommunications, as well as the creation of a number of controlling and executive bodies. The National Council of Telecommunications (CONTEL) func-

Communications Policy and Planning

tioned directly under the President as a regulatory and policy-making body, responsible also for broadcasting. A special public company, EMBRATEL, became responsible for the installation and operation of the planned national telecommunications system, the national television network and the Brazilian participation in international systems.

A major reorganization took place in 1972 with the establishment of a Ministry of Communications. All telecommunications enterprises were grouped under a new entity, TELEBRAS (Telecomunicações Brasileiras), in the form of a holding company which is mainly responsible for planning, co-ordination, training and research. Other telecommunication enterprises are being set up in each state for the developments of local telecommunications while EMBRATEL continues its work on the inter-state networks and in the international sector.

Advisory bodies

Of a different kind are permanent bodies that serve as advisers to governments on various aspects of communications.

Such bodies have been set up in both industrialized and developing countries. Their functions show great variations in underlying concept and approach. Some are mandated to advise on telecommunication matters; others deal with 'the media' in general, and still others with all audio-visual means of communication from cinema and broadcasting to cable, videograms and community video.

Even granting national differences in requirements and priorities, these advisory bodies reveal the lack of a generally recognized theoretical framework. Moreover, there does not seem to be one example of an advisory body which provides guidance in terms of a comprehensive communications policy.

Other specialized bodies

In recent years there has been a growing recognition of the need to deal in a coherent way with the use of communications in support of development planning and projects. A number of countries have established—or are moving towards—more formalized structures for 'development support communication'.

In some cases the development support communication bureaux are centrally located in the Ministries of Information and/or Planning (operational in Indonesia and Iran; proposed in Guyana, Jamaica and Jordan). In others, these activities have been given a base in sectoral ministries, such as rural and agricultural sectors (operational in Mexico, Peru and Iraq; proposed in Cameroon, Gambia, Ghana, Bolivia, Colombia, Egypt and Morocco); or population/health/family planning sectors (Kenya and Thailand). In Nepal and Sri Lanka it is proposed that both the planning and agricultural sectors be involved.

Temporary bodies concerned with policy formulation

In many countries the required policy formulation has not been achieved through the kind of institutions mentioned above. This seems to be true whether a single ministry or several ministries are responsible for policy and planning or whether there are special regulatory or advisory bodies.

The appointment of Committees or Commissions of Inquiry into a specific area of national activity for the formulation of policy and planning proposals is well known in many countries. One of the earliest attempts at the formulation of a national communications policy was made in the USA. In a message to Congress on 14 August 1967, President Johnson transmitted recommendations concerning the American position with regard to Intelsat as well as a number of domestic communications issues. A Task Force on Communications Policy was established which was requested to study, *inter alia*, which new technology could meet present and future communications requirements in the most effective and efficient manner. The relatively wide range of subject matters covered by this Task Force made their report an ambitious attempt to come to grips with at least part of the new communications landscape.

Of great general interest is the Telecommission in Canada,

Communications Policy and Planning

which represents the most thorough, open-minded and lively investigation on telecommunications undertaken anywhere. In September 1969, the Minister of Communications announced plans for a comprehensive study of the present state and future prospects of telecommunications in Canada. The more than forty separate studies organized by the Directing Committee were grouped under eight headings:
— legal considerations
— economic considerations
— international considerations
— technological studies
— information and data systems
— telecommunications environment
— telecommunications and government
— special studies.

The general report was published in 1971 under the title 'Instant World'. It sets out the background to the problems facing policy-makers and discusses the social aspects of telecommunications, the history of telecommunications in Canada and its importance for the development of the country. It defines government responsibility in protecting public interest in the communications field.

The Telecommission and its report remain an exemplary but unfortunately rare attempt to provide the basis both for public discussion and for policy formulation. It says much for the foresight and unorthodox attitude of the Canadian authorities that the Telecommission includes such aspects as telecommunications and the arts and that a major effort was made through seminars, conferences and meetings to involve large segments of the population in the discussion.

Following the report of the Telecommission and the publication of its policy proposals in April 1975, the Federal government, through the Minister of Communications, has taken steps to implement a number of proposals made. The Provinces have been invited to join in the establishment of a Committee for Communications Policy, consisting of the Federal and provincial ministers responsible for communications. This Committee deals with such matters of common concern as system planning, inter-provincial and international services and technical standards. In addition, the Federal government will help to support an Association of Communications Regulatory Bodies which would study such matters as economic criteria for regulation, and harmonization of regulatory practices. Parliament will be asked to enact measures to revise and consolidate existing Federal legislation concerning communications. The first stage, for which legislation has already been introduced, will concern the establishment of a single regulatory body to exercise the powers and functions of the CRTC and the Telecommunications Committee of the Canadian Transport Commission (which exercises regulatory authority over telephone and telegraph companies). The intention is to streamline the Federal machinery for communications policy and regulation. A second-stage legislation would entail a complete revision of existing statutes with a view to clarifying their application to contemporary and future modes of communication and to establishing a coherent body of federal law on communications.

International organizations

In the communications and media field, a number of international organizations play an increasingly important role in policy formulation, adoption of international legal principles, planning and research.

United Nations

The United Nations involvement in matters related to communications and information concerns a number of vital issues, mainly with regard to political, legal and development-related aspects:

(a) Work in the field of human rights is exemplified by the Universal Declaration of Human Rights (1948), the covenants on Civil and Political Rights (1966) and on Economic, Social and Cultural Rights (1966). The relevant dispositions in these conventions concern various aspects of freedom of information. Within the UN framework, efforts have also been made on a

Communications Policy and Planning

draft Convention on Freedom of Information; this work, however, has not advanced for over a decade due to conflicting ideologies.

(b) The formulation and adoption of space law has taken place exclusively in the UN. The basic text is the Outer Space Treaty of 1967, which is also applicable to satellite communication. Important principles are also to be found in a number of General Assembly resolutions, and in the current work on legal principles for satellite broadcasting.

(c) In conjunction with such organizations as the United Nations Development Programme (UNDP), the World Bank and the International Telecommunications Union (ITU), the UN is actively engaged in projects and studies concerning the planning and development of communications infrastructure, media institutions, etc., in developing countries.

(d) The UNDP as well as such agencies as FAO and UNICEF also take an active part in projects concerning development support communication.

International Telecommunications Union

The activities of the ITU concern mainly regulation, planning and development.

(a) The bases for ITU's regulatory action are the decisions made by various Administrative Conferences, the Plenipotentiary Conference and the IFRB (International Frequency Registration Board), one of its permanent organs. The most obvious features of this activity are the allocation of frequency bands and adoption of procedures and other rules incorporated in the Radio Regulations.

(b) The planning aspect is handled by a number of bodies established within the ITU framework. This work concerns the establishment of regional networks and also planning of a world network. Special conferences deal with the use of certain frequency bands such as the 1977 conference on satellite broadcast systems in the 12 GHz band.

(c) The ITU acts as the executive agency for telecommunications projects in developing countries, and also undertakes other projects on its own.

Edward W. Ploman

United Nations Educational, Scientific and Cultural Organization (UNESCO)

UNESCO's mandate in the communications field covers a number of different aspects.

(a) 'Normative' action mainly concerns the 'free flow of information': a number of agreements have been concluded under UNESCO's aegis such as the so-called Florence and Beirut Agreements on circulation of educational, scientific and cultural materials.

(b) In its communication programme, UNESCO includes activities related to the promotion of national communications policy and planning, as well as a research programme intended to support these activities.

(c) In terms of assistance to member states, UNESCO acts in such areas as training and research, studies on various aspects of communications development and planning, activities related to the use of new media and technologies in education, etc.

(d) Applicable to the media is also another field of UNESCO activities concerned with cultural policies. Of particular relevance to the media are resolutions adopted by the Inter-Governmental Conferences on Cultural Policies, held in Venice, Helsinki and Accra.

World Intellectual Property Organization (WIPO).

Another field of great importance concerns intellectual property rights. The organization primarily responsible in this area is WIPO which, with regard to certain conventions, co-operates with UNESCO and ILO. The main applicable conventions are the Berne Convention, the Universal Copyright Convention and the Rome Convention; special conventions have also been concluded on the protection of phonograms and of television programmes transmitted via satellites.

Developments in new technologies have led to a growing realization of a need for a major reappraisal of legislation in this field and the introduction of new and more adequate concepts and laws.

Communications Policy and Planning

Recent Measures: Legislation, Public Inquiries

General

Whatever the actual structures in communications—whether telecommunications or media—recent action taken in many countries seems to prove that they have been found inadequate.

Much of the policy formation and planning effort have gone into providing new legislative frameworks for the operation of various communication services. This activity has been particularly obvious in broadcasting but has also included the reorganization of telecommunications structures, new mass media legislation, intellectual property rights, protection of privacy in connection with the use of data-banks, etc.

There have also been important policy statements as a basis for regulatory action, generally on some specific aspect of communications: for example, in the USA the Federal Communication Commission (FCC) policy statements on cable television and President Nixon's policy statement on domestic satellite systems, and in Canada the Government Green Paper of 1975 dealing in overall terms with the entire regulatory machinery in communications. In a number of other countries official commissions are presently at work on different sectors or aspects of communications.

Some examples follow of these activities, with particular emphasis on broadcasting, since in this area there have recently been a number of attempts at solving major policy and planning issues in new ways.

Recent legislation

Mention has already been made of the restructuring of telecommunications in Brazil. Another kind of reorganization was introduced in 1975 in Australia, where the Australian Post Office was divided into two organizations, one responsible for postal services and the other for telecommunication services.

Broadcasting has recently been restructured in a number of countries such as the UK (introduction of commercial local radio) and Sweden (establishment of a special corporation for local radio). In New Zealand, Austria, Italy and France the entire broadcasting systems have been reorganized; the most radical change occurred in France where the previous highly centralized system was broken up into separate organizations, each responsible for certain aspects of broadcasting, and into a number of controlling and advisory bodies. A move in the opposite direction has been announced in Nigeria: the present television system with both Federal and provincial stations will be 'federalized' so as to provide for more co-ordination of resources. Another step has recently been taken in India, where television has been taken out of All India Radio.

Many of the concerns that have found expression in actual or proposed legislation also form the basis for the mandates of public inquiries.

Current investigations

A few examples of current investigations will be mentioned in order to show differences in approach and concepts.

Three Committees of Inquiry into media and media-related questions are currently at work in the United Kingdom. The Royal Commission on the Press is 'to inquire into the factors affecting the maintenance of the independence, diversity and editorial standards of newspapers and periodicals, and the public's freedom of choice of newspapers and periodicals, nationally, regionally and locally'. The Annan Committee, named after its chairman, deals with the future of broadcasting. A third committee is considering possible changes in copyright legislation in view of new technical developments and recent revisions of international conventions.

In Germany the authorities decided on another approach: namely to concentrate on the development of the telecommunications system. The commission set up for this purpose in 1973 reported at the beginning of 1976.

In Sweden, official enquiries on the media have proliferated and now cover new legislation on freedom of expression in all the media, the future role and structure of both educational and general broadcasting, the financial condition of the press, the effects of business concentration in mass media, the role and use of advertising and a number of more specific issues.

Communications Policy and Planning

Issues

Technological

The opportunities and challenges of new communications technologies and services provide the immediate reason for a re-examination of policies and systems.

Several attempts have been made to provide an overview of current technology and services with a forecast of possible and probable developments. Typical examples are the technological parts of the already mentioned studies performed by the President's Task Force on Telecommunications in the USA and the Telecommission in Canada. Other recent examples are the Television Advisory Committee in the United Kingdom, the Finnish expert committee on communications policy, the studies undertaken by the National Iranian Radio and Television and the report known as Telecom 2000 in Australia.

(a) Much of the recent policy and planning efforts have been in relation to satellite communication whose dimensions, both in practical and institutional terms are such as to require a comprehensive approach. Among them should be noted:

— the preparation for the Satellite Instructional Television Experiment (SITE) which started in India in August 1975;

— the comprehensive study undertaken by the Spanish-speaking countries of South America with the assistance of UNDP, UNESCO and the ITU, on a regional educational system, using advanced technology including satellites (SERLA—Sistema Regional de Teleeducacion para los Paises de America del Sur). This feasibility study is expected to be published in 1976;

— studies aimed at the establishment of a regional Arab satellite system conducted by a number of Arab regional organizations, partly with the assistance of ITU and UNESCO;

— studies, both official and private, concerning various forms of satellite communication in the United States, Canada and Japan, particularly with regard to domestic systems;

— policy and planning studies conducted in Europe with regard to a common European satellite system (ESRO, CEPT, EBU, etc.), the joint French-German system Symphonie, and national level studies (Federal Republic of Germany).

(b) The development of computer technology and the issues raised by the integration of computers into the telecommunications network, data transmission and processing have led to considerable planning efforts in the technical field.

As an example of policy issues of major concern, those discussed at a recent OECD Conference on Computer-Telecommunications Policy may be mentioned:

— what are the implications of computers and telecommunication systems for social development?

— if countries are to derive maximum social benefits from the applications of computer-telecommunications, what are the implications for the allocation of national resources?

— could the public be better served by new market structures for computers/telecommunications?

— what is required to ensure harmonious development of these technologies and to avoid disparities among countries?

(c) The advent and rapid growth of cable television in the United States and Canada has led to the adoption of policy guidelines and has had a considerable impact on the whole field of mass communication.

Apart from such incidents as cable and politics in combination causing the downfall of a government in Italy, cable television has not been a major issue in Europe until recently. A number of European countries have authorized limited experiments in the use of cable television for purposes other than distribution of regular broadcast programmes (France, Netherlands, Sweden, UK), but so far the results of these experiments have been inconclusive.

France may be mentioned as an example. Following certain policy statements by the ORTF and the PTT, a number of experiments in local programming and other more advanced cable activities were to be undertaken in six cities. However, priority has now been given to the improvement of the telephone system and to the total coverage of the national territory by all radio and television channels as well as completion of the conversion from the 819 to the more widely accepted 625 CCIR standard.

Communications Policy and Planning

In Germany, cable television and teleprocessing have been specifically mentioned in the mandate of the 'Commission for the Development of the Telecommunications System'. In the Netherlands, a recent note by the Minister of Communications to Parliament gives an overview of developments in the cable area and points to probable developments and possibilities in the medium and long-range perspective.

The only other country where cable systems have been extensively introduced is Japan, where authorities support some of the most comprehensive experiments anywhere and where a great number of new and advanced communication services provided through cable systems are being tested.

(d) Since videocassettes and videodiscs do not need a telecommunications network for their distribution, there has been a tendency to deal with them more or less according to the rules and policies which are applied to the press and publishing. This has generally meant leaving them to the private sector, subject to generally applicable legislation.

In Sweden, however, it is felt that steps ought to be taken to prevent this new medium from becoming exclusively exploited by commercial enterprises. The government has set up a public company which, if required, could initiate videogram production and distribution, particularly in the educational field. Moreover, the government has called for an inquiry into issues raised by advertising in videograms, which is part of a major study on policies concerning advertising in general.

National communications plans

It is hard to discover a national communications plan which merits that name. As far as is known, no plan in any country encompasses the entire range of activities relevant to communications. The plans that exist are generally more modest in nature. In many countries there are 'telecommunications plans' which deal with the technical infrastructure and equipment and the foreseen extension of various services. A typical example is the Venezuelan Five-Year Plan for telecommunications, 1969-73, which covers such aspects as networks for telephony

Edward W. Ploman

—local and long-distance traffic—telex, telegraphy and the needs in terms of finance, human resources, buildings, equipment, etc., to achieve a certain growth rate. Broadcasting is not included within it, nor is there co-ordination with the educational or other sectors. There are examples of a more comprehensive approach having been adopted in recent years. The Canadian experience has already been mentioned. Of great interest is the report Telecom 2000 prepared by the National Telecommunications Planning Branch (NTP) of Telecom Australia and made public in March 1976. This report, which was conceived as an examination of the capabilities and the role of telecommunications in the society of the future, is not seen as a blueprint for the planner. Its scope is wider: the purpose is to provide a guide to possible directions in Australia's future and to likely trends in demand for telecommunication facilities which the early twenty-first century will impose.

NTP was thus requested to identify future communication service needs and recommend long-term policies, strategies and plans to meet them, to recommend the role of the Australian telecommunications authority in providing services in the years ahead and to prepare the guiding technical framework. As the programme evolved, a fourth important objective was added: to foster a continuing exchange of views between the Australian Telecommunications Authority and society about the future development of telecommunications services in the country. In keeping with this comprehensive approach, the report begins with a study of social, economic and technical futures and only then proceeds to a discussion of different services and technologies: the radio frequency spectrum and mobile services; cable television, computers and communications, visual telecommunications; it also includes sections on the economic, research and planning aspects.

Media policy and planning

While concerns and issues vary from country to country, it is possible to distinguish certain main patterns and problem areas.

(a) *Definition of media: scope and role.* Broadcasting may be

Communications Policy and Planning

used as a relevant point of departure. Despite the fact that in ITU regulations broadcasting refers only to over-the-air transmission, in a number of national legislations the definition of broadcasting has been widened to include cable distribution (Canada, Sweden, etc). Even so, present broadcast legislation does not adequately cope with the implications of new technical systems such as satellites, cable, videocassettes.

Already most broadcasting organizations carry out activities which are related to, but go beyond, broadcasting: publishing of printed material for programme information and records are obvious examples; in education, broadcasting organizations have followed the trend towards a multi-media approach which has extended their activities into new fields.

Further policy issues arise from new uses of television. In the UK, new techniques for the distribution of text and graphic material such as the CEEFAX and ORACLE systems have been developed by broadcasters and are operated by them. In Germany the press argues that these techniques are not broadcasting and belong to the press. In proposals for new legislation covering all mass media, a Swedish Parliamentary Committee suggests that telefacsimile systems such as the American Homefax and the Japanese Telenews should follow the rules for printed matter, while CEEFAX and similar systems should fall under broadcasting.

(b) *Regulation, control and supervision*. The interpretation given to such expressions as media regulation and control differ, depending on political and social context. This is particularly true about rulings which relate to freedom of expression, censorship and other control measures. There are, however, a number of areas which seem of general concern.

Problems of regulation and control in the technical field arise in the relationship between telecommunication administrations or agencies, broadcasters and the operators of new communication systems such as cable television, particularly in countries where broadcasters or other communicators do not own the transmitter network. Despite the distinction which has been established in most countries between telecommunications function and media function, there remain areas of contention:

speed of introduction of new services, tariffs, operating practices.

Control in the financial field also presents difficult problems. Any system for financing broadcasting implies some kind of control, whether it be by advertisers, regulatory authorities, governments or parliaments. This issue has taken on a new and serious aspect for the public service organizations in Europe which depend on licence fees for all or a major part of their revenue. Saturation levels in receiver ownership have been reached and there are no longer automatic increases in revenue to offset steadily rising costs.

Control of programming usually represents the most hotly contested issue. Basic rules concerning programming are laid down in law, administrative regulations, broadcast charters, articles of association, agreements between governments and broadcasting organizations. Control may be placed either inside or outside the broadcasting organizations. The official mechanisms depend to a large extent on the political and cultural climate. In Austria and France rather complex systems of controlling and supervisory bodies have been set up. In France a special role has been given to Parliament in the form of an advisory standing committee, whereas in Italy the new broadcast law of 1975 foresees a very strong role for a parliamentary committee whose powers go beyond supervisory and directive functions and include involvement in the actual running and management of the broadcasting service. Considerable attention is also being paid to complaint procedures. In Sweden a special complaints body outside the broadcasting organization has existed for a long time, and recently both in Austria and France special bodies have been created by law.

(c) *Centralized and decentralized patterns of organization.* Any analysis of present patterns of centralized and decentralized structures cannot go far if it does not recognize that centralization and decentralization often co-exist. The Swedish legislation of 1966 expressly provides for competition between two television channels within one and the same organization; Italian and Austrian broadcasting laws provide for various degrees and levels of autonomy within a centralized structure;

the new French system retains a broadcast monopoly, but divides responsibility among several organizations. Conversely, decentralized, pluralistic or federally organized systems may centralize certain programme areas or functions. Apart from the network affiliation as practised in North America and many Latin American countries, there are other examples: in the UK the news service of commercial television is provided by a single entity (ITN); similarly, the West German broadcasting organizations of each State share a common national news service.

In a number of countries, programming other than news is organized according to centralized and decentralized patterns simultaneously; particularly striking examples are to be found in Holland and the Federal Republic of Germany.

In many countries there is a trend towards decentralization, with local stations providing local programming. In the case of SITE, the Indian instructional satellite experiment, transmission to the satellite originates from one point, but programmes are prepared in a number of languages at production centres in various parts of the country. The long-standing pattern of regional radio in India has also been extended to television, and such centres as Bombay, Madras and Lucknow are or will become regional production centres.

(d) *Access and participation*. During the last decade an increasingly vocal criticism of present media structures has come to the fore.

At one level it has crystallized around the issue of editorial responsibility and control, or—expressed in another way—of the relationship between management and creative staff. In a number of countries this issue has been expressed in the specific form of 'internal media freedom' and the status of journalists or writers or producers. These problems have been tackled through statutory regulation or through organizational reforms which tend towards decentralization, less hierarchical structures, more autonomy for editorial offices and programme departments.

At another level, criticism of present media structures represents a challenge of many of the social and cultural assumptions underlying the various media models currently applied. This critique comprises two fundamentally different attitudes: whether to bring about changes within the framework of existing media structures, often with particular emphasis on the control of programme content, or whether to favour change of the structures themselves.

Established broadcasting organizations are becoming more sensitive to demands for greater public participation in their decision-making and programming and for direct access to broadcast time.

There are many examples of broadcasting organizations whose policy councils include representatives of the public or of listener organizations. This is a long-standing practice in Denmark, and another example is provided by the recent Austrian legislation. A Council of Listeners and Viewers, consisting of thirty-five members appointed according to complex rules, is mandated to submit recommendations concerning programming and proposals for technical installations. The Council also elects members to certain controlling and supervisory bodies.

The regulation of broadcasting activities implies that certain institutions have the right to decide who has access to the media and under what conditions. This may take the form of 'official access' by government and other authorities for various kinds of messages (emergencies, etc.); 'functional access' for purposes of education, charity appeals, public information, etc.; and 'civil access' to provide for 'right of reply' 'right of correction'. In addition, most broadcasters provide programme forums wherein citizens who are neither employees nor experts are given an opportunity to express their views.

What used to exist as an initiative of the programmer has now become a public demand. Current concern over increased citizen participation in democratic structures has already reached the point where specific and detailed rules concerning access have become law. In Italy, the new Broadcasting Act empowers a Parliamentary Committee to regulate the right of access accorded to political groups represented in parliament, trade unions, religious denominations, local authorities, ethnic and linguistic minorities, and so on.

Communications Policy and Planning

Participation and access are aspects of a whole spectrum of citizen involvement. At one end of the spectrum the established broadcasting organizations would maintain full control over the broadcast output. At the other end, citizens would bypass established media structures and develop new social systems of communications.

At the Annual Meeting of the International Broadcast Institute in 1974, many reasons were given as to why access and participation should be essential components of a broadcasting system: mass media represent significant concentrations of power and require checks and balances; participation and access can engender public involvement and help citizens to overcome the subject/object split inherent in mass media communication. Participation in production helps to demystify electronic journalism and to make citizens more critical and conscious users of mass communication. Finally, any established media organization can reflect only a certain range of social views. In a dynamic society there are always communication needs of which the organization is unaware. Opportunities must be provided for society to hear the messages of emerging groups, in the language of those groups.

Note

1   See R. G. A. Jackson, in *A Study of the Capacity of the United Nations Development System* (p.v.): 'Inquiries have revealed example after example where departmental ministers of state have advocated policies in the governing bodies of the particular agency which concerned them that were in direct conflict with their government's policies toward the UN system as a whole.'

3
The Cultural Compass and the Transmission of Values

Abraham A. Moles

Introduction

From now on, the human being will find himself within an environment which is for the most part artificial. Contact with nature—with trees and landscapes—has been reduced for most members of western society to a rejection of socialized behaviour, to wishful thinking, to a dream or to an activity managed and enclosed into social life itself. 'Nature' has become 'artifice' to the extent that this word 'natural' has acquired the meaning of immediate, permanent, determining what is simple, spontaneous and obvious. This artificial world of objects, pictures, sounds, rules, signs and individuals is what we have come to call 'nature'. Our true 'Nature' henceforth is 'Culture'.

The only 'natural' world is the artificial world: we live inside cubes, within time schedules, agendas, urban routes, employments. As to the 'Nature' referred to with deep feelings by the seventeenth-century Encyclopedist reformers and their romantic successors, it has become or tends to become a rare, precious, sought-after and distant value. Its approach is a conquest, a product of art for which the private car (for all) and the country house (for some) are the mediators.

Thus the individual culture is, on the one hand, the artificial environment man has created for himself and, on the other, the tool by which he is able to give value to actions in order to build his autonomy or his participation. It is an extraordinarily general meaning of culture that contemporary anthropology offers us. It goes largely beyond the classical definitions: 'all

The Cultural Compass and the Transmission of Values

that man will no longer be able to forget' proposed by Margaret Mead or Albert Schweitzer, or the 'definitions by contents' which saw in Culture the more or less redundant sum of cultural elements: museums, libraries, concerts, arts and sports, summed up in a never-ending list which currently encompasses the whole relational life.

Of these tools, television, radio and press are what is commonly called the 'mass media'. They broadcast from one source a multiplicity of copies, and by this service divide the cost of the message they produce by the number of contacts. They are the dominating—should we say domineering?—elements of the cultural experience. The individual finds himself within the social mass, more or less aloof from the other individuals whom he must make a bigger and bigger effort to contact. He is locked inside his personal sphere, his *Umwelt*, which includes the family microgroup, occupation relationships or week-end friendships. The elements really present, those which are the major tools of his cultural contacts, of the sedimentation of past experiences and of tele-events within his conscience are the mass media. Among them television plays a leading role as demonstrated by countless statistical and sociological surveys.

It is within this framework that the sociologist ought to interpret the role of TV. Nevertheless, some theoreticians already foresee its fall in view of the statistically limited but rapid rise of intermedia and the rediscovery of interpersonal relationships. After having been, for economic reasons, at the service of mass media (press and television), it seems that technology will now be at the service of intermedia.

Television is now at the pinnacle of its power and has become the major reference of socialized man. 'They said it on TV' is the ritual sentence (replacing 'I read it in the newspaper'), so much so that any man foreign to television is slightly anomic: the man who doesn't own a television set is like one who, in the past, could not read.

The behaviour of the televisional man is the 'normal' behaviour; it is he who should be the subject of the sociologist's attention, of the economist's and of the culturalist's. For a long time to come (even if one can imagine the end of it) 'To Be

Abraham A. Moles

There' (Kosinski) will mean to be present at the television set, to be a televisional man.

On the Analysis of Values

Living in society is more and more living within society, since society tends to become a framework rather than a thing: it means to react adequately (Spinoza) to this composite framework including, on the one hand, the real beings with whom one is in touch and the material world of objects and services the anonymity of which is nevertheless basically socialized, and, on the other, the imaginary beings, the fluorescent ghosts that appear on our TV screen which subtly invade our mind by realizing a domain which, despite its limitation, is extraordinarily dominating.

The Coca-Cola bottle carries, in addition to an image of sterilized bottled freshness, of status and daily banality (*Zeichenträger*), a certain symbol of the American culture which has exported it. To what extent is the appearance of this bottle correlated to the existence of modern bulldozers and to the construction of motorways? Is this correlation basically necessary or is it just a 'halo' effect of the influence of a too powerful culture?

These are the questions we have to develop in our approach to cultural mechanisms and to the influence of mass media as amplifiers of culture.

Three types of value are implied in rapidly developing countries.

(a) *The values which are specific to development*, i.e., those bound to development itself, which should be promoted by social dynamics if society does not want to enter into a series of international contradictions. One can mention some of its characteristics:

— Orientation towards the future, rather than orientation towards the past.

— Mastery of signs in writing, which corresponds roughly to the mechanism of literacy.

— Idea of merit or of a promotional society, well analysed by

The Cultural Compass and the Transmission of Values

Michael Young, who defines merit as the sum of the intelligence quotient (IQ) and of personal effort and sees in it the determinant of the place of the human being in the social pyramid: M = IQ + effort.

— Idea of participation in collective welfare, i.e., of an automatic mechanism of global redistribution of riches, underlying or regimenting the individual in the social pyramid, or of social mobility as discussed by Pareto.

— Idea of critical analysis of all traditions in order to judge and to assess their present and future value.

— Such values are the basic factors of evolution that cannot be reduced or fought against without contradicting the very idea of evolution in the western way of life. The analysis of these values is the task of the philosopher, the culturalist, the moralist, and perhaps of the politician.

(b) *The spurious values* that are constantly inserted within the socio-cultural framework are present as correlations which 'accompany' the main values, but are not functionally or organically bound to the main values. Thus we may wonder whether the TV image is inseparable from the cowboy film, whether the promotional society is inseparable from the soft drink, etc. In fact, it will be one of the tasks of cultural engineering to establish what correlations exist between these factors and to identify concealed tendencies. Reference can be made here to Inkeles's work, *Becoming Modern*.

(c) *The specific values bound to the civilization of the past*, but in no way incompatible with modern life. In all countries there are those who worry about the arising of phenomena that betray the very gist of their civilization. These spurious factors are unfortunate sequels of development itself which abusively standardize and reduce the specificity of civilizations. 'What is Persian', 'What is Spanish', 'What is Brazilian', etc., are phrases which demand objective content analysis by the cultural engineer.

Within our framework in which television is the major factor of contact between human beings and the collective environment, the problem has to do with the possibility of co-existence of a technological development universe and a 'Persian way of life', a 'Brazilian way of life', a 'Spanish way of life', as distinct from the 'American way of life' so clearly imposed by the very idea of development.

It is difficult in our present state of knowledge and of cultural technology to separate the second group of values from the first. To give a typical example, the problem of violence on television does not seem—according to the results of various recent conferences, among which is the RAI's in Florence in 1973—to be intrinsically bound to the broadcasting of the American Western or to detective films, but rather to the generalized violence of a western society which is vainly looking for the means to introduce sufficient feed back into a frame from which the ancient ways of social control are disappearing but where the new ways of control have not yet taken root.

While we may be unable to disentangle the often obscure bonds between the first two groups of values, and while therefore the action of individuals responsible in this field finds itself diminished and open to criticism, the third group of values, being relatively independent of the first two, may provide a balancing effect.

This mechanism of discovery within a universe of technical civilization may lead to a return to specificity, to a search for a style of life in which the word 'tradition' is not necessarily a conservative nor an old-fashioned term. For Iran, is the acceptance of oil energy incompatible with the respect and cultivation of the art of calligraphy or the enjoyment of Persian gardens? 'Only the really new is truly traditional,' T. S. Eliot said.

It is within this framework that the whole of the media, the whole mechanism of what may be called the 'self-teaching field', may play a new part which, up to now, has not been sufficiently acknowledged. How could we grasp them and sort them out?

The Cultural Compass

We shall call 'cultural compass' the idea of establishing a comparison between 'what currently is' and 'what is going to

The Cultural Compass and the Transmission of Values

be' in a global society concerned simultaneously with (a) promoting its development and (b) upholding or developing the specific characters which belong to its culture—its history and its linguistic genesis. The problem of the role and utilization of mass media in order to reach this balance is not unique to Iran. Many countries are facing the same question. They feel the need for a reference element within their cultural data base to provide policy guidelines and to control the different sociocultural cycles which at any point in time turn Culture into a dynamic system. 'What will be' is, partially but necessarily, determined by 'what currently is'. From the very point of view of individuals' creativeness and not from mere inheritance we do not live in a cultural vacuum.

The cultural compass is based on the comparison between two distinct types of data by the methods of content analysis which, while discarding the specificity of information, distills those general features that influence permanently the mental frame of whoever is submitted to them. These two types of data are:

1. The world of current culture: what exists within the cultural context, the continually increasing amount of knowledge and clichés, the experience of a country or of a civilization. At any one time they are stored, as we have already pointed out, in libraries, museums or art galleries as well as in institutes of anthropology, towns and countryside, and, more subtly, in legends, archetypes, ways of life, cooking, the achievements of the past and the present, architectural and urbanistic styles, occupation as patterns of space and time, and values which underlie the efforts of all individuals. This world changes, but changes slowly. It represents the cumulative sum of all environmental factors.

2. The world which we have called with Silbermann (1973) the 'socio-cultural table', i.e., the world of novelty, of news, of all that inserts itself in the *Umwelt* of each citizen and modifies it. It is the world of cultural production as distinct from the experience of everlasting creation with respect to the accepted. In terms of mathematical analysis, it is the derivative of the function.

Abraham A. Moles

Pre-eminent among the great cultural amplifiers is television: then comes radio, the press, the mass media in general, including manufactured objects distributed by mass production and marketing which play a subtler but more important role than the conventional media to which our scientific myopia has reduced the very idea of culture. This permanent flow, the intensity of which is, for better or worse, modulated by the gate-keepers of the media, is fabricated by the producers, the designers, the artists, the commentators. It comes out of television cameras, printing presses, radio studios, mass production factories. It enters the immediate sphere of each individual and is readily distinguishable from the 'spontaneity' now so strongly threatened by the standardization of over-pressured man. Most of its volume belongs to the universe of 'document', i.e., of materiality, of a testimony put in the varied concrete forms that our technology provides. One of the trends of western society is to try to catch what is new, to report it, to force it into containers of culture. This is the idea, the ideal, maybe the ideology, of the book library, the photographic library, the record library, even the newspaper library, the 'cultural conserves', as Moreno has called them. It is the abolition of the transient, the fleeting, the fickle, in favour of the document, of the trace. We are faced with a materialization of the socio-cultural framework, the 'canning' of culture. The few elements which escape from it (the live television production, the political speech without tape-recording) represent a tiny percentage of the daily flow of messages.

In this respect we must point out the impact of the magnetoscope or videotape recorders. Pictures no longer fly away, neither do the words, since the advent of the tape recorder into broadcasting production. This has disastrous consequences. First, the invasion of our lives by the cultural conserves and second, the abusive controls of the cultural bureaucracy.

What is most relevant to our discussion is the possibility of establishing in a concrete manner this cultural compass. The permanent but endlessly changing flow of the evolution of the individual and of civilization should be (it already is, but in a non-systematic manner) submitted to the algorithm of content

The Cultural Compass and the Transmission of Values

analysis. The 'cultural compass' can provide a permanent comparison between the cumulative culture such as it exists and slowly develops within a society and the socio-cultural table, i.e., what happens each year, what comes and joins the existing culture, the 'differential culture' in relation to culture itself. Comparing those two cultures using the same method of analysis, searching by highly sophisticated techniques for the difference between what exists and what is added in each

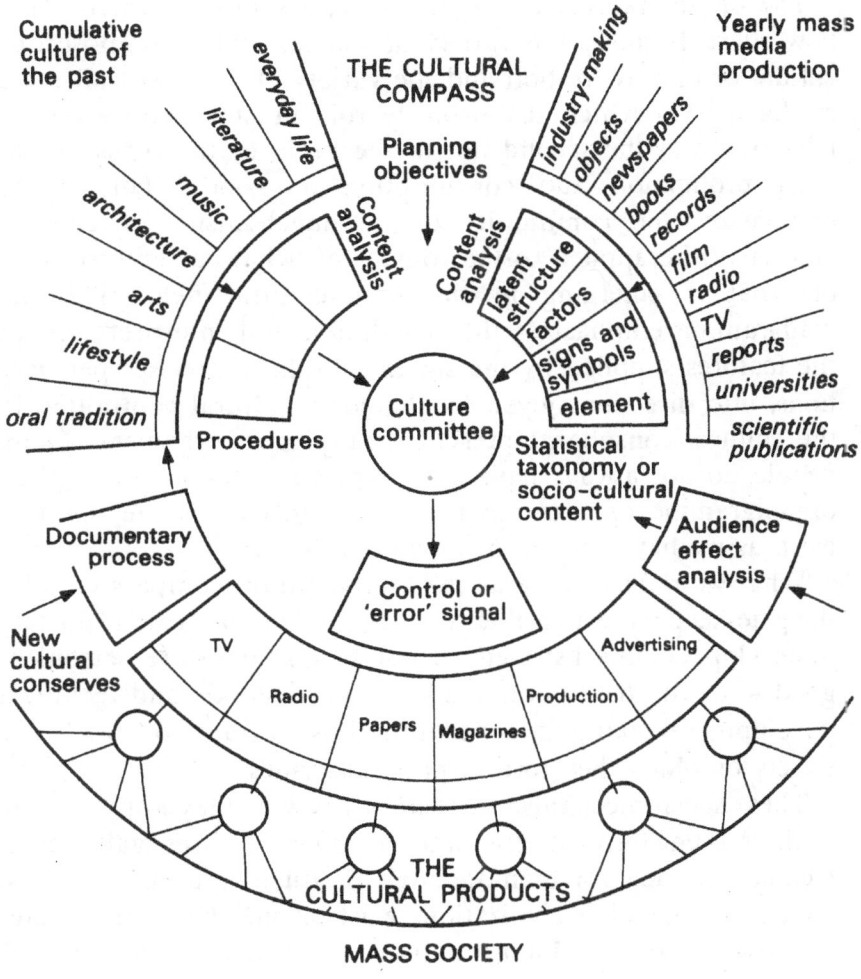

Figure 4 The socio-cultural compass

period of time will supply 'error signals'—what are called 'control signals' in system theory.

In other words, the comparison produces a signal which, according to the principles of systems analysis, can be injected as a regulating element of cultural activity to react, to rectify, to increase or decrease the flow, the influence or the style of particular media, taking into account their global role in the cultural integration of each individual at different levels of the social system.

The organigramme of Figure 4 depicts this argument in a flow chart. It shows the variety of sources which compose our culture or our civilization and the variety of what we call mass media among which the primary role must be conferred to television and the second not to the radio or the press but to mass production and consumption of goods. This figure emphasizes the community of the mechanisms of content analysis to be applied to the sources of 'what currently is' and of what is emerging in the socio-cultural field. The organigramme emphasizes the translation and interpretation of the features supplied by the signal into more precise specifications, into directions given by the socio cultural committee to the cultural consultants present in any great organism. These people do not always have a recognized status in the explicit organigramme of a company but in most cases they in fact exist, as we have shown in previous works.

What we refer to here as the socio-cultural compass enables the gate-keepers responsible for the mass media's role in society to develop a cultural strategy. These gate-keepers are persons of good will, who try to optimize cultural, scientific and technical development taking into account those values to which the society of which they form a part subscribes.

These social mechanisms are not as new as they appear to be in the present form. Radio, film and book libraries, galleries of technical models for manufactured products, museums of past epochs and of other civilizations exist in one shape or another in most rapidly developing nations. Indeed, these nations are thus classified because during a previous stage of their development (generally the nineteenth century), they estab-

The Cultural Compass and the Transmission of Values

lished the nucleus of these mechanisms necessary for the consciousness of their progress—breaking in this with the oral tradition. What is new in this concept of the cultural compass is the expressed intention of investigating by content analysis procedures the various aspects of these productions better to understand what is going on and better to determine what we can do within a collective conscience to make explicit the continuity of a civilization as a function of what already exists.

Summary and Conclusions

We shall sum up the elements of this report dealing with the influence of televisual culture and of its role in the development of a country.

1. Television is currently the leading element of the mass media, but its leadership and prestige can be established only by competition with other aspects of mass civilization.

2. Among the other media which contribute to the mediation between individual and society, we single out the manufactured object.

3. The television mediation consists of the emergence within the field of consciousness of images, phenomena, landscapes, characters and other events which interact with the real world in subtle ways to the point that the individual is less and less able to differentiate documents or news from a factitious universe which suggests to him roles and characters. This process corresponds to the projections made by a number of theoreticians of the cinema (Bazin, Morin, Cocteau, Boorstin, etc.). But the cinema never achieved the suggestive, hypnotic and continuous power of television.

4. Television is at the pinnacle of its power. It is one of the determining factors of social action and should be more than ever controlled by persons in charge of the evolution of society. But this power will not last for ever for at least two reasons:

(a) A cultural habituation of the individual can already be seen among children. It makes them reduce the status of the television set to that of a 'light-box showing pictures'. By phenomenological reduction, the television set loses its sanctified appeal and is reduced to a more modest role, an element among others in a diversified environment, a tool that we control, that we are able, if not to censor, at least to forget. Some surveys carried out in the United States and in Canada (Gerbner, Taylor) suggest that this phenomenon is indeed occurring.

(b) Many theoreticians foresee that the technology that has created and promoted electronic mass media will from now on put its overwhelming power at the service of intermedia—media which distribute pictures, sounds and cultural conserves to the private sphere. These intermedia would provide (a) means of interpersonal communication (of which the conventional telephone is an example, somewhat obsolete but in the process of renewal), and (b) selfmedia, i.e., communication of the individual with himself through time. The human being would find himself no longer submitted to a mass influence, but inserted into a relational structure where he broadcasts just as well as he receives thus establishing through this communicational autonomy (in itself a consequence of a communicational opulence—still to come, but already conceivable) a new independence from the Establishment.

5. The television mediation, such as we know it, is hampered by scarcity: the TV picture is much poorer than radio sound as improved by frequency modulation, and the contents of this picture are generally not good. With a restricted stock of characters and situations, most productions and messages are but a structural recombination of a finite number of types. Thus, television contributes to stereotype of thought and to a standardization which runs counter to creativity. There is a vast gap between what television programming could be like (and occasionally is: walking on the moon, recreation of Aeschylus or of great social events), and the profound dullness which is the diet of everyday televiewers.

6. Content analysis is an important tool that social sciences can put at the disposal of the television medium. It enables a permanent non-alienating evaluation of the message flow and identifies underlying structures such as intelligibility, rhythm, expressiveness, connotative feelings, etc. Content analysis has

The Cultural Compass and the Transmission of Values

developed techniques to bind latent factors to these values and thereby provides a tool capable of investigating whether social values (or even political values) fit or misfit the social action.

7. Among these values, some are specifically related to the needs of a developing society. Their analysis falls within the competence of the sociologist or of the culturalist. In order to build a television policy it is necessary to adopt an attitude congruent with its own values. For instance, to import for economic reasons programmes from countries with different linguistic or aesthetic structures may distort and deviate the cultural evolution.

8. Countries for which these arguments are likely to be important fall in two main categories:

(a) those where television, at least in theory, serves the collectivity in its institutional form, i.e., the Nation,

(b) those where television is split into a multiplicity of competing systems which, rather than produce programmes, try to produce televiewers in order to sell them products and, thereby, increase consumption.

Each system may claim certain advantages. With competing channels there is greater freedom. A centralized system under the sponsorship of the state is compelled to operate under a measure of censorship or control. But centralized channels, which do not have to dissipate their energy in an effort to hold on to evanescent audiences are, in principle, capable of greater unity and structural coherence. This puts them in a better position to promote mental or collective consistency. Culturalists have a tendency to consider this internal consistency one of the essential elements of western civilization.

9. Television plays different social roles depending on the situation of the viewer and his distribution within a territory. It is an element of unity, of contact, of coherence, of opening, of culture and of progress in countries or in the areas with low population density where individuals are distant from each other, held by this very distance on the fringe of the world (rural areas). It is also an element of superficiality, of dispersion, of withdrawal into oneself, of building a defensive wall, of closure and, finally, of indifference in dense societies or where

many programmes are competing for the communicational time-budget of the individual. This competition changes their character, making them entertaining instead of educative, thrilling instead of informative, shallow instead of instructive.

10. We shall call cultural compass a new tool of the social engineer based on the comparison by content analysis between what a culture is at a given moment and the contributions of new elements. Mass media, in the general sense of the word, constantly come and modify this culture. From the comparison between both there comes a signal of control which may be put at the disposal of those whom we may call 'the responsibles', the gate-keepers of messages or objects.

11. The representation of cultural modifications through the media picture which emerges is that of an individual going through space and time within the trajectory of his 'universe line', and subjected along this path to the successive flows of dissimilar sources (the physicist would talk of incoherent sources) each of them producing a programme that may be coherent in itself, but whose successive influences, juxtaposed by the hazard of the individual's paths through space and time, provide him with a whole mosaic of messages. These messages deposit inside him a kind of stratum, which we have called the 'individual mosaic culture', through a process of self-teaching or of permanent education. This process, within the urban society, competes with the more conventional process of concentrated education located in specific places of space and time—what we call school or traditional teaching.

If we are more and more obliged to live within a society of media gradually achieving communicational opulence, it is relevant to wonder whether it is not possible to put a remedy to the mosaic aspect of this sedimentary culture by introducing into (1) the messages, (2) their distribution, and (3) their programming, certain semi-aleatory elements of regularity which will allow the establishment of a relation between what is broadcast and vital experiences, building up what we may call a programmation of the self-teaching field. Is this a task that is assigned or assignable to media leaders? It is high time that this question was raised.

The Cultural Compass and the Transmission of Values

References

Frank and Moles, A. (1970), 'Motivations adultes à la structuration de la pensée', in *Education Permanente*, Publication du Conseil de l'Europe, Hachette.

Inkeles, Alex (1966), 'The modernization of man', in *Modernization: The Dynamics of Growth*, New York: Basic Books.

Kosinski, Jerzy (1973), *Being There*, London: Pan Books.

Moles, Abraham. *Sociodinamica da Cultura*, Sao Paulo: Editora Perspectiva.

Moles, Abraham, 'Ecologie communicationnelle: un nouvel aspect de l'économie des media', *Revue Économie et Société*, Cahiers ISEA.

Moles, Abraham. *La Communication*.

TV et Culture, Cahiers RTB 17, 1970.

'Systèmes de media et système éducatif', *Perspective*, 5(2) pp. 176-98

Moles, Abraham and Oulif, J. *Le Troisième Homme: Vulgarisation Scientifique et Radio*, Diogènes.

Moles, Abraham (1974), 'Société et télévision', Travaux du Conseil de l'Europe, *Comptes Rendus du Colloque de la Gestion des Télécommunications dans les Sociétés Démocratiques*, Munich, June.

Silbermann, A. (1973), *Soziologie der Massenkommunikation*, Cologne: Kohlhammer.

4
An International Survey of the Future of Broadcasting
Farhad Hakimzadeh and Donald Meals

Introduction

This article reviews the findings of an international survey conducted by the Prospective Planning Project of National Radio Television. The purpose of the survey was, first, to obtain a worldwide perspective on the evolving future roles of broadcasting institutions and second, to establish what general relationships exist between environmental factors (political, economic, cultural, financial, etc.) and policies/strategies adopted by broadcasting organizations. A revised Delphi method was used for this investigation. The first part consisted of interviews with public broadcasting experts from seventeen countries. These interviews served to identify key issues and trends that characterize probable future broadcasting missions as well as organizational structures required to support them. With these world-views as inputs, a questionnaire was constructed to test and analyse a second and third round of judgments from a selected group of the experts interviewed in the first round plus a few additional experts which were later added to the list.

The Delphi Method

Recognizing that judgmental factors play an essential role in all planning processes, it is natural to want to make the procedures for obtaining such 'soft' data as reliable and efficient as possible. The Delphi method is designed to pool the opinions of experts on a particular issue. In view of the practical and psychological drawbacks of attempting to reach a group position through round-table discussions, the Delphi method seeks

An International Survey of the Future of Broadcasting

to retain the stimulating give-and-take of conventional debate while preserving a measure of anonimity for individual contributors by having an intermediary question the participants individually and repeatedly by questionnaire or interview while proving continual feedback on the opinions stated by others in previous phases of the questioning without revealing the authorship of a particular opinion.

For the present study the following procedure was used. A set of specialists was contacted and interviewed. General topics were outlined but otherwise the interviews were unstructured, allowing the respondent to concentrate on any issue that he or she felt was important. Based on these preliminary findings, a questionnaire was prepared and mailed to a selected group of the initial interviewees plus a limited number of experts not contacted in the interview round. The replies to this first questionnaire were returned to the respondents together with a slightly revised questionnaire, again soliciting their judgments. The details of these three rounds are as follows.

Round 1: Interviews

The purpose of this 'open-ended' initial round was to delineate the subject matter of the inquiry so as to obtain a listing of the major challenges/opportunities which broadcasting institutions will be facing in the next decade.

Round 2: Questionnaire I

Based on Round 1 results, four major broadcasting policies/issues were selected. Respondents were asked to evaluate present conditions in their country with respect to each policy and try to predict 1983 conditions. They were also asked to judge the effect of a list of environmental conditions on these broadcasting policies/issues.

Round 3: Questionnaire II

The results of Round 2 were returned to the respondents in summarized form. Respondents were asked to reply to a second set of questions consisting of a simplified version of those of Round 2, taking Round 2 results into account.

Farhad Hakimzadeh and Donald Meals

Panel Composition

Since one of the goals of this inquiry was to study how different environments affect the form, structure and role of a broadcasting agency, a heterogeneous group of countries was visited, selected from among those with useful and extensive experiences in the field of broadcasting. These countries (Table 1) enjoy full radio coverage and various degrees of television coverage. With one exception, they are served by public broadcasting organizations. Several have internal or external privately-owned competitive radio or television stations. In some, over-the-air broadcasting is supplemented by urban cable television systems. In most, AM and FM radio service is provided.

TABLE 1   List of countries

Australia*, Belgium, Canada, Denmark, Egypt*, Federal Republic of Germany, France, Hong-Kong*, India, Israel, Japan, Poland, South Africa, Spain, Sweden, United Kingdom, United States of America
---

*Interviewees were contacted outside their own country.

In over fifty separate interviews, each lasting from one to three hours, we had opportunity to solicit the opinions of seventy-five mass-media professionals and experts. Our primary contacts were with the management of the broadcasting establishment(s), frequently the director general and managers involved in long-range planning for their organization. We also contacted professors active in communications research, representatives of the press, or members of professional or international organizations related to broadcasting.

Thirty-nine of the interviewees were chosen for Round 2 and another seven experts not interviewed in Round 1 were added. Criteria for selection were breadth and depth of knowledge of broadcasting conditions in their own country. Round 2 questionnaires were returned by twenty-four (52 per cent) of the participants. These twenty-four also received Round 3 questionnaires and sixteen (67 per cent) responded.

An International Survey of the Future of Broadcasting

Findings of Open-ended Initial Round

There is considerable communality as to objectives, organization, technology and social environment of broadcasting agencies. Yet, despite these similarities, broadcasting agencies differ from one another depending on national culture, history, political system, etc. These differences show up more in the content of broadcasting than in organizational structure.

Agency life cycle

In the organizational life cycle of broadcast agencies one can distinguish four phases:

1. *Innovative and entrepreneurial start-up.* In this phase engineering and technology are predominant.

2. *Expansion and growth.* With nationwide expansion of coverage, production facilities and programming, production executives share control of the agency with engineers in an uneasy alliance.

3. *Maturity.* This phase is characterized by full geographical coverage, high percentage of set ownership and large audience size, both in terms of percentage of population and in actual numbers. Control of the broadcast agency lies with those responsible for programmes. Competition emerges within the broadcast medium, from other media such as the press, from movies and from new technological delivery systems such as cable or video-cassettes.

4. *Decay or survival.* In their mature phase, many agencies fail to exhibit adequate sensitivity to the needs of their audiences. Their base of support is eroded and governments may be pressed to exert more direct control. Under such circumstances, broadcasting agencies face serious strategy decisions and questions concerning their primary role. Since their responsibility encompasses technology and transmission facilities as well as programme content, they are frequently faced by basic conflicts/issues.

National versus individual needs

This basic conflict in broadcast programming and content has important technological and organizational implications. It opposes the individual's desires and need for leisure, distraction, entertainment and relaxation to the nation's need for literacy, education, technical skills, and shared commitment to national objectives.

All national public broadcasting agencies began in the capital and gradually spread countrywide. They tend to reflect central authority and the value system of the power elite. This centralization is diminishing, but a shift toward regionalism and localism is often hampered by shortage of creative talent. There is an increasing trend toward special audience programming and away from broadcasting to mass audiences, reflecting an awareness of heterogeneity of tastes, preferences and interests. There is the issue of feedback from the audience as a prelude to two-way communication between broadcasting agency and audience. Feedback raises the question of who, besides the audience, ought to provide constructive criticism for broadcasting agencies which enjoy a national monopoly.

Triangular dependence and inter-dependence of broadcasting agency, government and public

This area of tension emerges from the sometimes conflicting needs of government, agency and audience as separately and together they try to serve their needs and the more general shared missions and objectives of society. Most national broadcast agencies seek a measure of independence from control by governments and audiences. Governments, without exception, seek to control public broadcast agencies. Audiences seek responsiveness and satisfaction from broadcasters. Two questions are basic for a national broadcast agency:

1. How to remain politically responsible, and, consequently, acceptable both to government and public.

2. How to be financed so as to remain politically responsible, and yet at arm's length from the government, in order to serve the information and entertainment needs of the public.

Broadcasting competition

This issue involves both inter-media competition for audience and financial support, and intra-medium competition in programming and audience building. Both types of competition have proved helpful in societies rich enough to encourage them. Even in less wealthy societies inter-media competition has desirable results.

Intra-broadcasting competition has been the norm in the privately owned broadcasting systems in the United States, between private and public stations in Canada, England and Japan, and between public agencies and private peripheral 'pirate' stations in France, Belgium and England. It is largely unknown, however, in countries with national broadcasting agencies. In recent years there has emerged great public and government discontent with the continued existence of monolithic national broadcast agencies. This public dissatisfaction is forcing the breakup of broadcast monopolies, usually into component radio and television networks—generally with an overall agency to manage and referee the hoped-for competition between the newly 'independent' units.

Impact of social attitudes and new technology

In western Europe and in the United States a social evolution is rapidly changing the triangular relationship between government, broadcast agency and audience. The historic reasons for broadcast monopolies are being increasingly questioned. Massive monopoly agencies along with their monumental, centralized production and operation facilities, are giving way to organizational forms based on new technologies and new information delivery systems such as satellites, cable television, cassettes, computers, and low-cost lightweight film and video recording systems. These technologies, combined with changing public opinion, presage a change in availability of broad- and narrow-cast information, a change from scarcity to abundance, from mass to specialized programmings, from studio to location production, from agency monopoly to intra-broadcasting competition, from in-house production to supplier production, from one-way transmission to two-way communication. Programming and social objectives are taking precedence over engineering and technology. In the process, professional creative ability is replacing civil service as the basis for a career in broadcasting. One observes a growing tendency for what were once distinct systems of electronic commmunication to become interconnected and integrated.

Questionnaire Findings

Based on the Round I findings described in the previous section, four broadcasting issues were chosen as particularly significant at the present time:

1. Approach to Audience: Integration vs. Segmentation
2. Control of Broadcasting: Controlled vs. Autonomous
3. Treatment of Values: Single Value vs. Active Encouragement of Multiple Values.
4. Organizational Structure: Centralized vs. Decentralized.

Respondents were asked to provide the following information for each of the above policies/issues:

(a) Present conditions (1975) in their country (rating their judgment on an eleven-point scale from −5 to +5).

(b) Perception of conditions in their country in 1983.

(c) Relative importance of 'environmental conditions' (audience heterogeneity, financing methods, broadcasting structure, etc.) on these policies/issues in their country.

Approach to audience

Broadcast systems take different approaches to their audiences. At one extreme is the hypothetical system that makes no differentiation whatsoever in its programming between audience location, interest, age, etc. Although it may respond to the interests of its audience, it presents programmes that are appropriate for the audience as a whole and never, or rarely, caters to interests held by a minority. At the other extreme

An International Survey of the Future of Broadcasting

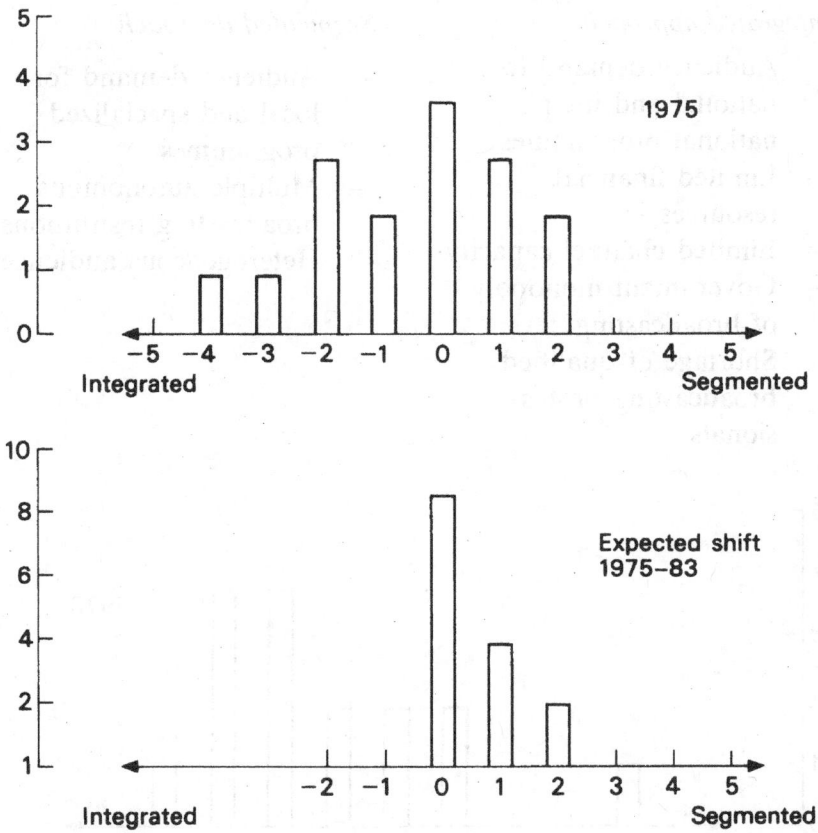

Figure 5   Approach to audience

—also hypothetical—is the broadcasting system that rarely or never presents programmes designed for the interests of the majority. All programmes are related to the interests of particular groups of listeners. The continuum between these extremes may be represented by a scale with a midpoint that stands for a relationship to the audience that gives equal emphasis to integration and segmentation.

The responses of Round III are summarized in Figure 5 which shows the extent to which conditions vary from country country and which suggest that the trend appears to be toward greater audience segmentation. The principal factors favouring an integrated or segmented approach are:

Integrated approach
— Audience demand for national and international programmes
— Limited financial resources
— Limited channel capacity
— Government monopoly of broadcasting
— Shortage of qualified broadcasting professionals

Segmented approach
— Audience demand for local and specialized programmes
— Multiple autonomous broadcasting institutions
— Heterogeneous audience

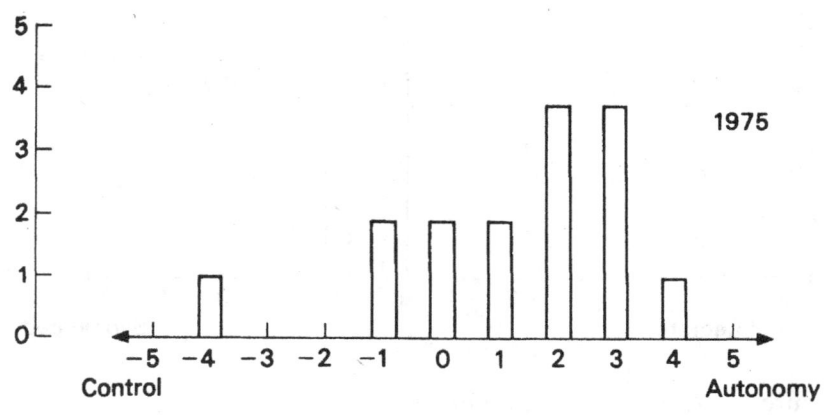

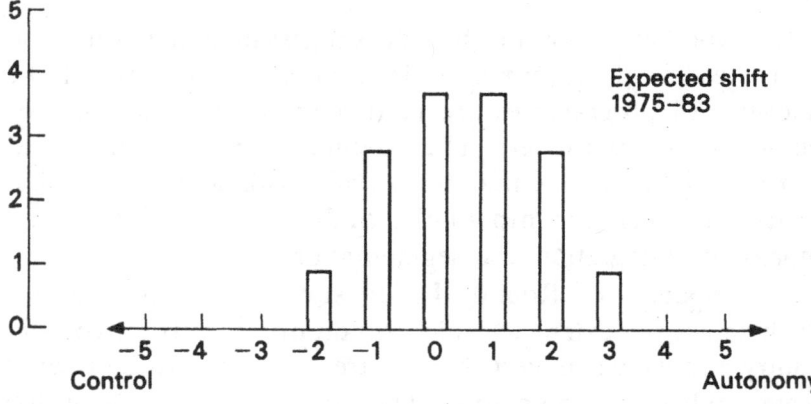

Figure 6 Control of broadcasting

An International Survey of the Future of Broadcasting

Control of broadcasting

Broadcast organizations differ as to the degree of control exercised over them by governments or other pressure groups. At one extreme are broadcast organizations which are part of the government—a bureau or division of a ministry. Programming is subject to day-to-day control and operators are directly accountable to the government. In some instances, equally strong control is exerted by apparently independent broadcasters who, however, rigorously apply standards which are equivalent to those favoured by the government. At the other extreme are independent broadcast organizations which set their own standards, formulate their own programme policies and select their target audiences.

Respondents indicate that in their countries broadcasting operates relatively autonomously as shown in Figure 6 which peaks toward the right end of the pectrum. Opinions as to future trends range rather widely with a comparable number of respondents foreseeing greater control or greater autonomy.

The main factors tending to foster broadcasting autonomy are:
— Stable political environment
— Ample channel capacity
— Multiple broadcasting institutions
— High level of audience education and sophistication

Treatment of values

Wide differences exist among broadcast organizations in the way values are treated in their programmes. Some broadcasters reflect a single dominant set of values while others actively encourage diversity.

Programming that reflects a single dominant set of values contains themes, commentary and even artistic forms that are rigorously consistent with a particular political philosophy, religious orientation or specific cultural view of life. The content of news and public affairs broadcasts may be slanted or selectively presented to conform to a single set of values. Alternatively, many different values and points of view may be presented. Programming oriented towards pluralism promotes and even stimulates the expression of values that are in conflict with each other and with those that are dominant. Audience participation is encouraged. The reporting of public affairs may take the form of investigative reporting designed to expose and examine events, even if it leads to public reaction against governmental positions or against respected public figures.

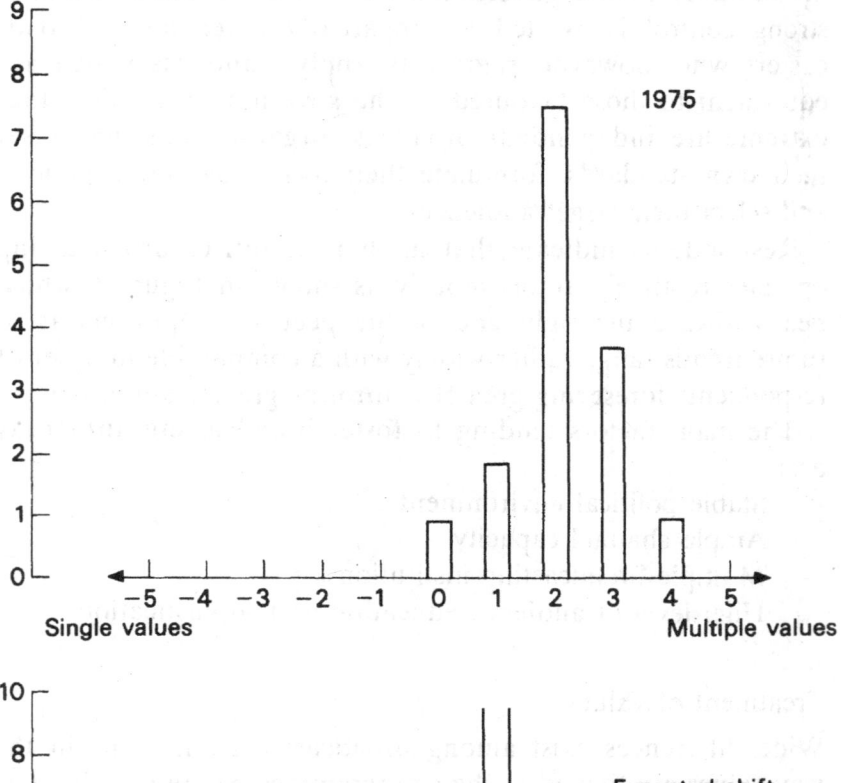
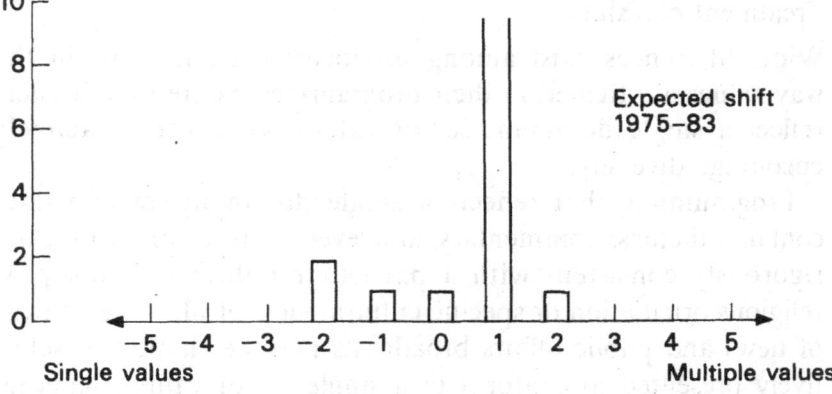

Figure 7 Treatment of values

An International Survey of the Future of Broadcasting

With regard to this issue, respondents agree that in their countries a moderate pluralistic value system prevails in broadcasting (Figure 7). The direction of change seems to be toward a further strengthening of the pluraristic position.

The following environmental conditions are favourable to broadcasting characterized by 'multiple value' systems:
— Autonomous broadcasting institutions
— Emphasis on regional audiences and special interest groups
— High level of audience education and sophistication

Organizational structure

How broadcasting institutions organize to manage their activities is currently a very lively issue. At one extreme one has highly centralized structures with a single organization controlling all broadcasting activities along functional lines. At the other one finds division of the total broadcast capability into multiple and independent organizations competing with each other for audiences. Some organizations may achieve a balance between centralization and decentralization by adopting divisional structure with a functional organization within divisions, each autonomous but subject to central control.

According to the results of this study, many countries appear to have struck a balance between decentralization and centralization by providing decentralization within a single organization. This is reflected in Figure 8, which shows a concentration toward the middle of the scale. The expected direction of change is toward slightly greater decentralization.

Impact of New Technological Developments

In trying to understand how broadcasting policies/issues are resolved one cannot neglect the impact of new technological developments. Nine such developments were chosen for review, since they are the ones considered most likely to become readily available in the coming decade:
  1. Point-to-point satellite transmission and reception.
  2. Direct reception of satellite signals by end-users.
  3. Localized satellite transmission.

4. Transmission via cable or optical means.
5. Recording and playback capability (e. g., video-cassettes).
6. Playback capability only (e.g., video discs).

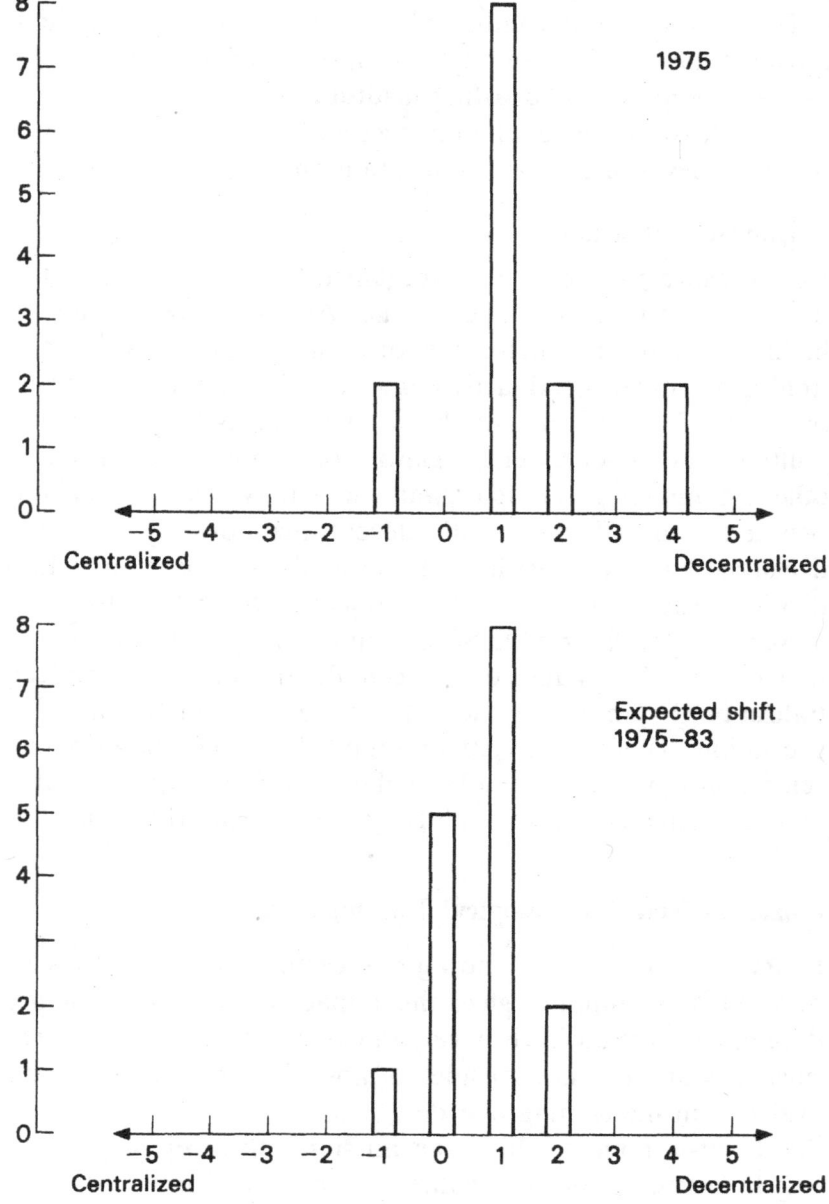

Figure 8 Organizational structure

An International Survey of the Future of Broadcasting

7. Portable studio equipment.
8. Individual access to large data and programme storage.
9. Transmission of specialized programmes to interested audience only.

Asked to assess the likely effect of these technological developments on the four broadcasting policies/issues discussed above, Round 3 respondents agreed that the overwhelming impact is likely to be towards a more segmented approach to audiences, towards more pluralistic values, more autonomy and more organizational decentralization. They also proffered these additional comments:

— Transmission via cable or optical means will not see a rapid expansion in the coming decade.
— Satellite transmission and reception on a point-to-point basis will be widely used but its impact on the four broadcasting policies/issues will not be great. Direct satellite reception and localized transmission will have limited applications.
— Lightweight portable studio equipment will result in greater organizational decentralization, and may influence the content of programmes by permitting a more segmented approach towards audiences.
— Video-cassettes, video-discs and individual access to data and programme storage will permit the delivery of programmes to audiences with very specialized interests and needs.

Conclusion

The purpose of this study has been to obtain a worldwide perspective on the evolving future conditions of broadcasting institutions in order to establish some relationships between the social and technological environment on the one hand and the structure of the agency and the content of broadcasting on the other. The experience in the countries visited suggests that there is sufficient similarity, of objectives, organization, technology and social environment, among broadcasting agencies to permit generalizations relevant to Iran.

Farhad Hakimzadeh and Donald Meals

This is a useful lesson since it implies that broadcasting agencies, whether operated as private organizations or government monopolies, in countries which differ widely in economic development, cultural traditions, political institutions and technological sophistication, share common problems and can benefit from each other's experiences. The world of broadcasting, it would seem, cuts across national boundaries and is truly global in scope.

II
The Role of Mass Communication in National Development: Facets of Innovation

5
Cultural Continuity and Change
The Role of Mass Media[1]

Elihu Katz

Theorists and policy-makers, on the subject of modernization, have held high two hopes for broadcasting. One is that broadcasting should contribute to the process of integration, helping to forge a nation from regional, tribal and ethnic loyalties. The other is that broadcasting should contribute to socio-economic development, helping to motivate and to instruct in the problems that beset the peasant population of developing countries. To the extent that the mass media have been given a chance—that is, in those nations where radio and television networks have been extended to cover the countryside—there is a record of achievement, though very uneven, with respect to these two hopes.[2] Apart from coverage, however, very few developing countries have harnessed the media seriously to their developmental goals.

Where the processes of national integration and economic development have taken hold, the side-effects of modernization have become increasingly apparent to the planners and policy-makers. Modernization brings in its wake a standardization and secularization of culture, such that the traditional values and arts, those that give a culture its character, are being overwhelmed by the influx of western popular culture. Rock music and comic books and Kojak threaten not only local tribal cultures but the Great Traditions of societies such as Thailand, Israel and Iran.

The traditionalists knew all along that this would happen: that is why they opposed modernization, and often the idea of the nation-state itself. The technocrats simply ignored the problem, and some of them remain untroubled by it even today; to them emancipation from tradition is a price worth paying. For those who dream the dream of liberal democracy, there is too much restraint implicit in a commitment to the continuity of tradition. But for a lot of people in between—those concerned with modernization, on the one hand, and with authentic identity, on the other—the problem is serious. (Geertz, 1973: 24) states it this way:

> Now that there is a local state rather than a mere dream of one, the task of nationalist ideologizing radically changes. It no longer consists of stimulating popular alienation from a foreign dominated political order, nor with orchestrating a mass celebration of that order's demise. It consists in defining, or trying to define, a collective subject to whom the actions of the state can be internally connected, in creating or trying to create, an experiential 'we' from whose will the activities of government seem spontaneously to flow.

The dilemma, according to Geertz, is in finding a proper balance between the cosmopolitan, future-oriented 'spirit of the age'—what he calls 'epochalism'—and the common experiences that inhere in tradition—or 'essentialism'. The sources of the latter, says Geertz, are parents, traditional authority figures, custom and legend, and, of the former, secular intellectuals, the oncoming generation, current events and the mass media. For Geertz, the mass media seem inexorably opposed to 'essentialism'.

We ask here whether this is necessarily so. Can not broadcasting give voice to culturally authentic forms of expression? Looking at the screen, or listening to the radio, it certainly seems as if they can not. But let us permit ourselves, at least, to ask the question.

Mass Media and the Continuity of Culture: a New Promise

Asking the question is not simply an academic exercise. The nations' leaders, too, are asking and it has not occurred to them, unlike the anthropologists, that the media may be unable to do

Cultural Continuity and Change

it. Governments are demanding that broadcasters help to solve the problem. Language is the most obvious means; in Algeria, for example, since 1971 radio and television have substituted Arabic for French as the language of programming. Governments are insisting that broadcasters sharply decrease the proportion of programmes which are purchased abroad: Peru, Nigeria, Algeria are ready examples.[3]

Increasingly, one hears explicit statements of policy on this subject. Thus, in establishing the expanded NIRT in 1972, the Council of Ministers named as the first aim of Iranian broadcasting 'to assist in safeguarding, developing and propagating Iranian culture'. 'The raising of the cultural level,' says the Algerian Quadrennial Plan of 1970, 'which depends in the first instance on the educational effort, is equally dependent on the activities of the broadcasting system and on giving as many citizens as possible access to the national cultural heritage.' More consistently than in other countries, official Brazilian statements on broadcasting refer to the importance of cultural goals. But the first set of legal documents following the adoption of the Brazilian Code of Telecommunications in 1962 goes even further. The goals of broadcasting, it says explicitly, are educational and cultural 'even in their aspects of information and entertainment'.

What is happening, in effect, is that a third area of promise is being accorded to the broadcast media. In addition to national integration and socio-economic development, leaders are proclaiming that radio and television should promote the continuity of traditional culture.

The call for more indigenous self-expression in broadcasting is being sounded loudly in the developing world. It is, as we have said, the voice of those concerned with modernization but not at any price. The earliest broadcasting in Indonesia and in Brazil was organized by 'cultural associations' interested in cultural creativity as the basis for national integration. The voices being heard today for mobilizing the mass media in support of cultural continuity are not concerned only *intrinsically* with authentic creativity for its own sake or for the sake of national respect. Some of them are concerned with the *instrumental* use of the themes of traditional culture as a more effective means of reaching people with the message of national integration and modernization. Peruvian rediscovery of their Inca ancestry, for example, relates to the fact that the Incas did have, in fact, a certain form of primitive socialism. Or again, there is a legend which tells how the participation of the people can 'help' in the mending and resurrection of a great Inca king who was decapitated by the Spanish. Peruvian planners have created a festival around this revived legend to promote the idea of 'participation'.

Whether the motivation is intrinsic or instrumental, the call for more indigenous creativity on the part of those committed to modernization poses serious questions. First there is the question already noted of whether the media are capable of answering the call. Second comes the question of which tradition to promote? There are Zoroastrian and Islamic elements in Iranian culture, Indian and Spanish elements in Peruvian culture and French and Arab elements in Algerian culture. Which should be emphasized? The choice, of course, is related to the ideological and developmental goals of the decision-makers. But even within the tradition, there are problems of selectivity. Certain elements are more compatible with modernizing values than others; indeed, certain elements of the religious tradition are obviously antithetical to modernization. Related to this is a question also alluded to earlier: whether promoting the renaissance of traditional arts and values is not giving undue support to repressive elements in society which would deny freedom to others. Champions of pluralism and freedom of expression in their 'epochalism' may be no less committed to the search for a national identity than the 'essentialists', although each group is fearful, justifiably, of the other.

Global 'Peyton Place': the Homogenization of Broadcasting in the World

While those who favour freedom of expression cannot help but fear the call for an 'essentialist' emphasis in broadcasting, study of the programme schedules of radio and television in developing countries will at least serve to place the problem in an empirical—not just ideological—perspective. By convention, broadcasting in Britain limits imported programming to 14 per cent. By contrast, in the eleven developing countries we studied, this proportion ranges from 30 to 75, averaging about 55 per cent, and the proportion is even higher if one examines only prime-time hours. The United States, of course, is the major supplier. It is commonplace to point out that television programmes around the world are densely populated by American detectives, cowboys and conniving housewife heroines. Two or more of our eleven countries were showing 'Gunsmoke', 'Ironside', 'Family Affair' and 'Streets of San Francisco' in July 1975. Summer Saturday nights on the national channel in Iran, for example, featured 'Family Affair' at 1930 and 'Days of Our Lives' at 2100, while the second channel was offering 'The Bold Ones' at 2005 and 'Kojak' at 2200. Cyprus, increasingly, is tending to balance US imports with programmes from Greece, even though Cyprus television considers its cultural level higher than that of Greece and was established several years earlier. Algeria, despite its Arabizing policy, still imports heavily from France, and Thailand is importing an increasing proportion of its programmes from Japan. Nevertheless, the United States is predominant almost everywhere.

It is not simply the 'imperialism' of the suppliers that explains the high rate of imported programmes. Television stations, even small ones in poor countries, broadcast some 6-10 hours per day (totalling a minimum of 2,000 hours per year), and professional pride, if nothing else, requires it. All things considered, it costs at least $1,000 to produce even a rudimentary programme of one hour, while the cost of buying an hour of foreign programming is a function of the number of sets in the country, and of whether other countries in the same language or geographic region have adopted it. Thus Iran can buy 'Ironside' for $300-400, Thailand for $250-350, and Peru can buy it for $250.[4] Even if these figures are doubled to make allowances for extra costs such as subtitling, the fact is that they are able to broadcast 'Ironside' for less than the cost of producing the most modest of their own programmes and for a small fraction of the price it costs to make originally in Hollywood (about $200,000). Even if the money were available for so many hours of local production, the talent is not, nor is the infrastructure in the other arts—film, theatre, graphics—well-developed. For the same reasons it is not unusual for small countries in Europe to import as much as 50 per cent of their programmes.

So the problem is as much one of demand as of supply. While radio is often more indigenous than television, the ravenous local demand for music to fill the hours is as good an explanation for the worldwide success of rock (or whatever else happens to be in fashion) as is the eagerness of the recording companies to sell their product. The complexities of television production—even where fewer hours are involved—makes the demand even keener.

In examining the situation of broadcasting in the developing countries, one must look beyond the importation of tape and films to the importation of programme ideas and formats. What is not directly imported may be—at second glance—imported as a model or 'stimulus' for local translation. Salesmen for the international television marketeers come equipped not only with packages of videotape but with catalogues of ideas which are also for sale. Thus quiz, the variety show, the soap opera are locally produced according to imported models although they may sometimes be adapted quite creatively—as we shall illustrate below.

The standardization of television around the world is further reflected both in the format of the programme schedules and in the proportional distribution of programmes by category. International travellers have very few surprises in store when turning on the TV in their hotel rooms. Wherever they go they will find that news occupies about 10 per cent of television time, with an added 10 per cent of current affairs and documentaries. Series and serials share about 20 per cent of the time and children's programmes, light entertainment and feature films are each assigned somewhat more than 10 per cent of the

Cultural Continuity and Change

schedule, while sports and adult education of all kinds are each given somewhat less than 10 per cent. Religion, music of all kinds and plays each take about 2 to 5 per cent of television time. But there is about a 30 per cent chance of seeing 'Kojak' at about 2100 some night in the week. The variations by country are only slight: the French tradition (Algeria, Senegal) includes more talk and current affairs while the South American tradition gives prime time to its home-made, and sometimes original, soap opera, the *telenovela*. Countries like Cyprus and Algeria make more deliberate selections of foreign material in order to give explicit emphasis to their cultural ties.

The demand for local programming, and even more, for local programming rooted in tradition, is better understood in this perspective. It is not simply an expression of ideological commitment but a question of whether one wants one's culture to be overwhelmed and homogenized. The world is indeed becoming a 'global village' in the sense of being exposed to the same television programmes. The name of this global village is 'Peyton Place', so to speak.

This problem is all the more urgent in view of the fact that television has hardly been launched in many developing countries. Typically, it has been established in and around the capital city, but has spread no further yet, and the huge cost of extending television coverage can be justified, if at all, only in terms of its potential contribution to development—political, economic and cultural. Why then impose an alien formula? As the Brazilian Minister of Education says, 'Commercial television is imposing on the youngsters and children of our country a culture that has nothing to do with Brazilian culture ... Thus, instead of being a creative element in the diffusion of Brazilian culture, television appears as a privileged vehicle of cultural import, a basic factor in the "decharacterization" of our creativity.'[5] Or, as Peruvian planners and educators are saying, if the Indians of the Sierra are to benefit from the introduction of television—now that the network is being expanded—the universal programming formula should not go with it. The Indians' expectations of development plans appear to be positive: health, education, agriculture and the Spanish language:

115

expectations which can be promoted in some measure, by the broadcast media. Why not, they ask, provide a broadcasting service which will meet these expectations? Why ask these people to *change* their expectations so that when television finally arrives they will be looking at their watches expectantly on Saturday nights at 2100 wondering why 'Kojak' is late?

Taking Entertainment Seriously

It is interesting to note that this concern over the display of alien values on television and the demand for increasing attention to the promotion of indigenous creativity reflects a changed conception of the broadcast media on the part of policy-makers. In proclaiming the goals of integration and modernization, attention usually focused on the informational and educational role of the media. News, current affairs, and programmes for the farmer or the housewife were subject to close surveillance, while entertainment was usually perceived as trivial or neutral or, sometimes, more functionally, as a source of escape or relief from the strains of social change. Recognition of the promise of the media in connection with the problem of cultural identity leads to the realization that entertainment is not neutral but an active force in the communication of values.

Politicians and planners are not alone in this discovery. Like them, students of mass communication have also tended to give more attention to the role of the media as agents of information and persuasion than as agents of entertainment, and it is ironic that there are very few television viewers who would make the same mistake. Perhaps not all viewers are aware or concerned that 'Peyton Place' or 'Sesame Street' contain alien values; but they surely know that the primary function of broadcasting, almost everywhere, is to entertain.[6]

The implication of all this—for planners, for broadcasters, for academics—is to take entertainment more 'seriously'. If broadcasting is to be harnessed to the goal of promoting indigenous values, it is important to understand how entertainment works. That means understanding what message is

Cultural Continuity and Change

implicit in 'Hawaii 5-0', what people perceive in it, why they enjoy it, what it 'gives' them, and then, by contrast, analysing the experience with home-made broadcast entertainment and with entertainment in traditional culture. Doing so will immediately suggest that the performing arts in many traditional societies make no room for the distinction between information and entertainment. The Peruvian revolutionaries who want to harness the media to their ideas for creating a socialist society based on the rehabilitation of traditional Inca values insist that it is 'alienating' to make the conventional western distinctions among information, education and entertainment.

Incidentally, it is not true that American thrillers and Westerns are the most popular programmes in any country, although it is fascinating, admittedly, to see how easily such programmes cross national borders. Visual action, not words, is part of the answer. It would be of great value—now that entertainment is being taken seriously—to study the meanings these programmes carry in different cultures and the functions they serve. But their popularity notwithstanding, the fact is that certain home-made programmes—especially the home-made soap opera—almost always outdraw them in popularity. This kind of indigenous competition does not often satisfy the 'essentialists' or developmentalists either. Very often, as we have said, they are based on imported models, but they may contain some clues about how to make more authentic television. We turn now to consider some efforts in this direction.

Indigenous Programming: Some Creative Efforts and the Issues They Raise

Everywhere, there have been attempts to create at least some programmes which give expression to cultural authenticity and continuity. Programmes for holidays are often of this kind. But before rediscussing special events we wish to marshal examples from several countries of relatively more continuous kinds of programming, from which certain generalizations will suggest themselves.

Elihu Katz

South America is a good place to begin. From Mexico to Argentina, the 30- or 60-minute *telenovela*, five-days-a-week and hundreds of episodes long, is the most popular form of television.[7] Its origin, apparently, is in the American soap opera translated and exported by pre-Castro Cuba and now made-for-television in Mexico, Venezuela, Argentina, Brazil and elsewhere. Mexico television thrives on the export of its *telenovela*, the form of which is also being creatively used. In Mexico itself, the *telenovela* has been adapted to the presentation of historical drama, telling the story of Mexico's march to independence. It is interesting to note that during our visit in Algeria, broadcasters were debating this very question: how to translate Algeria's epic struggle for independence into television terms.

In Brazil, the largest of the networks, Globo, has commissioned some of the country's best writers to create stories in the *novela* form. The late-evening *novela* in particular (there are three *novelas* each evening) is now a 'serious' affair, relating to real-life people (rather than escapist dreams) and to contemporary social issues. It is an interesting example of a carefully considered and costly initiative to improve the quality of product on the part of an oligopolist. It is also possible that the move is better interpreted as a response to the increasingly vocal concern of a government with matters of television: but whatever the motive, the achievement is real.

There are several lessons to be learned here, the first of which reminds us that, in its various forms, the serialized soap opera seems to be the most popular genre of television all over the world. It is much more widespread than the action-adventure story, for example, which is limited to the US, England, France and Japan. Indeed, the first dramatic production attempted by many a new television service is a serial story set in a family or village, incorporating heavy doses of folk wisdom and morality. Britain's 'Coronation Street' is probably the closest western analogue to this theme. Thus, Iran's most popular programme is colourful Morad Barghi's discourses to his family, while the story of a moralizing taxi driver, his clients and comrades, is one of Senegal's leading programmes. Cyprus and Israel both

Cultural Continuity and Change

began their dramatic presentations with a family soap opera. The characters are familiar, the setting is recognizable, the problems are real (if somewhat exaggerated and sentimentalized), and wherever there are measures of popularity, these home-made programmes out-draw the most famous of American imports.

Second, it is worth noting—in connection with the Brazilian case—that the status and authenticity of broadcast art can be considerably enhanced when the best writers and directors are incorporated into the media. The glamour of broadcasting—even of television—is by no means uniform throughout the world. In certain traditional societies journalists and broadcasters are held in rather low esteem because they are associated with an irreverence for authority and a bohemian style: in other places they are dismissed as mere civil servants.

Still another implication of the Brazilian experience is that the media cannot be genuinely creative unless they cultivate and exploit the other creative arts in society. It is extremely difficult to establish a western-style system without good writers, a tradition of theatre, a local film industry and experienced craftsmen in the other graphic arts. As we shall note below in discussing Thai television, many of the Asian countries have highly productive film industries. In Senegal, we found that the active local theatres and film studios were a great asset in the introduction of television, although the lack of formal agreements with writers' and film-makers' guilds have impeded optimum cultivation of these alliances.

The introduction of television in Colombia, on the order of General Rojas when he took office, made early use of a tradition of theatre in the country, and the report of these early plans sounds interesting, if dictatorial (Fox, 1974). Thai television immediately employed the dubbing troupes which, for years, have ad-libbed translations of imported foreign films in the movie theatres (and still do). Patronage by broadcasting of these allied arts is of central importance to creativity and authenticity on radio and television.

South American television has another original aspect: the ebullient celebrity presiding over a variety show of great duration, sometimes six or seven hours long. While this form seems to be on the decline, it is interesting to take note both of the folksy quality of these shows and of their open-ended character. It is curious that television came to the new nations complete with stop-watches, so that time could be divided into 15-, 30- and 60-minute segments. It is worth asking whether creativity in broadcasting in the new nations would not benefit from more freedom from the rigidities of western time frames.

Thailand, too, has an interesting story. Like Brazil and other countries, the earliest days of Thai television contained a much higher proportion of indigenous creativity and of televised material based on traditional art forms such as the shadow play, the dance theatre, puppeteering and so on. The decline in the proportion of these original productions in Thailand and elsewhere followed the increase in the number of hours of broadcasting, the importation of foreign films and serials, the invention of the videotape, and perhaps just plain exhaustion. The fact is that Thailand has several classic dramatic forms which have not yet found their place in television; the national theatre for example is the last preserve of the dance-drama. Instead Thailand is importing gory Japanese thrillers at very high rates, vying with the importation of American series, and causing one to wonder why the native traditions of theatre find no real expression in the broadcast media. On the other hand, Thailand has a film industry which produces over 100 films per year. Television does show its share of these films, many of which are reminiscent of the *telenovelas*. Indeed, one wonders how much of these 'Easterns'—which are similar, we are told, to the films produced in Iran, India, Turkey and other Asian countries, each of which has a substantial film industry—are based on indigenous themes and how much influenced by western models.[8]

One of the traditional Thai forms has made it, both on radio and television. This is the *mau lum* folk opera or song-story of which Dr S. J. Tambiah (Goody, 1968) writes:

> A measure of the contemporary appreciation of it is that wherever the radio has spread into villages, the programme

Cultural Continuity and Change

most avidly listened to is *mau lum*. The entertainment appeal of *mau lum* stems from the fact that much of its content is drawn from the pool of northeastern tales and myths ... rather flexibily constructed rhyming songs (with) room to improvise. The *mau lum* singers not only preserve and propagate religious traditions; they are also the channel through whom certain stories and epics, popularly known and appreciated in northern and central Thailand, are passed onto the northeastern villagers. They sing stories about the life of the Buddha which are nationally known and in a different form are heard in the temple ... The repertoire includes courtship and love poetry, burlesque and earthy, bawdy jokes: it echoes and stimulates the romantic sentiments of the young men and women.

Traditionally, these singers travel widely, particularly in the north-east of the country, appearing at all-night sessions of fairs held in the temple grounds. Efforts have been made to expand their repertoire to take account of campaigns of rural development, anti-communist propaganda, and other contemporary and development topics. 'To the extent to which singers take to them' (the new texts), writes Dr Tambiah, 'a truly grass-roots propaganda machine will have been harnessed by the government to promote its political and socio-economic policies.'[9]

Other broadcasting systems, too, have successfully incorporated traditional media. The *Griot* of Senegal, for example, who sing of lineages and history as chroniclers of an oral tradition, are on the regular payroll of ORTS, Senegal.

Here, too, are several important principles for us to consider: (1) The distinction between information, education and entertainment is of no relevance to these artistic traditions. (2) An art form, the *mau lum*, which is associated with festivity and holiday has been sufficiently secularized and routinized to fit the time-slots and production formats of radio and television. (3) The incorporation of contemporary references apparently has a share in the goodness of the fit between traditional and modern media. (4) Art forms which traditionally take place out of doors have been successfully moved into the studio.

Why is it so difficult, then, to marry broadcast media to classical arts?

One reason is that classical arts are dying in the developing countries and, as far as we are able to judge, this is not typically *because* of broadcasting. The traditional story-teller of the Iranian teahouse or the Ruhozi theatre-on-the-pool began to disappear before the rise of television, even in places to which television has not yet penetrated. Perhaps radio is to blame, but local informants were uncertain on this issue. The classical dance-drama of Thailand, one of the great achievements of its high artistic traditions, survives only under the patronage of the national theatre; and the theatre is the only training school for artists. Similarly, the national theatre in Japan is the only remaining school for Kabuki actors; the family tradition which passed the art from father to sons has been broken.

We do not know where to place the blame. Richard Hoggart (1972) blames the tourists for the westernization, if not the decline, of the dance-drama in Bali. It is not primarily a *performing* art, he claims; and the same may be true for other art forms related to religious traditions: they do not survive the process of secularization. And modernization, in its various aspects including literacy—but not just the broadcast media—is to blame.

A second reason for the difficulty in transposing these traditional forms has to do with their limited repertoire. Many of these traditions are built on a very small number of classical themes, which are rapidly exhausted by radio or television. Those artistic traditions which do succeed over radio or television tend to have modes of refreshing themselves such as the contemporary allusions in the *mau lum* or the *Griot* song histories.

Broadcasters and artists in several countries called our attention to the traditional location on the village square of some of the best-liked of their performing arts and the constraints of the radio or television studio. This problem was emphasized in both Algeria and Nigeria. Part of the problem, of course, is in the lack of professional training and the dearth of equipment

Cultural Continuity and Change

for outside broadcasting. Part of it is in a bias which leads professionals to think that the studio is where broadcasting belongs. But the problem goes deeper: there is a certain incompatibility between 'inside' and 'outside' because of the communal and participatory nature of the 'outside' audience, on the one hand, and the freedom of movement of the artists, on the other. Perhaps there is more to it than that; we do not know enough of these traditional arts to be able to judge. The communal viewing of television may be of some use in this connection. The communal TV set is a necessity in any event in the developing countries, and perhaps it has certain advantages over individual viewing. Coffee-house discussions of the content of the newspaper were, and in some places still are, the breeding-place of western public opinion (Speier, 1950; Trade, 1901). Perhaps a certain kind of television deserves to be seen in the tea-house or the village square.

Still another difficulty in the transplantation of the traditional arts is the 'festive' character of so many of them, which cannot easily be made into just another programme on a Tuesday evening. Here, the broadcast media are caught in a basic paradox: the best—the most authentic—of their materials are appropriate for special occasions, yet the professional goal of broadcasting is enshrined in 'continuous performance'. Perhaps television would be better if it were less continuous; perhaps the aim should not be to be on the air every day for as many hours as possible. It is no coincidence that broadcasting is often at its best on holidays when it has something special to say. The media often rise to these occasions with special bursts of creativity in which they manage to catch the mood, and enhance the celebration, of both traditional and modern holidays. In the 'engineering' of new national holidays, governments often show acute awareness of the potential role of the media.

On the 'Translation' of Tradition

Our entire discussion of the problems of broadcasting and culture is anchored in the fundamental question of whether the media are capable of contributing to 'essentialism' in Geertz's phrase—or whether they are its sworn enemy, agents of 'epochalism' or worse. It is clear that the media are capable of 'opening a window to the world', even if the view is distorted and, in the opinion of some, demeaning. It is clear that they are natural allies of the forces of modernization and development, however casually or unintentionally they pursue those goals. What is not clear is whether the values and artistic traditions of the society must also make way—along with the methods of subsistence farming—for the homogenized popular culture of the West.

In the last few pages we have given some examples of successful coping by the broadcast media with the challenge of cultural continuity, and we have said something about the ingredients of these successful efforts: joining forces with the traditional performing arts through cultivation and patronage; drawing on those arts which can handle contemporaneity in the context of tradition; building on special occasions such as holidays; and going 'outside' the studio and the home for both production and reception. But the problem goes beyond specific programmes, or even special programmes. There is a sameness in the style of television and radio presentations which has come packaged with the technology, almost as if the microphones and camera came wrapped together with instructions for presenting a news programme, or variety show. Indeed, we noted that these formulae are for sale as well, and tend further to standardize the broadcast media around the world.

One wonders whether this has to be: cannot Nigerian, or Peruvian or Senegalese television be more indigenous, not just in programming, but in style? What is needed are more radical suggestions for making radio and television relevant for traditional people who have more important problems than those which can be solved by Chief Ironside. Tanzania is an example of a country that has tried this, and Peru is another which is talking about it. Their ideas are not based only in the content of specific programmes but on a different conception of the role of the media. Radio and television need to be 'reinvented' in a

Cultural Continuity and Change

sense. But how? How can tradition be translated into the language of the broadcast media?

One idea is to make certain that producers have a deeper grounding in their *own* cultural traditions and not only in the traditions and technology of metropolitan broadcasting. Informants in several countries told us how ill informed broadcasters are about the traditional arts of their own societies and about the ceremonies and values of their own cultures. The techniques of producing and directing are mistakenly thought of as content. Sorting this out may lead to a more creative blending of the old and the new.

This idea, perhaps, can be further developed. A society concerned over the use of broadcasting for cultural continuity might try to experiment with the establishment of an 'institute for the translation of tradition' whose members would give serious thought to traditional forms and content, on the one hand, and to the language of the media, on the other. Experts in the tradition, scholars and researchers, could sit together with producers and directors in an effort to find solutions to the problem of *domesticating* the broadcast media. What is needed are not programmes about tradition but a series of creative acts which will take the 'mood' or style of a culture and translate it into broadcasting terms.[10]

For example, broadcasting systems everywhere have to solve the problem of how to mourn: there are holidays of mourning such as punctuate the calendar of Islam, or commemorative mourning on the anniversary of wars, or mourning as on the death of a leader or a great man. All cultures provide rules for such occasions. There are rituals to be followed and symbols to be displayed, pleasures to be denied, and a variety of enabling means through which people can commune with the living and the dead. These rules are not readily translated into the language of radio and television, yet the more modern a society becomes, the more broadcasting is expected to take the lead on such occasions. Spontaneously, or by imitating foreign models, broadcasting stations do their best, simply transmitting the rituals and ceremonies as they are enacted outside the studio. The celebration of Shi'ite Islam of the deaths of Ali and

Hussein, the death of John Kennedy in the United States, the mourning for the dead of the wars in Europe, the commemoration in Israel of the holocaust which brought death to six million Jews are all improvised by the media. For example, replacing scheduled radio programmes by the broadcast of classical music is the accepted form of broadcast mourning in Israel. But little or no systematic effort is given anywhere to finding 'authentic' solutions to the problem of how broadcasting might capture the *mood* of the tradition.[11]

Celebrations of the Sabbath is another example. Christianity and Judaism have a day, each week, which is not simply a 'day off' but one which is endowed with spirituality. Other cultures have similar days; Islam has an entire month of Ramadan. The challenge to broadcasting is to discover the forms that capture the spirit of these occasions, more for the modernizing groups in the society than for the traditionals. The standard solution for the Sabbath is to broadcast a music-and-variety show for the family, or sometimes, a programme that is a little more highbrow than usual. An institute of the sort outlined above might find a more 'authentic' solution.

Creativity based on the interaction of research, tradition and the media would be the primary charge of the institute, and within its context producers could also be trained in their own cultures. They could be sent out into the countryside to observe and record the traditional performing arts. They could be assigned to view television-in-deed, to view their own programmes—together with families and groups in traditional settings. They could be asked to analyse the meanings and the functions of different sorts of programmes for these groups. They might study and observe the teahouse as a form of community centre in which communication goes on. And thus the issue of differentiating information, education and entertainment in programme schedules could be thrashed out.

Conclusion

The performance of broadcasting in the realm of cultural continuity falls very far short of the promise held out for it.

Cultural Continuity and Change

Indigenous self-expression in broadcasting is often little more than a copy of metropolitan models. There is a need to link the media with other arts, traditional and modern, from which ideas will flow. There is a need to create programmes that will give authentic expression to the culture in the process of its confrontation with modernity. But more than this, there is the need to employ broadcasting in ways which will better fit the moods and styles of the national heritage and of its special occasions. Perhaps the luxury of immersing producers in their own cultures, and forming creative groups of broadcasters, scholars and carriers-of-the-tradition to plan schedules and invent programmes together holds out a fragile hope that broadcasting might live up to its promise of contributing to cultural continuity.

It is all too easy, of course, to suppress free expression in the name of culturally authentic creativity. That is obvious. But even for men of good will, as was noted earlier, the commitment to authenticity in the media poses a dilemma: how does one reconcile this commitment with the equally compelling commitment to promote mass communications which permit the exchange of ideas among individuals and among nations? The dilemma is a genuine one, and therefore cannot be perfectly resolved. Rather, rapidly developing societies must steer a practical course which refuses to sacrifice authenticity to modernity and refuses to sacrifice freedom to authenticity.

Notes

1   The thoughts and observations in this paper are from a research project on Broadcasting and National Development under the joint direction of the writer and Professor E. G. Wedell. The project, financed by a grant from the Ford Foundation to the International Broadcast Institute, is based on an extensive survey of developing countries as well as intensive field work in a sample of eleven countries: Algeria, Brazil, Cyprus, Indonesia, Iran, Nigeria, Peru, Senegal, Singapore, Tanzania, Thailand. The full report of the study is to be published, along with the series of case-study monographs by Katz, Wedell, *et al*. Fieldwork was carried out during 1973-5 and no effect is made here to update the

observations made at the time of the case study. I should like to add that the discussion in this paper profited greatly from the debate in the Working Group on 'Cultural Continuity and Change' at the Mashad Symposium.
2. Most developing countries have achieved full radio coverage, some only recently, but television tends to be limited to urban areas, even when the system is government operated and essentially non-profit. Direct measures of the effects of exposure to broadcasting are not usually available, nor does our own study include such measures. A strong case for the influence of broadcasting on modernizing attitudes is made in the recent book by Inkeles and Smith (1974). An earlier statement is in Rogers and Suenning (1969).
3. These, and the examples that follow—except where otherwise noted—are from the case studies in Katz, Wedell, *et al.* (1976).
4. Latest figures from *Variety*, 8 January 1975, p. 96
5. Lecture of the Minister of Communication, Quandt de Oliveira, on 'Television as a Medium of Mass Communication', at the Anhebi Faculty of Social Communication, Sao Paolo, 19 November 1974, pp. 18-19.
6. We are taking no account here of the eastern European countries or of China, where the situation may be different: we simply do not know.
7. Based on survey data. Recent analysis of the US soap opera as a genre may be found in Katzman (1972) and in Newcomb (1974). The South American *telenovela* is studied in Marta Colomina de Rivera (1968) and E. A. Arriaza Camero *et al.* (1972).
8. This is an important area for study. The story-within-a-story form together with the implausible coincidences which bring protagonists together seems unwestern, at least in modern terms, but the saga of the village girl who flees to the city in quest of the lover who deserted her, etc., seem familiar. But these are mere impressions and the content analysis of popular Asian film and television stories well deserves attention.
9. The harnessing of traditional performers to development and other instrumental goals is not, however, our primary interest here. For other examples of this phenomenon, see Rogers and Shoemaker (1970) and publications of the International Broadcast Institute.
10. The example of the Children's Television Workshop, which created 'Sesame Street' through the interaction of a team of producers, child psychologists and media researchers, is relevant here. So are the working teams of Britain's Open University.
11. Grunebaum (1955) poses the same problem with reference to the 'spirit of Islam as shown in its Literature' (chapter 5) and even

gives an extended example from an epic poem on mourning (pp. 104-9). Analysing what is 'peculiarily Islamic' (not just Arabic) about this poem, he uses criteria of content (continual 'need to live with one's death', 'heedlessness'), outward form (the manqama), inner form ('abrupt transitions' of mood), attitude toward literature ('as a display of philological erudition and prosodical virtuosity ... in invention of incident, repartee, or argument').

References

Arriaza Camero, E. A. *et al.* (1972), 'Estudios sobre Algunos Aspectos de la Imagen de la Telenovelas en un Sector de la Poplicacion de Caracas', *Orbita,* cuarto semestre, Caracas, Venezuela.

Colomina de Rivera, Marta (1968), *El Huesped Alienante,* Maracaibo, Venezuela: Editora Universitaria.

Fox de Cardona, Elizabeth (1974), Report to the International Broadcast Institute Meeting in Mexico City.

Geertz, Clifford (1973), *The Interpretation of Cultures,* New York: Basic Books.

Goody, Jack, ed. (1968), 'Literacy in North-East Thailand', in *Literacy in Traditional Societies,* Cambridge University Press.

Grunebaum, G. E. von (1955), *Islam: Essays in the Nature and Growth of a Cultural Tradition,* London: Routledge & Kegan Paul.

Hoggart, Richard, (1972), *Only Connect,* London: Chatto & Windus.

Inkeles, A. and Smith, D. H. (1974), *Becoming Modern,* Cambridge, Mass.: Harvard University Press

International Broadcast Institute (1974), Seminar on Motivation, Information and Communication for Development in African and Asian Countries, London: International Broadcast Institute.

Katz, Elihu, Wedell, E. G., *et al.* (1976), 'Broadcasting and National Development', an unpublished report with eleven case studies.

Katzman, Nathan (1972), 'Television soap operas: what's been going on anyway?', *Public Opinion Quarterly,* summer, p. 200.

Newcomb, H. (1974), *TV: The Most Popular Art,* New York: Anchor.

Rogers, Everett and Shoemaker, Floyd (1970), *Communication of Innovations,* New York: Free Press.

Rogers, Everett and Suenning, Lynne (1969), *Modernization Among Peasants,* New York: Holt, Rinehart & Winston.

Speier, Hans (1950), Historical development of public opinion, *American Journal of Sociology,* 55, 376-88.

Trade, Gabriel (1901), *L'Opinion et la foule,* Paris: Alcan.

Variety (1975).

6
The Governance of Mass Communication
The Government, the Audience and Social Groups[1]
Ithiel de Sola Pool

How a nation's broadcasting system should be organized depends on what one wants that society to be. Electronic communications are the nervous system of a modern society. They are bound to both reflect and shape people's lives, relations with each other and with their government. Thus, in order to consider alternative ways in which a broadcasting system might be financed, governed and internally organized one ought to start by considering how broadcasting relates to the plural social groups that make up the society, what they believe, what other modes of communications are available to them, and what are their development goals.

These are big questions. They are questions of social and political philosophy. Technical questions that social research can answer may be embedded in them, but the full answers involve judgments of value and also the exercise of wisdom in the presence of uncertainty. In short there is no 'state of the art' about how to organize a broadcast system. There are the experiences of different countries many of which are well documented. Outstanding among these descriptions is Asa Briggs's multi-volume history of the British Broadcasting Corporation (1961-70) and the reports of the Royal Commissions on Broadcasting. The Canadian Ministry of Communication has produced a particularly reflective commentary in its Report of the Committee on Broadcasting (1965). The U.S. experience has been reviewed by Erik Barnouw (1966-70). Comparative studies of television in various countries are also available (Pige, 1962; Dizard, 1966; Emery, 1969; UNESCO) dealing with questions of monopoly, decentralization, government or commercial control, taste and quality. Yet, in the last analysis,

The Governance of Mass Communication

the issues involve fundamental political theory. What kind of a state does one want? What kinds of autonomous initiatives contribute to or obstruct national policy?

A nation is too complex an organism to be moved by a single decision centre. The relationship of the parts to the whole in a polity has been the subject of a large literature by such authors as Rousseau, De Tocqueville and Weber (de Sola Pool, 1967). The most important recent contributions to this field have come out of organization theory which has once more reaffirmed the awareness that the power of any organized unit (be it a firm or nation) is a function of the multiplied initiatives of its many members and therefore depends on their motivations. Innumerable studies by organization theorists have shown lateral and informal communication and multiple initiatives to be the condition of effective achievement of goals defined for the entity by its unifying leadership (March, 1965). These studies have also shown that the key role of the leadership of an organization is most often not its exhortation of the many subordinate leaders who must act, but the presentation of a role model to them. Although these findings have many implications for broadcasting, they lead to no simple solution for broadcasting policy. They are guidelines that must constantly be kept in mind, whatever organizational structure one chooses.

The Place of Broadcasting in the Total Communication System

In developed societies an integrated communication system serves a multiplicity of purposes. It serves government, business, education, public health and private life. All of these have legitimate communication needs. All of them require an easy flow of messages among all points in the land and among all its citizens. They all share in the use of telephones, printing presses and broadcasting. One problem confronting developing countries is how to overcome fragmentation by building a comprehensive communication system in which all can talk to all and which serves a variety of social needs.

There is the danger that a communications system designed by one set of institutions and with one set of purposes in mind will fail to meet other needs, i.e., that it will be 'sub-optimized' for one narrow set of purposes. A number of historical examples can be given. In the US, where it started, the telephone system was designed as a business service to provide calls for paying subscribers. Communal needs were not adequately considered. Consequently, fire and police alarms had to be set up on separate and less adequate networks. Phone circuits were not available, as they could have been, as an all-point alarm system instantaneously accessible to anyone from anywhere. Similarly, broadcasting in some countries has developed as an entertainment medium to serve advertisers, in other places as a propaganda medium for the government. In the former case there is the danger that no provision will be made for allocating some portion of spectrum time for serious broadcast purposes. In the latter, there is the danger that the commodity distribution system of the country will be denied access to the most effective means of informing consumers about the products that business is trying to make available. In both situations, education is likely to get inadequate allocations of broadcast facilities. Somehow, communications facility planning—whether through a market or through consultative processes—should be based on inputs from all institutions as to their prospective needs.

Communication system decisions made today will affect what will be available fifty years hence and will influence how every element of society functions and performs.

Broadcasting is a growing component of a modern communications system. Even in the most advanced countries, where broadcasting has been a live activity for over fifty years, studies show that every year a larger portion of the people's news consumption comes from broadcasting as compared to print media. Educational use of broadcasting is growing almost everywhere. In developing countries where literacy is not universal and where a powerful independent press has yet to take root, broadcasting is even more important. Since the transistor revolution, radio has been their main news source.

But even if broadcasting is a country's main source of information and entertainment, it cannot function in isolation

The Governance of Mass Communication

from other media. Broadcasting provides a means for support and dissemination of the work of film-makers, traditional artists and journalists, and it depends upon the prior existence of such cadres and their skills. Without them, broadcasting stations would have little to broadcast.

Furthermore, broadcasting is only one of the many kinds of communication that a society needs. Being few in number, broadcast channels must necessarily address mass audiences. A vital role remains for print media, film, field agents, posters, telephone, mails and traditional arts that transmit specialized messages to groups both large and small and to individuals. Broadcast planning should take into account its relationship to all these other media.

Comprehensive communication planning requires that broadcasters and the post/telephone/telegraph co-ordinate their long-range planning activities. By working together they can reduce duplication of facilities and avoid investment in incompatible equipment that may later present obstacles to interconnection. Currently, the principal areas which require close broadcast-telecommunication co-operation are microwave and satellite systems for nationwide message distribution. In the near future, particularly in rapidly developing countries like Iran, there will be other areas of overlapping facilities between broadcasting and point-to-point transmission. As spectrum limitations force broadcasting, especially for such purposes as education, on to broad-band enclosed media such as cables or optical fibres, both broadcasting and point-to-point transmission can share the same networks. Conversely, to reach isolated villages with message traffic, the airwaves and broadcasting receivers may be the most economical means, using off-hours or sidebands or regions of the spectrum which are otherwise unexploited.[2]

In short, planning for broadcasting is an integral component of planning for a total communication system and should be carried out with the country's total communication needs in mind.

Not very many countries have done a satisfactory job of comprehensive communication planning. *A priori* one might assume that such planning would be best done in countries with centralized planning and nationalized communications monopolies, but this is not the case. In such societies broadcasting falls under the jurisdiction of politicians who are not much interested in engineering questions while telecommunications falls under the jurisdiction of engineers. With two powerful national monopolies at the helm one tends to find warring baronies rather than co-ordination. Thus, in the Soviet Union, the most extreme example of a centrally planned society with nationalized service monopolies, broadcasting is a Party matter under the All Union Committee for Broadcasting, whereas telecommunications are handled within the normal ministerial structure. The relations between them are remote. In Canada, on the other hand, and to a lesser extent in the United States, a loose, decentralized system provides for greater interplay between the two electronic communications sectors. In Canada broadcasting is handled at the Provincial level and 40 per cent of all homes receive their television signals by cable. Phone companies have assisted in cable-laying, but most cable systems are independent. In parts of Canada the phone company is publicly owned; elsewhere it is private. This variety of patterns has allowed for constructive experimentation with all possible relationships between broadcasting and telecommunications. These experiments are monitored by the Canadian Radio and Television Commission which, like the American Federal Communication Commission, regulates both broadcasting and telephony.[3]

The most typical pattern, worldwide, comes closer to the Soviet than to the Canadian extreme. A government department runs telecommunications. A separate government department or public corporation has a monopoloy on broadcasting. There is little interaction between them at the policy level except for the fact that the broadcast network may be a customer of the PTT.

The Relationship of Broadcasting to Society

In any highly pluralistic society such as Iran, it is essential both for the different groups themselves and for national integration

The Governance of Mass Communication

that broadcasting present over the air the activities and interests of the various social groups. Radio and TV are mirrors of the society. It is important for the self-esteem of citizens who belong to different social groups that they see themselves in that mirror. It is important for mutual respect and, therefore, for social peace that others in the society see prideful images in that mirror of social groups whom they might otherwise disdain.

The presentation of pluralistic images is more likely to contribute to national unity than to fission. The appearance on the air of figures with whom individual citizens can easily identify contributes to the acceptance of the messages conveyed. In many developing countries fear of regional divisions has prompted governments to centralize all broadcasting in the capital and to present on the air a single style of person with a single accent. The result has been to deprive provincial authorities of a major tool for implementing regional programmes and to give broadcasting an alien, elitist image.

The face and voice of the person on the television screen does not command instant authority by virtue of his role. Unlike the father of a family, the policeman on the block or the mayor of a city, he has no other relations with the audience that draws their respect. His appearance, his style, his way of talking, must somehow draw him out of the crowd. He cannot be characterless. He must be a striking human being with distinctive features that become his hallmark. Features that groups can identify with are particularly important if he is to act as their spokesman. And he must also stand out as a man of exceptional character. In short, a popular broadcasting system with mass appeal requires stars.

This may seem ironical. Simplistic popular political theorizing sometimes presents a polarity between democracy in which all are equal and which is, therefore, leaderless and aristocracy in which there are elite individuals. However, since ancient times sophisticated political theorists have understood that in some respects the opposite is true. It is oligarchies that most strenuously combat 'the cult of the individual'. Competing oligarchs do not wish any one among them to develop a mass following. Conversely, democracies, as Plato, Aristotle, Ibn

Ithiel de Sola Pool

Khaldun, Moise Ostrogorski and Max Weber pointed out, require 'demagogues' (in the Greek sense) or charismatic leaders to mobilize a popular following. Thus, if broadcasting is to serve as an initiator and mobilizer of public action it must do it through distinctive stars with whom people can identify.

A nation is too large an organization to function with all initiative taken at the centre. There are limitations of time and attention as well as limitations of imagination and empathy both by those at the centre and those out at the grass roots. Emotional attachments are strongest to persons with whom one has some human contact, as every politician knows.

Television does not change these facts. It should work with them. To be seen on TV is a useful halfway step to being seen in person. However, the face seen on TV but who no one whom one knows has ever met in person, who has no shared relatives with one's own relatives, who has no known private life like one's own, is simply not as credible as the TV spokesman who is also part of one's own circle. Consensus about the purposes and programmes of the centre is more likely to be achieved by diverse elements talking to each other than by appeals from the centre itself.

For effective broadcasting by different social groups it is not enough to present pictures of different regions, costumes and tribes. There is a limit to the extent to which even the most talented producer can create programmes which are meaningful to people who differ greatly from himself unless he draws them directly into the production process.

Members of the relevant social groups can usefully be involved in the planning and creation of programmes. Mechanisms for such participation include advisory committees, local origination, and feedback programming in which local activities are used for programme material and members of the group are invited to express their reactions. Such programming can contribute to credibility and offers the opportunity of presenting the unity in diversity of the nation.

Credibility

Without credibility among its audience, a broadcasting system

The Governance of Mass Communication

is at best a bulletin board for notices and a conduit for entertainment trivia. If a broadcast system is to activate a people it must be trusted.

Credibility is a serious concern, for credibility is a fragile matter. It is easily compromised and hard to regain. Credibility requires that the broadcaster can be counted on by his audience to tell the truth in regard to the things he discusses and also to address himself to matters which the listener considers important. Evasion as well as distortion compromises credibility. Credibility can also be served by putting spokesmen on the air whom listeners already trust and feel related to.

One type of programming that helps maintain credibility is 'town meetings' in which real daily problems are discussed and different views and suggestions as to their solution are put forth. Credibility is aided by the broadcaster having a status that is recognized as independent from government pressures, discussing issues impartially, presenting alternative views on controversial issues, airing problems that really trouble people and providing a channel between people and government.

Three additional points need stressing. First, if television is perceived as just a part of some remote elite status or of the government, the suspicion may arise that the medium does not give relevant information or the whole truth. To counter this, the role of television as a professional, free and independent journalistic medium must be assured by its charter. Second, viewers must not think of television programmes as shows produced by an insular metropolitan clique. On the contrary, viewers should consider themselves as active participants. This can be achieved in part by a programme policy which encourages as much as possible participation by ordinary men and women. For such fieldwork programme production special training should be provided for the programme staff. Third, the image which the communicator projects on the screen makes a difference. The broadcast organization should analyse what kind of communicator is desirable in the current political and socio-cultural context.

In many field experiments an attempt has been made to create programming that is credible in rural areas. Senegal, for example, has a weekly programme in which an issue is discussed by villagers and tape recorded. The announcer invites letters from other villages about the same problem which are then read over the air and answered by a high government official. Experience has shown that when development plans are discussed at the village level and broadcast over the air the interest is greatly enhanced.

The Role of Broadcasting in Social and Economic Development

Social and economic development is development of people. To achieve it requires learning, motivation and effective communications. A broadcasting system provides the government with means to promote and explain development plans and their implementation, to provide a link between the government and the people.

Too often those who engage in developmental planning think only of providing the economic prerequisites of development such as capital, or, if they think of motivation at all, of economic incentives. While these are important considerations, attention should also be given to psychological planning for mobilization. Broadcasting organizations should be attuned to fulfilling that role. It is one of the main contributions they can make to development. Broadcasting organizations can explain to government departments and other authorities the potential of electronic mass communications in support of development as well as their limitations. They can advise government and other development agencies on the psychological dimensions of programmes and can advocate before planning and other development agencies the requisite communication aspects and resources for persuasion.

Developmental broadcasting demands close co-ordination with the concerned government departments and other institutions responsible for implementation. It would be pointless, for instance, to promote a new seed variety if it is unavailable in the localities where it is to be used.

Broadcasting for developmental purposes requires very

The Governance of Mass Communication

special skills that not all broadcasters have. Development broadcasts should have entertainment value as well as other qualities. Broadcasting organizations in rapidly developing countries must provide training which goes beyond classical broadcasting training and includes an understanding of all aspects of the development process and the use of communications media for it.

As a development agency, a broadcasting organization has the critical responsibility of activating the human potential of the country and its cultural development. This contribution to development can be provided not only by serious educational programmes but also by those whose primary aim is entertainment. Entertainment programming can present audiences with role models for new ways of life and can fulfil an informative role as well as, or even better than, programming which is more purposively informative.

So far we have laid out some basic considerations for the governance of broadcasting in a rapidly developing country. These included the structure of a total national communication system of which broadcasting is but a part; the social structure of the country; the need to establish credibility with a diverse audience; and the priority of the goals of rapid development.

We now turn to some conclusions that seem to follow.

1. *Value of non-broadcast activities to the broadcaster.* Broadcasting cannot be developed in isolation. Along with broadcasting stations, a successful system depends upon the existence of electricity, distributors, and repair shops around the country. Broadcasting requires performers, writers, journalists and directors.

The development of national cultural institutions must move forward on many fronts simultaneously. If there is to be appreciation of the country's ancient art, textbooks must teach about it in schools, museums must exhibit it, universities must train historians and archeologists document it. TV producers must have a source of material available to them. The development of culture is more than development of radio and TV.

Ithiel de Sola Pool

Because of their mass appeal, radio and TV are apt to move ahead faster than other cultural institutions. They do not require literacy and reach everywhere at low incremental cost. For its own well-being, the broadcasting industry ought to help develop other cultural institutions which would otherwise lag behind. Since such related activities are not central to the organization, a broadcaster might perhaps spin them off when and if they acquire the ability to become self-sustaining. This would be a wise exercise in self-restraint and a way of avoiding the atrophy that often accompanies excessive growth. The unique capability of a broadcasting network to start the ball rolling should be recognized. It knows its audiences. It has the experience. If a broadcasting organization is to fulfil its role as promoter of economic and social development, it must inevitably branch out into auxiliary activities. To teach courses over the air it must distribute associated printed matter. To engage in agricultural advice programmes it must maintain liaison with field agents. Its activities must be defined by its substantive goals rather than by a particular means of transmission.

2. *Research provides policy guidance.* Broadcasters need a two-way relationship with their audiences. Credibility as well as effectiveness in promoting development depends upon an understanding of and interaction with the many social groups that make up the audience. Research is an instrument for getting to know the audience better. It is a voice of the audience. It helps the broadcaster avoid the danger of transmitting only the limited views of his own social milieu.

Research takes many forms and requires a variety of skills.
— Library research contributes to the content of programmes.
— Audience research provides data on audience composition, size, type and interests and helps broadcasters to be responsive to their audiences.
— Effects research reveals audience attitudes, values and behaviour.
— Needs analysis at both the national and audience level specifies programme requirements.
— Organizational and systems research on the broadcast institution itself serves to identify the best combination of

resources and their management for responding to changing requirements and opportunities.
— Programme testing and evaluation of pilot material contribute to the development of innovative concepts.

In view of the importance of research and its potential but fragile capability for objectivity, we should consider how research activities ought to be linked to programming and operating policy. Research organizations need budgetary and other flexibility to allow them some freedom of initiative. Autonomy serves both to sustain the creativity of researchers and to stimulate research ideas the best of which are likely to come out of the researcher's own experience and expertise. At the same time, if the research is to prove of practical use, researchers must maintain close liaison with policy makers. A number of conclusions follow:

(a) Research ought to report to the highest policy levels.[4] While programming departments may have some internal research requirements, research in general will not be objective nor will its results be properly applied if it is not lifted above the pressures of day-to-day production.

(b) There should be rapid dissemination of research results to all levels of the organization where they may be used.

(c) Researchers within the broadcasting organization should maintain contact with professional colleagues in other institutions and should act as translators of research results into terms the policy makers can understand.

(d) Research provides background information and *post facto* evaluation. In addition, by operating iteratively in the production cycle it should answer questions raised by producers as they arise.

(e) Research may at times provide useful programme material by identifying people's interests and concerns.

Relationship of Broadcasting to the Government

Throughout the world one finds a variety of arrangements for the governance of broadcasting, ranging from pure government monopoly to purely commercial systems. Other arrangements include broadcasting by public corporations, by universities, by churches, by voluntary associations and by combinations of the above. There may be a single broadcasting organization or several competing ones.

The relationship between management of programming and of transmission also varies. In France and Holland, for example, one monopoly operates the transmitters for several broadcasting organizations. In Holland a number of producing organizations share studios, wavebands and transmitters. In the United States, on the other hand, each broadcasting organization owns its own physical facilities.

The only aspect in the hardware-software relationship that is universal is that in broadcasting software considerations are dominant. Whereas in telecommunications systems engineers are generally in charge, in broadcasting organizations political, marketing, and cultural specialists have the upper hand.[5] The top men may be drawn from the fiscal or marketing areas, from programming or from politics. There may be one production organization or several. The production organization may be an integral part of, or distinct from, the broadcasting stations which create the daily schedule, and also from the transmission organization. Broadcasting stations may be loosely federated into a co-operative network or run by a national organization. There may be one network or several competing ones. Where there are competing networks there may be a mixed system, as in Britain and the United States where some networks are private and some are public.

At the structural level there is no single answer as to what is the most desirable system for all countries and for all times. The structural form of broadcasting organizations is determined by particular socio-economic, cultural and political factors operating in any given society, the resources available and the number of channels. Relationships between media and government change as new social, economic and technological environments emerge.

In all circumstances, however, broadcasting has relations with government. Government needs channels through which to talk

The Governance of Mass Communication

to the people; the people for their part, need information about their government. Furthermore, it is the government which, by law, determines the basic policies and structures under which the national communication system operates. Government allocates the scarce spectrum. In most countries government provides all or most of the funding for broadcasting. And governments may, by their controls, undercut the effectiveness of broadcasters.

There is need for strong protection of the autonomy of broadcast organizations, whether broadcast monopolies or competing networks. This need follows directly from the importance of credibility. To win its listeners' confidence a broadcasting organization must show that it is devoted uncompromisingly to doing its job and is not the agent of outside forces.

Autonomy means independence of broadcasters in their professional role, not autonomy of a social elite. This latter form of autonomy develops easily because broadcasters are inevitably drawn from the better educated, professional strata of the population. The autonomy that is desired is that of broadcasting professionals acting responsibly. To achieve it while resisting the temptation to become 'a happy few' requires continuous interaction of the independent professionals with their audience by the various means mentioned above: research, feedback and participant programming, and decentralization of the system. Autonomy is fostered by professionalism, protected financing, strong traditions of broadcast independence and an appropriate structure of the broadcasting organization. Organizational mechanisms that protect broadcasting autonomy include tenure for broadcasting staffs, high position in the state structure for the director general and governance by a board independent of both the government and the broadcast organization. Such a board of directors can act as an intermediary between the government and the director general in the case of disputes. Its membership may be drawn from universities, journalists, associations, arts and business, or may have members appointed or elected by interested parties such as recognized national associations and the government.

Ithiel de Sola Pool

With autonomy goes responsibility. Broadcasting organizations must provide access to the air for diverse elements of the population. This can be done by making available specialized channels, or specialized programmes within general channels, through advertisements, public service announcements, interview programmes—and, most important of all, by local and decentralized programming.

Discussions of relationships between power centres such as government and the broadcasting organization often degenerate into assertions of formal authority. It is easier to engage in legalistic definition of roles than to describe how two large organizations interact. The relationships between large social institutions are polymorphous and occur at hundreds of different organizational levels. The symbiotic relations at these levels often determine whether and how policies will be implemented. If intervention and control between government and broadcasting organization were to occur only at the summit level, the real power of one institution over the other would be small because effective exercise of power requires many points of linkage. What is likely to happen if the top authorities are the only point of linkage is a deadlock (not unlike negotiations between superpowers) with each head official unable to yield any point that might open up unforeseen troubles in the large structure below him. Only when middle and lower level personnel interact with one another in the carrying out of programmes can effective action be taken. In other words, joint programmes require that authority be delegated to interagency links.

Financing

A successful broadcasting organization must have an adequate and sufficiently stable source of funds to retain its autonomy. There are various ways in which this could be achieved. Licence fees seem to provide broadcasters with a stable source of income. But legally imposed fees tend to remain unchanged in the face of inflation and, under usual circumstances, do not provide a satisfactory solution.

Part of the broadcasting revenue may come directly out of

The Governance of Mass Communication

the government budget. In the United States, where this is the case for the fourth network, there is currently a lively discussion on how to protect broadcasting funded by the government budget from congressional pressures. A proposal which may be adopted provides for three-year funding, with Congress voting each year on the appropriation for the year three years hence. Since control of events three years in the future is not likely, this scheme would minimize the risk of political interference. To meet the problem of unanticipated inflation, the formula for broadcasting revenue could be related to a fixed percentage of the national budget or to those components of the national budget relevant to communication.

But a system fully supported by the government runs the great risk of becoming boring and reflective of the tastes and views of the civil service. There is no incentive to attract audiences, since the revenue does not decline if the audience falls off, and the only people who must be satisfied are those who hold the purse-strings.

A broadcasting system fully paid for by advertisers, on the other hand, tends to produce mass entertainment exclusively since entertainment programmes have been shown to achieve much higher audiences than any other offering. Advertisers are not interested in the intensity of viewer enjoyment as long as the viewer watches at all. Even when faced with competition on the air, an advertiser is not prepared to double or triple production budgets to gain a few extra audience percentage points. In the United States he restricts himself to what can be done for about 2 cents per hour per viewer.

The viewer may be willing to pay substantially more if he feels he is getting his money's worth and may be prepared to subscribe to pay-by-the-show schemes for the sake of quality programming that meets his particular taste. Collecting from the audience programme-by-programme involves, of course, some additional costs. A scrambling and unscrambling device has to be used, along with record-keeping. This is technically easier on a cable system than over the air, but the latter is also feasible.

Such a device is not necessary where customers pay a flat fee by month or year, as for example paying a licence fee at the post office. But under such a system the customer loses his influence over programming. The broadcaster is in control of what is offered and the viewer must accept it. Besides, in a country whose population is not affluent, the fee may slow down TV penetration.

The choice between having payment by the public, the advertisers or the government is partly a function of who can best afford it. In a poor developing country multinational corporations that wish to advertise may be the readiest source of funds. A pay-by-the-programme system requires the potential customers to be reasonably affluent. In some countries the greatest concentration of wealth is in the hands of the government.

The best solution is probably a mixed system, part of which is responsive primarily to audience tests and thereby provides a standard of comparison as to audience receptiveness, part serves primarily government objectives and part is purely commercial. With broadcasting deriving its revenue from a variety of sources it is important that a substantial portion of the revenue be for general purposes not tied to the special interests of the sponsor. If each government agency—each university, for example—supports programmes exclusively in a particular field such as education, health, national culture, etc., and inadequate resources are provided for unsponsored activities, distorted programming will result.

Internal Organization of the Broadcasting System

Just as there is no single formula for the overall structure of a broadcasting organization or its relation to other authorities, so there is no single formula for its internal structure. That depends on the practices of the country, the past established traditions of the organization, its stage of development, and what makes the people who are doing the job feel comfortable.

If there is any one guiding principle it is that broadcasting is a creative activity which must allow scope for a variety of

The Governance of Mass Communication

approaches and pluralism of initiatives to avoid the ossification that arises from traditional bureaucratic structures.

Of great importance is decentralization in the broadcasting organization—and not necessarily or exclusively on a geographical basis. There may be functional divisions with each unit responsible for different types of programming, e.g., educational or ethnic. There may even be separate units set up with no clear difference in their characteristics for the explicit purpose of promoting a spirit of competition among similar but independent creative groups.

Regional distribution of creative and production activities remains, however, the most important form of decentralization. It serves to overcome the serious problem of gigantism in primate cities which draw to themselves all intellectuals and persons of ability.

Geographical decentralization of broadcasting is also important because state and local authorities need access to broadcasting just as much as central authorities do. In education, public health, business enterprise or government the echelons which deal directly with people are those at the local level. Local school authorities, local merchants and local officials must reach people directly. It is they who can make the most and best use of broadcasting for social purposes.

Notes

1. Ideas in this paper were drawn from a panel discussion at the Mashad Symposium of NIRT's Prospective Planning Project.
2. The BBC's CEEFAX, which sends news and information direct to television sets, is an illustration of what is possible.
3. In the USA there is an Office of Telecommunications Policy which does not regulate but advises the government about broadcasting and telecommunications policy. There is also the Federal Communications Commission which oversees both broadcasting and telecommunication with regard to licensing of spectrum use and regulates rates.
4. There is often antipathy between researchers and producers. The 'critic' role of the researcher makes this inevitable. No solution is ideal. Sometimes researchers are 'protected' by the top leadership by being put in an ivory tower away from the action. Neither this

alternative, nor co-opting the researcher into a responsible policy-making position is desirable. In the end a fruitful tension based on mutual respect and recognition of the need for some conflict depends upon the top leadership keeping close to both parties and insisting on their collaboration.

5   In the mid-1920s when this issue had not yet been settled in England, Lord Reith recounts in his diaries the attempt by the telegraphic industry to get control (as ATT also attempted unsuccessfully in the USA). In an entry for 19 March 1925 he notes: 'The trades unions are a nuisance so long as they think they can control the BBC ... Noble said nobody else could manage the BBC as well as they did, because of their knowledge of wireless, which was of course humbug. It is not a knowledge of wireless that is required.'

References

Barnouw, Erik (1966-70), *A History of Broadcasting in the United States,* 3 vols, New York: Oxford University Press.

Briggs, Asa (1961-70), *The History of Broadcasting in the United Kingdom,* 3 vols., Oxford University Press.

de Sola Pool, Ithiel (1967), *Contemporary Political Science,* New York: McGraw-Hill, ch. 2.

Dizard, Wilson (1966), *Television: a World View,* Syracuse.

Emery, Walter (1969), *National and International Systems of Broadcasting,* East Lansing.

March, James G., ed. (1965), *Handbook of Organizations,* Chicago: Rand McNally.

Report of the Committee on Broadcasting, (1965), Ottawa, Queen's Printer.

Pige, F. (1962), *La Télévision dans le monde,* Paris.

UNESCO, *Communication Policies,* Studies on Ireland, Yugoslavia, Sweden, Hungary and Germany.

7
Multi-Media Education
Ivor K. Davies

Perceptions tend to vary widely, according to the perceivers and their sensibilities. So it is sometimes with the role of mass communications and multi-media in national educational development; different perceptions of the two forms often lead to quite different conclusions regarding their particular roles. Unless these perceptions are made public and openly discussed, problems are likely to arise, for we are handicapped by implicit assumptions and expectations.

All of us make assumptions of one kind or another, and nowhere are these likely to be more problematical than in the field of communications policy in developing countries. The role of mass communications (such as radio, television, newspaper, books, magazines, periodicals and people[1]), and the role of individualized multi-media (such as 16mm educational films, slides, transparencies, tapes, long-playing records, wall-charts, workbooks, working models, laboratory equipment, class-handouts, specimens, video-tapes and people) which are more traditionally associated with formal education, seem so obvious as to leave little room for further discussion. All of them seem to be nothing more than two broad categories of items that are increasingly being referred to amongst teachers as examples of media or educational technology. The main purpose of such technology is somehow to enhance efficiency. In other words, mass communications and multi media, in the educational context, are viewed as two different forms of technology that will enable teachers to do something that could not be done without its help. Such an assumption invites discussion, since it is critical to the overall role of these two types of media.

Ivor K. Davies

Media Technology

The term media technology (or as some would prefer, educational technology) generates some confusion, since it means different things to different people. In the literature of education, three very different meanings are discernible which have been designated by Davies (1972) as Media Technology I, Media Technology II and Media Technology III. Since media technology is an important element in modern educational policy-making, it is essential to appreciate both the various meanings, as well as the several consequences, of these quite different points of view. Most of the differences stem from alternative nuances of the word 'technology'. To some it implies hardware or machines, to others software or materials, and to still others know-how or process. Of the three usages, know-how (which is the oldest dictionary meaning) is the developing definition, and hardware (barely 100 years old in dictionary terms) the oldest and by far still the most current.

Media or Educational Technology I

Media Technology I is the hardware approach. It stresses the importance of *teaching aids* such as television, teaching machines, radio, simulators, equipment, language laboratories, etc. The origin of this particular approach lies in the application of engineering to the perceived problems of education. This is the classical meaning of the term 'media technology'. Perhaps because it is so concrete and easily understandable, it is what most developing countries have been tempted to purchase, often with embarrassing results. The mere expenditure of vast sums of money on machines is not necessarily the best way of expanding and developing educational programmes in developing countries, as dusty and rusting piles of unserviceable equipment in some schools indicate.

Media or Educational Technology II

Media Technology II is the software approach. It stresses the importance of *learning aids,* such as film and videotape, behavioural objectives and evaluation, individual worksheets,

Multi-Media Education

slides and transparencies, books, newspapers, resource materials, etc. The origin of this approach lies in the application of psychology to the problems of learning. Currently, this is fast becoming the fashionable meaning of the term 'media technology', especially with the growing emphasis on curriculum development and instructional development in Europe and North America.

Media or Educational Technology III

Media Technology I and II can be usefully encompassed by a more embracing view which combines the separate hardware and software approaches of the other two perspectives. Media Technology II stresses the importance of viewing teaching and learning as a whole, as a *Gestalt*, not to be confused with either electronic gadgetry or new ways of designing and producing educational materials. Media Technology III is as wide as education itself, and is concerned with the design of *appropriate* learning environments. The origin of this particular approach lies in the application of the strategies of the behavioural sciences to the problems of education. It has a design orientation, a problem-solving emphasis in which an attempt is made to look sceptically at a teaching-learning situation so as to determine its possibilities. In this way we will find means of releasing or liberating ourselves from self-deception or delusion, and be able to reject the idea of *one* overall panacea for educational problems.

Media Technology III is a much more demanding technology. Its sensitive, yet sceptical, orientation frees it from many of the constraints that seem to operate in the case of Media Technology I and Media Technology II.

Efficiency and Effectiveness

In allocating resources for learning, politicians, planners and educators have one prime responsibility. They must ensure that both they, and their projects or programmes, are effective. In the past, there was a tendency to emphasize efficiency, but today *effectiveness* has become the central issue.

Ivor K. Davies

Efficiency involves doing things right; effectiveness involves doing the right things, as illustrated in Table 1. Well-designed classrooms, up-to-the-minute modern facilities, the latest television studios, superb motion picture capabilities, the newest language laboratories, etc. are all commendable in themselves as outward and visible signs of efficiency, but they do *not* guarantee effectiveness.

Effectiveness, in the context of Media Technology III, does not necessarily involve hardware or software capabilities, nor the personality of the teacher, the length of his training, the elegance of his teaching. Effectiveness is a function of what is achieved, as well as the appropriateness of the means by which that achievement is attained. If an educational programme fails to achieve its objectives, then it is ineffective—no matter how efficient it may be. Mass communications and multi-media can and do contribute to education in two significant ways. First, they play an important role in ensuring that education be efficient; more importantly, they also can help ensure that education be effective.

TABLE 1 Effectiveness and efficiency (from Davies, 1971)

EFFECTIVENESS is doing the right things		EFFICIENCY is doing things right
this involves		*this involves*
creating alternatives	*rather than*	solving problems
optimizing resource utilization	*rather than*	safeguarding resources
realizing responsibilities	*rather than*	following procedures
meeting criteria	*rather than*	increasing pass-rates
satisfying needs	*rather than*	reducing costs
using a systems approach	*rather than*	treating things separately

Multi-Media Education

Effectiveness is rarely a quality that is brought to a situation. It is something consciously achieved by learning how to manage effectively a situation. This means taking into account not only the needs of the task, but also the needs of the society and of the people involved. People are the raison d'être of an educational system; indeed, they are the very system itself. As Richard Peters (1966) reminds us, education involves initiating people into worthwhile activities, activities that are thought to be valuable enough to pass on. Media has an essential role in this initiation process, whilst technology (in the dictionary sense of 'know-how' rather than in the more restricted sense of machines) has an important role in assisting us to identify. design and evaluate worthwhile means and ends.

In order to achieve effectiveness, educators and planners concerned with questions of national educational development must possess four main skills:

1. They must be *sensitive* to the needs of the total situation; not only to tasks but also to people, not only to ends but also to means.

2. They must be able to *diagnose* the requirements of the total situation, creating alternatives rather than just solving problems with ready made solutions.

3. They must have sufficient professional expertise to be able to choose and implement the right strategy at the right time.

4. They must be flexible enough to be able to put into effect whatever the total situation demands. This involves sensitively balancing both people and task needs, as well as national. cultural and religious concerns.

But sensitivity, diagnostic ability, professional expertise and flexibility are not enough. Effectiveness also involves empathy for the value system that underlies a nation's identity, particularly as this can, all too often, come into direct conflict with the value system underlying a western interpretation of what mass media is really about.

Alternative Approaches to Educational Planning

In engaging in educational development at either the national or the local level, most developing countries are faced with the problem of making decisions about the possible use of mass communications and multi media. Indeed, in many countries, plans have revolved around the utilization of mass media, particularly radio and television. Other countries, less favoured with material resources, have developed plans around the use of more conventional and less costly audio-visual methodologies.

In a very real sense, planning is little more than anticipatory decision-making. It involves deciding what to do, and how to do it, before any concrete action is taken. It involves deciding the nature of the relationship between the *ends* desired and the *means* available. When both ends and means are known, little planning is necessary for no decisions of consequence have to be taken. All that is necessary is to derive a set of methods or procedures that will assist in the implementation. When the ends have not been determined, and the available means are unknown, creative, sensitive and careful planning is needed, not only in terms of the task to be accomplished but also in terms of the people and culture involved.

The usual advice given to educators and media specialists involved in planning activities begins with the apparent truism that the first step ought to be to define goals or objectives, since once these are identified everything else will fall into place. This advice outlines a systematic form of planning. Other alternatives are available. The means–ends model is richer in possibilities than might appear at first sight. Figure 9 illustrates some of the options available. For the sake of clarity three paths are highlighted: path 'X' which implies a *systematic* view of planning; path 'Y' which implies an *expedient* approach to planning; and path 'Z' which implies a *piecemeal* or successive approximations approach towards educational planning and development. In actual practice, of course, it is unlikely that planning can be so neatly cut and dried as the three modes presented here. Combinations and compromises inevitably take place in real world situations. But, as we shall soon see, the systematic view of planning is closely related to a Media Technology I view of the world, expedient planning to a Media

Multi-Media Education

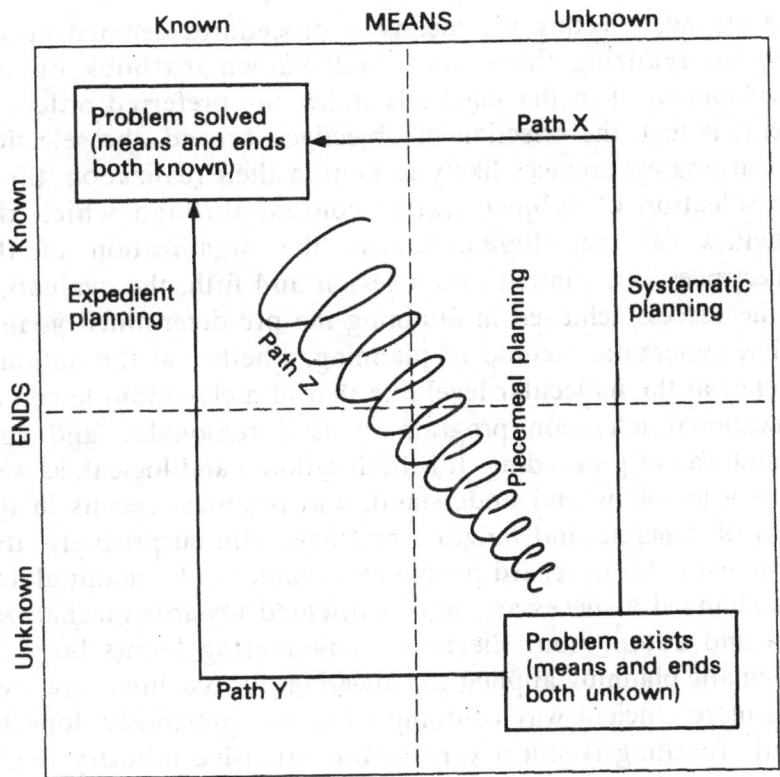

Figure 9 The means–ends model of planning (from Davies, 1966)

Technology II view, and piecemeal or successive approximation planning to a Media Technology III set of assumptions.

Systematic planning

Path 'X' in Figure 9 represents a systematic approach towards educational planning, whether it is at the national or local level, or whether it simply involves the development of a curriculum, course, lesson or module. This particular approach is highly commended in textbooks concerned with audio-visual instruction, curriculum development, instructional development and the development of educational materials for educational television, radio or printed texts. Basically, systematic planning consists first, of defining the ends or objectives to be realized, and second, selecting the means or procedures deemed necessary for realizing them. As a well-known textbook on the development of media materials states, the preferred orders of events is first, the selection of objectives, second, the selection of learning experiences likely to help in their realization, third, the selection of subject matter content through which the activities can be offered, fourth, the organization of the experiences and content into a lesson and fifth, the evaluation of the success achieved in attaining the pre-determined goals.

The systematic method of planning, whether at the national level or at the molecular level like that of a classroom lesson or educational television programme, is a reasonable and successful way of proceeding. It is both rational and logical, as well as easy to follow and understand, and produces results in the form of concrete and tangible products. Not surprisingly, this approach tends to regard people as variables to be manipulated and changed as necessary, and is oriented towards mechanization and automation. Electronic engineering looms large in systematic planning applied to education, for machines are seen as a more efficient way of doing what was previously done by hand. Teaching is still a very labour intensive industry hence the temptation to use radio and television, language laboratories and simulators, teaching machines and computer-assisted instruction.

While systematic planning is an excellent strategy to adopt when one has a clear set of goals and feels reasonably confident that they are attainable, it is of little use when the future is unknown. For this reason, the approach has a number of serious drawbacks (see Oakeshott, 1962; Popper, 1966). The major criticisms seem to centre on the fact that means are isolated from ends, rather than seen as heads and tails of the same situation and that ends are viewed as unchanging rather than as capable of evolving during the planning and implementation stages of educational development.

One of the best known examples of systematic planning involving media technology is that of the Open University in Britain which, from many points of view, has been a successful venture. It has attracted worldwide attention, receives a well-

Multi-Media Education

deserved favourable press, has a waiting list of students wanting to enrol in its programmes and—in a stringent economic climate—is the only British university to have its financial grant increased. Yet the Open University has largely failed to fulfil its charter of being a university of a second chance (a significant proportion of its students have already had some form of higher education), and it has not used mass communications in really innovative ways. Only the distribution role of the media has been exploited, rather than the actual power of the media. But above all it appears to see the human mind as a vessel of varying capacity into which knowledge can be poured via television, books and tapes, rather than what its first chancellor saw as 'a fire that has to be set alight and blown with the divine efflatus'. In other words, mass communications have been used for their efficiency role, rather than for the twin roles of efficiency *and* effectiveness.

Educational technologists at the Open University who are responsible for developing and designing courses appear to see mass communications as a means of transmitting information to largely passive students. As Harris and Holmes (1975), both former members of the faculty, point out, a great deal of 'the curriculum design work has involved getting the messages clear, simplifying them, removing ambiguities and doubts, and then packaging these messages attractively in logical sequences. Such "rationalization" of the teaching material is done solely because of the one-way technologies of print, television and radio.' What is unfortunate is that not only does the criticism seem to be true, though there have been some brilliant exceptions, but that two experienced technologists appear to see television and radio as necessarily one-way technologies.

Expedient planning

Although this method of planning is presently unfashionable in education, at least in print, it is still widely practiced. Expedient planning, as typified by path 'Y' in Figure 9, is particularly advantageous when the situation requires a development or change in attitudes, sentiments or values (see Davies, 1976). In such circumstances, the very act of defining the ends to be achieved can contaminate the values and sentiments one may wish to change. It is worth nothing that some of the most creative changes in education, involving media in a highly innovative way, have stemmed from this approach. Some of the functional literacy campaigns have been based on this model, as have some of the non-formal educational programmes in Asia involving hygiene, family planning, agricultural development and current or national affairs. In these cases an attempt was deliberately made to avoid pre-stated objectives (despite the fact that they are almost de rigueur in these days of accountability).

An interesting example of the expediency model with systematic overtones is to be found in Thailand in the area of family planning. Using primary field research in a range of different religious communities, supplemented by more formal interviews and structured surveys, a compendium of socio-economic characteristics of the rural communities in different regions of the country was compiled. This was used as a means of determining the most expedient way of introducing an effective (and, the compilers hoped, efficient) programme of family planning in each of the regions. It suggested that a multi-media approach using mobile audio-visual units was likely to be more successful in delivering messages to specific communities than either national television or local radio, both of which have too broad a range and are unable to deal with local differences. Films made by urbanized personnel prove to be next to useless for rural audiences, and highly professional foreign films are inferior to amateur films made in Thailand. Most important of all, media (whether films, flip-charts or television) have their increased effectiveness when used by, or in tandem with, trained local people working as agents of change.

Piecemeal planning

Whilst paths 'X' and 'Y' represent two of the choices available to educational planners and technologists, the means–ends model suggests that there is at least one other way of proceeding. This involves what Popper (1966) calls a piecemeal approach, which he recommends as being methodologically sound without the dangers often implicit in systematic planning. In the path 'Z' model, rather than defining the ends or the means as the first step in planning, a cyclical approach is employed involving successive approximations. Such a model involves no blueprint or master plan. Rather than adopting a reconstructionist or utopian approach to educational planning, one searches for, and deals with, the greatest and most urgent evils.

As Karl Popper (1966) points out in the wider context of society at large, piecemeal planning

> is the difference between a reasonable method of improving the lot of man, and a method which, if really tried, may really lead to an intolerable increase in human suffering. It is the difference between a method which can be applied at any moment, and a method whose advocacy may easily become a means of continually postponing action until a later date, when conditions are more favourable. And it is also the difference between the only method of improving matters which has so far been continuously successful, at any time, and in any place ... and a method which, whenever it has been tried, has led only to the use of violence in place of reason, and if not to its own abandonment, at any rate to that of the original blueprint.

In following this approach to educational planning, a developing country might start with a rough definition of the more important and pressing needs, such as education of girls or expansion of secondary or vocational education, and then consider the resources available, as well as those that could be made available. While in some cases money may not be a constraint, in all cases the shortage of skilled manpower will be a limiting factor. Once this analysis has been completed, an attempt is made to define more precisely the goals that might realistically be achieved. Then one reverts once more to the means available and considers how they might be best employed.

Ivor K. Davies

Piecemeal planning has many advantages from the point of view of mass communications and multi media. Instead of setting out on vast spending sprees involving the purchase of all kinds of media and the construction of expensive buildings, a number of pilot or pathfinder projects are attempted in order to determine what is likely to be successful. There is no reason, of course, why pilot projects should not be conceived within an overall conceptual plan, but piecemeal planning does imply that projects should cover a wide range of possibilities, should involve phased implementation, should be watched over and directed by responsible task-forces and should allow for both centralized and decentralized forms of organization. A team or project approach is also preferable, rather than a specialist type of operation. Camera men, television producers, script-writers, teachers, curriculum developers, evaluators, subject-matter experts and textbook writers should work as a team. It is thus preferable to gradually create a resource base with every type of production capability (from television, audio-visual to printed materials), rather than to think in terms of a separate television station, a separate audio-visual centre, and a separate printing plant.

An example of a rapidly developing country using this method of planning is the Kingdom of Saudi Arabia which is undertaking a major expansion and development of its educational programmes. Working on the premise that educational technology III will be essential to the whole scheme, they have planned for a National Centre for Educational Technology in Riyadh, for associated District Resource Centres in the major population centres, and for educational technology co-ordinators in the larger schools. The national plan involves curriculum development, media design, development, production and distribution, pre-service and in-service training of teachers, evaluation and educational research of the applied variety. It is envisaged that all types of media production and utilization will be available and that whatever media mixes are appropriate to the situation will be employed. A project team type of operation is also central to the concept. Each team will be given a specific responsibility for realizing a particular project, and the

Multi-Media Education

members will work together for its achievement at both national and local levels. In this sense, there will truly be *educational* television and radio, as integral parts of an overall curriculum, rather than self-contained, 30-minute type programmes produced by entertainment orientated television personnel. The plan will unfold over twelve years and has such flexibility built into it (including the concept of a temporary national centre on a reduced scale) that it may be reduced or expanded at any time, that its direction may be changed, and that priorities may be altered as the need arises (see Davies and Platt, 1966).

Identifying Educational Needs in Developing Countries

One of the most important problems facing developing countries arises not so much from the use of media in education, but from the difficulty of identifying worth-while activities. Certain educational objectives can be demonstrated to be of high priority. Amongst them are programmes in teacher-education, primary education, pre-school education, rural education, vocational education, primary education and the education of girls, as well as campaigns in functional literacy, hygiene and family planning. Having identified the broad programmes is but a small step. More difficult is the identification of the activities which ought to make up their respective curricula. The nature of these activities will determine not only the cost of the programme, its length and the resources necessary to sustain it, but also its feasibility, appeal, appropriateness and indeed its very effectiveness in meeting both individual and national needs. Yet, all too often, particularly in developing countries, there has been a tendency not to consider the full range of choices in the excusable haste to get things moving. Large quantities of hardware are purchased without either the means to maintain it in working condition or enough materials or programmes to use with it. Hardware is useless if it won't work or if there is insufficient software like films and programmes to feed into it. It is also ineffective if the material has not been developed in such a way as to form an integral part not only of the content but also of the teaching strategies associated with the design of the curriculum.

One of the basic assumptions typically made by Westerners arriving in a developing country is that there is an overwhelming educational need. Since illiteracy rates are high and since there is an obvious lack of schools and teachers, it is felt that people are desperately in need of education. Their remedies, therefore, are simple: build schools (usually in some variant of the western mode), train teachers (following some American or French model of teacher-training) and use mass communications (particularly television) as a ready and obvious delivery system. In one sense this is a reasonable way of proceeding, as it involves the implication that it is best to start afresh and to destroy what went on before.

But if the different assumption is made that one is dealing with an experienced, mature, educated but largely illiterate society, then the problem takes on a rather different dimension. A sophisticated yet illiterate people require a rather different type of solution. Schools, trained teachers, television, etc. may be still necessary, but the curricula, subject matter, activities and emphases are likely to differ both in character and kind.

Aspects of achievement

Two concepts will probably make the point clearer. Any type of deficiency in human performance typically tends to revolve around two aspects of achievement. These can be identified as 'accomplishment' and 'acquirement'. The distinction between these two terms, while seemingly pedantic, is an important one and has consequences both in terms of perceived educational need and the nature of the activities likely to fill that need. It also has consequences in terms of teaching and learning, schools and schooling, media and technology (Gilbert, 1967; Davies, 1971).

Quite simply the two aspects of achievement are:

1. *Acquirement.* This refers to what a person has learned or acquired. It denotes achievement in the sense that certain things have been gained, won or acquired as a result of learning. Acquirement is what is reflected in the lists found in most

syllabuses, and these lists represent the seemingly never ending things that have to be mastered.

2. *Accomplishment.* This, on the other hand, refers to the value or worth of what has been achieved. Different values, of course, can be placed on achievement, depending on the context, people and culture involved. Western society, for instance, places an enormous value upon literacy as the outward and visible sign of an educated person, whereas the Moslem world has traditionally placed a high value on its oral tradition, in which some of the world's greatest poetry looms large.

The important thing to recognize is that a person's level of acquirement, in terms of knowledge or skill, may be high but of little value if the level of accomplishment is low. An example may help. A western child may be unable to tie his or her shoelaces. Inquiry might soon establish that he can carry out each of the *separate* actions involved in tying a shoelace. What he lacks is, first, knowledge of the correct sequence in which each of the actions must be performed, and, second, practice in carrying out the sequence. Thus a relatively small deficiency in acquirement (correct sequence and practice) leads to a very large deficiency in *accomplishment* (successful tying of shoelaces).

Turning now from the relatively trivial act of tying shoelaces to the more complex procedures involved in learning the job of a bank-teller in Nairobi, Dr Gilbert (1967) points out:

> You will probably say that you know nothing about bank tellering. I say this is not true. If you study all the operations a bank teller uses to balance his books, you will find that you have already acquired most of them so that your deficiency in acquirement is quite small. In other words, the difference between what you and the bank teller have acquired is quite small. Nevertheless, the few operations you have not acquired prevent you from accomplishing the objectives of the teller's job. In terms of what you and the bank teller know about his job, there is very little difference between you; in terms of the value of what you know, you are worlds apart. However, a small change in acquirement can often

produce an enormous change in accomplishment. If someone were to teach you the few bank tellering operations you don't know, you would soon accomplish the objectives of the tellering job as well as the veteran teller.

In terms of a curriculum and of resources for teaching and learning, the consequences of this distinction between acquirement and accomplishment are very great indeed. A traditional training programme would assume that someone who cannot do a job must start from the very beginning and learn each operation in turn. This might require a lengthy training course, expensive resources, a great deal of teacher time, and, above all, treating adult trainees as ignorant and inexperienced. A more perceptive training programme would consider the possibility that a short and inexpensive course might realize the desired objectives by concentrating on only a few deficiencies.

Conclusion

This chapter has ranged over a wide field. In almost all of the topics discussed, the plea has been made for sensibility, strategic decision-making, and a willingness to proceed with caution. Mass communications, and more conventional multi media, are all too often perceived as panaceas, universal magical wands, that can bring about revolutionary educational change and immediate progress in developing countries. If care is not taken, the developing world is likely to be strewn with the sad remains of highly expensive communications equipments, unused and unloved as far as teachers and students are concerned, while education continues in an expanded, but still traditional and perhaps impoverished manner. But it does not have to happen. Success depends upon ensuring that media technology fulfils the needs of learners, teachers, employers and society, rather than dictating what those needs should be. It also depends upon a willingness to use a reasonable method of educational planning to improve the lot of people, rather than a much more dramatic or revolutionary method for which the blueprint may be poorly conceived. Above all, however, it depends upon people feeling involved, being involved and acting involved. But care still has to be taken, as Sa'di reminds us, to ensure that we do not overlook perennial wisdom in an age of change. We must ensure that we:

Crush not yon ant, who stores the golden grain;
He lives with pleasure, and will die with pain:
Learn from him rather to secure the spoil
Of patient cares and persevering toil.

Note

1 People, especially opinion leaders, can be regarded as another medium of mass communication. In a very real sense, it is possible to study their 'coverage', effect and 'content'. See Katz and Lazarsfeld (1955).

References

Davies, I. K. (1966), *Objectives in Curriculum Design*, London and New York: McGraw-Hill.
Davies, I. K. (1971), *The Management of Learning*, London: McGraw-Hill (published in the USA as *Competency-Based Learning: technology, management and design).*
Davies, I. K. and Platt, W. A. (1966), *An Operational Plan For the Development of an Educational Technology Programme for the Ministry of Education in the Kingdom of Saudi Arabia*, Riyadh, Saudi Arabia: Ministry of Education.
Davies, I. K. (1973), *The Organization of Training*, London and New York: McGraw-Hill.
Gilbert, T. F. (1967), 'Praxeonomy: a systematic approach to identifying training needs', *Management of Personnel Quarterly*, 6(3), 20–33.
Harris, D. and Holmes, J. (1975), 'Open to Martha, closed to Mary', *The Times Educational Supplement*, 14 April, P. 21.
Katz, E. and Lazarsfeld, P. F. (1955), *Personal Influence*, Chicago: Free Press.
Oakeshott, M. (1962), 'Rational conduct', in M. Oakeshott, ed., *Rationalism in Politics and Other Essays*, London: Methuen.

Ivor K. Davies

Peters, R. S. (1966), *Ethnics and Education*, London: Allen & Unwin.
Popper, K. R. (1966), *The Open Society and its Enemies*, vol. 1, London: Routledge & Kegan Paul.

8
National Development Support Communication[1]
Edwin B. Parker and Ali Mohammadi

Communication has been widely viewed as a major force for national development, at least in the years since the early pioneering work of Wilbur Schramm (1964). The early work on the relationship between communication and development focused on the messages in the mass media and how they could be utilized to create a sense of national identity, foster attitudes favourable to modernization, or fulfil the goals of such particular campaigns as family planning, disease prevention or agricultural development projects. While drawing on that rich tradition, this paper shifts the focus of attention to the technology of communication and to the institutional structures supporting or made possible by the communication technology. Rather than assume that present technologies and institutions are immutable, we start with the assumption that technologies and institutions, as well as messages, can be planned to support the goals of national development. The following sections begin with a general discussion of the goals of national development, the factors and constraints influencing development and the general strategies open to rapidly developing nations (or nations wishing to develop rapidly). The discussion then turns to the specifics of communication in support of development, including communication technology, institutional structure and choice of messages. A concluding section summarizes the policy and planning issues associated with national development support communication.

Goals of National Development

In order to have effective policies for communication in support of national development, it is important to have a clear picture of the national development goals that the communication policy is supporting. Although different nations have differing goals, we can begin with a general statement of goals that might apply in more or less modified form to most nations seeking rapid development.

Economic development

Rapid economic development is often defined in terms of economic development or standard of living, with Gross National Product (GNP) or *per capita* GNP as the basic indicator of economic development. Although the improved quality of life that economic development brings is usually the major goal of development, economic indicators are imperfect measures of the quality of life for which they are surrogates. Human development is a better label for the implicit underlying goal of improved human happiness and quality of life. In any society of human beings, economic development is a means to the end of greater well-being for the members of the society. It would be a perversion and confusion of means and ends to use conventional measures of economic growth as the sole indicator of that greater well-being, especially if in the process important human values are subordinated to the economics. A major difficulty leading to this potential confusion is the fact that we lack satisfactory national measures of quality of life and human development; nations are compared with other nations or their own prior state on the basis of the sometimes misleading economic indicators. Denis Goulet, in his book *The Cruel Choice*, speaks of bread, dignity, and freedom as the three goals of development, none of which should be subordinate to the others, important as bread (his shorthand for economic development) may be.

Equitable distribution

Even a very high rate of economic development, or perhaps especially a high rate of economic development as measured by conventional indicators, may lead to some sectors of the population being relatively or absolutely worse off than they

National Development Support Communication

were before. There is a suspicion that the economic development plans of some countries are designed not to create the maximum economic growth for the country as a whole, but to maximize the increases in the wealth of that sector of the society that is already relatively wealthy. Some try to justify the widening economic disparities between rich and poor by claiming that it is an inevitable and necessary consequence of economic development. If this were true, then humane governments, remembering that the purpose of economic development is to improve the quality of life of their people, would place compensatory programmes high on their list of development goals. The development goal could be stated as reduction of economic disparities by improving the well-being of less privileged people through full employment, equitable distribution of services, and equitable access to resources necessary for economic advancement.

The claim that widening gaps between rich and poor are necessary may be false and self-serving, even when it is a well-intentioned honest belief. The goals of rapid economic development and equitable distribution may not in fact be in conflict. What may be in conflict is the choice of an appropriate time scale for measuring the growth and the question of who receives the benefits from the required investment. The natural resources of any country are fixed, even though they may not be fully known or fully exploited. What is variable is the human knowledge, labour, and initiative that is brought to bear on those resources. Investing in the human resources of the society in order to increase the level of knowledge, the productivity of labour and the incentives for initiative may lead to greater return on national investment than much direct investment in physical facilities. But the return on the investment may not show on the financial statement of the immediately following fiscal year. The economic payoff from improved health of babies or improved education for children may come in decades rather than years. Plans intended to maximize economic growth over a twenty year period are likely to include more such investment than plans designed only to maximize growth in short intervals. Private investment in the development of human resources is always less than needed to optimize the potential, even the most conservative economists admit (Friedman, 1962). The society has more to gain from educating and motivating the least well educated and cared for members of the society because the gap between their actual and potential contributions is greatest. But these are precisely the people who are least able to invest in their own self improvement. And, at least in societies that prohibit human slavery, it is difficult for individual members of the society to obtain a full return on any investment they make in the education of others. Because the society as a whole is better off when the brain-power and labour-power of all members of society are mobilized effectively, investment in the equitable distribution of such services as health and education may be the most promising investment a society can make, even when judged on narrow economic criteria.

National cohesiveness

One of the prime goals of most developing nations is to create a sense of national identity within a society often composed of disparate ethnic, tribal or linguistic segments. Although militant nationalism leading to hostility between nations can be deplored, few question the value of integrating and interconnecting in co-operative fashion the diverse cultures and interests within a society. Nationalism is preferred to tribalism, even by idealists who hope for an end to competitive nationalism in a world in which the sense of family of humankind predominates.

The economic historian and communications scholar Harold Innes (1950) was one of the first and most persuasive in drawing attention to the role of communication in linking together a nation. Maintaining political control over any geographic area requires a communication technology permitting messages to be easily transmitted over the entire area. Just as communication through space is essential, so a satisfactory technology for communication through time (for example, writing on stone tablets) is essential for the continuity of a nation over time. He also cites historical evidence to show that

National Development Support Communication

communication capability linking together the members of a society is essential to national survival. He points out that no national governmental structure can survive indefinitely without at least the acquiescence of the people who are governed by it. If the communication system of the society is monopolized by a minority class (even a powerful ruling minority) that does not have adequate communication linkages with the rest of the society, then, over time, that minority may grow sufficiently out of touch with the rest of the society that the nation cannot survive without major upheavals in governmental structure.

A communication system linking together the members of a society and permitting continuity through both space and time does not guarantee national cohesiveness. Such a communication system is a necessary, though not sufficient condition. If the messages transmitted over the system lead to mutual adaptation and co-operation among the different regions, tribes, ethnic and linguistic groups or classes, then a national identity results from the mutual accommodations. On the other hand, if the messages are part of a process by which one segment of a society is exploiting another, then improved communication may merely expose that pattern of exploitation and hasten a polarization that will destroy hopes for national cohesion.

It is misleading to think of messages as causes leading to the effect of national cohesion. National cohesion should be defined as a state in which the diverse elements of a society are interconnected so that they can and do communicate with each other. If one segment of a society maintains monopoly control over the messages of the communication system in an attempt to impose national cohesion on the rest, the result may well be the opposite of that intention. Thus, the goal of national cohesion is, by definition, not an effect of the messages in the communication system. The goal of national cohesion is synonymous with the goal of creating a communication system through which people in every segment of the society have bi-directional communication with other people in the society.

Human development

Many people, including the writer, consider the goals of human dignity and human freedom of choice to be as important as economic development and national cohesion. Economic development is extremely important because it can enhance human development. Those who argue that economic development should be given precedence assume that the goal of economic development is contradicted or impeded by other values and point out, quite rightly, that starving people have no freedom or dignity. In fact, there is no contradiction or conflict between economic development and enhancement of human freedom and dignity except in the case of exploitation of some members of the society for the benefit of others. If the benefits of economic development are being equitably distributed, the improved economic well-being contributes to human freedom and dignity. At the same time, when they know that they will share fairly in the benefits of economic development, people who have maintained their human dignity and free choice will be more strongly motivated to contribute to the economic development that benefits all. Only when some humans are being exploited for the benefit of others does a conflict arise. In which case the conflict is not between economic development and human dignity. Rather, it is a conflict between one segment of the society getting more economic benefits and dignity, and another segment of the society getting less of both.

Information as a Factor in Development

In a fundamental sense there are only two factors of production. These are conventionally labelled as land and labour. In this sense, land means all of the natural resources of a society. It includes the land, forests, water, climate and existing stock of seeds and animals that form the resource base for its agriculture. It includes oil, coal and sunlight or flows of water that can be used to create energy. It includes the ores and minerals that can be shaped into products desired by the society or exported in exchange for such products.

The second factor of production is the human labour that must be applied to these natural resources to make them useful to meet human needs and desires. This factor includes human knowledge and brainpower as well as physical labour. As Buckminster Fuller has pointed out (1970), the physical resources of a society are finite, but the human resources are potentially infinite because human brain-power can be used to discover or invent improved techniques for processing the available material resources. Some societies that lack an abundance of natural resources have been able to achieve economic growth through improving their techniques for acquiring and processing natural resources. Japan is the most frequently cited example of such a society.

For some purposes it is useful to discuss capital as an additional factor of production, even though it could be subsumed under the two-factor definition. Capital is that portion of natural resources and human labour that is not used to produce output for current consumption or trade, but is used instead to build tools or factories that are then used to produce the goods and services of the society. Even a society that is not developing must allocate some portion of its land and labour to capital rather than consumption, because the tools, buildings and machines of the society, however primitive, need to be periodically replaced if the society is not to regress to a more primitive and less productive state, with consequent decline in the products available for consumption.

Viewed from another perspective, the chief factor of production in modern times in both developed and developing countries is information. This factor is sometimes referred to as knowledge, education or human capital. Much economic development depends on improvements of techniques whether or not new technologies are involved. The level and kind of education or skill required in an advanced technological society is much different from that required in a poorer society. With adequate information it is often possible to find substitute materials rather than import scarce and expensive materials. If sufficient information is available, a society with much underutilized and relatively unskilled labour can develop production techniques requiring less expensive imported equipment and taking advantage of the available labour. With sufficient information and a sufficient level of education or skill on the part of the labour-force, it may be possible to import only the blueprints or the ideas for a new factory or industry without the expense and foreign exchange cost of importing the technology itself.

A highly developed telecommunications infrastructure will permit a society to have more efficient co-ordination of its productive resources (whether in a capitalist or socialist economy) because it will be easier to make the appropriate quantity of needed goods and services available when and where they are most needed. A competitive economic system requires perfect information to reach optimum production, according to neo-classical capitalist economic theory. Planned economies must have accurate information to substitute for the flow of money that signals, to capitalist producers, how much of what goods should be produced. Effective use of a highly developed communication system will permit improved co-ordination in the distribution of goods and services as well as in their production. More equitable distribution, coupled with information about examples of more productive behaviour, may change the incentive structure such that more members of the society become motivated to increase the productivity of the society.

A developing country with a sufficiently well educated labour force may be able to adapt better the ideas of more developed societies to the local culture and conditions. Some of the technology and some of the institutional structures of developed societies may be quite harmful to the indigenous culture if they are imported together with the ideas imbedded in them. It often may be preferable to import and adapt the ideas to local culture and circumstance than to import all the trappings of another society. This is particularly true in the case where the technology and institutional arrangements may be harmful even to the societies they are imported from (Schumacher, 1973).

In the most highly developed societies a large investment in scientific research may be a major factor in stimulating economic productivity gains. In less developed societies, it may be efficient to invest in scientific research at a level that facilitates the understanding, the importation and the adaptation of ideas to local conditions.

These examples of the role of information, broadly defined, should indicate how information itself may be the key factor of production. Economic theories devised to deal with a stable set of technologies which fail to assume changes in the information structure will be quite inappropriate to developing societies. In developing societies the very nature of development requires that the level of knowledge itself be changing as well as the rate at which existing knowledge is applied to the enterprises of the society.

Information Policy Choices for Rapidly Developing Countries

There are four dimensions of development strategy on which developing countries make significant information policy choices. In each of these dimensions the choice is not an either/or dichotomy, but a matter of how to strike a balance.

Information vs. capital

Societies with insufficient financial capital resources have no choice but to emphasize an information strategy if they wish to develop. Tanzania, Cuba and China might be cited as examples where heavy emphasis is placed on education and mobilization of the human resources of the society. In cases where adequate capital is available (for example, through export of oil), the constraint limiting development will be the level of education and the degree to which the labour-power and brain-power of the society can be mobilized. Construction of telecommunication systems that facilitate the education and mobilization of the human potential is thus an essential development requirement within capital-intensive development strategies. Similarly, within information-intensive development strategies, the prime task is, by definition, to discover and implement procedures that more effectively train and mobilize the human resources. Since there are always shortages of teachers and field-workers to implement such information-intensive strategies and there is great difficulty in co-ordinating their work in areas lacking effective telecommunications facilities, even capital-poor societies need to examine carefully the possibility that what little capital resources they have might be best allocated to the telecommunication infrastructure. Better communication capability may be more important to an information-intensive development strategy than direct investment in transport or irrigation facilities. This is because, with effective communication, it may be easier to mobilize the labour and create the incentives that lead to the implementation of other needed facilities.

Infrastructure vs. projects

The infrastructure of a society is that set of facilities that does not directly produce agricultural or industrial products, but is essential for their efficient production and distribution. For a country or region to develop there must be transport facilities (railways, roads, air transport, etc.), electrical power, water supplies and communication facilities (telephone, telegraph, mass media, etc.). For example, in countries or regions lacking adequate supply or distribution of water, dams, canals and other facilities necessary to ensure the availability of water for consumption for agricultural irrigation and for industrial use may need to be given high priority. Without these basic infrastructure facilities it is difficult to carry out many desirable specific projects.

The development of a society can occur only as rapidly as the availability of the infrastructure permits, and in only those locations where the infrastructure exists. Successful mass-media campaigns require that media be available to the people the campaign is trying to reach. Industrial development is impossible without development of the power, water, transport and communication infrastructure. Sometimes short-run success can be accomplished by particular projects in locations with pre-existing infrastructure, but sustained rapid growth will require extensive infrastructure development. Much of the payoff from the investment in infrastructure may not occur until specific projects are implemented making use of that infrastructure. For example, agricultural marketing co-operatives may depend on

National Development Support Communication

better communication to determine demand and on better transport facilities to be able to deliver produce to locations of greatest demand. Development strategies looking for immediate benefits may foster projects utilizing existing infrastructure, but this may hamper later development if project investment is at the expense of infrastructure. Development of a telecommunications infrastructure permitting the flow of information throughout a society may be the single most powerful engine of sustained development.

National vs. regional development

One of the major strengths of the United States and German economies relative to the economies of such nations as France and the United Kingdom is the strong regional character of the USA and Germany. Regional centres of business, government, and culture may permit a more rapid development than a single national centre. Regional pride may foster regional development activities that would be less likely to occur if each region remote from the capital felt inferior, reflecting the reality of being dependent on distant decisions for development within their region. The move of the capital of Brazil to the new capital of Brasilia in the interior was part of the strategy for developing the interior region of that country. Regional differences in geography, resources and level of prior development may require somewhat differing development strategies that can only be implemented within a framework of more regional autonomy than is possible in a country with only one national centre of business, government and culture.

In order for a regional development strategy to succeed it is necessary to have excellent communication and transport facilities linking together the regional centres. Within each region, it is also necessary to develop communication and transport infrastructure in order to facilitate regional access to the services of the city serving as the regional centre. A decision to stimulate regional development implies a commitment to develop the communication facilities essential for regional interconnection.

Edwin B. Parker and Ali Mohammadi

Urban vs. rural development

The development experience in the last few decades has made it clear that an industrial development strategy does not automatically bring about improvement in agricultural productivity or rural incomes. When successful, industrial development strategies lead to gross disparities between the quality of life in urban and rural areas, with consequent migration from rural areas to urban slums. The resulting congestion strains the available urban services and threatens to reduce the quality of life in urban areas (Vakil, 1975). Compensatory programmes to improve the quality of life in rural areas are required, not only out of considerations of social justice, but also to influence migration patterns.

Agricultural development is a key factor in the plans of any country aspiring to rapid development. Even if exports of minerals and the development of manufacturing capability produced sufficient foreign exchange to permit imports of food-stuffs on a major scale, it would be a major policy mistake not to have local food sources to guarantee at least a minimal level of food supply for everyone in the country. At a period in history when worldwide food shortages are to be expected, a strong domestic agriculture may be a major national policy requirement, even if the country's land and water resources do not make it an ideal agricultural nation.

A large peasantry or nomadic subculture living not far above the subsistence agriculture level of existence will be a major drag on the economic and social development of any country, making it much harder to reach national goals for a higher average quality of life. If rural life is improved only by compensatory programmes without rural productivity gains, the rural sector will be a drag on the rest of the economy. Only if the brain-power and labour-power of those living in rural areas are also mobilized for national development can rapid development be achieved.

Nations trying to maximize economic development on a year-to-year basis may be tempted to invest only in short-term high-payoff urban industrial projects. The World Bank now

National Development Support Communication

officially recognizes that urban industrial development strategies are hard pressed to keep a growth rate sufficient to compensate for population growth and consequent declines in *per capita* productivity in many rural areas. The World Bank's officially stated development policy is to support projects that will aid the most disadvantaged 30 per cent of the population—in other words, the rural poor (World Bank, 1974).

One reason sometimes cited for lack of investment in rural areas is a supposed lack of profitable investment opportunities. This, in turn, follows from the poor state of development of infrastructure in most rural areas of developing countries. To break this vicious circle of rural poverty will require commitments to development of rural infrastructure, especially the telecommunication infrastructure. The absence of rural infrastructure may have to be treated as a major investment opportunity rather than as an excuse for lack of investment. The relative underinvestment in rural areas that is typical of developing countries may also be the result of two few examples of successful rural development as models to follow.

Recent changes in communication technology may now make it economical for many countries to plan a rural development strategy based on the implementation of a rural telecommunications infrastructure and the utilization of that technical capability for human development strategies (e.g. education and facilitation of local initiative). For a detailed discussion of the potential role of telecommunications technology for rural development, see Hudson and Parker (1975).

Development Support Communication Goals

The specific goals for development support communication must, by definition, be in support of the development goals of the nation and consistent with the choices made by the developing nation on each of the strategy dimensions outlined in the preceding section. For example, if the country decides on a regional development strategy, then regional television and radio stations or networks would be required. Messages in support of regional development all emanating from a centralized national media channel would be ineffective because the nature of the source would inherently contradict the message. If the national policy is to encourage local initiative, then national or regional messages to that effect will be less effective than arrangements that permit local access to broadcasting facilities. As these examples indicate, both the goals of development support communication and the process by which they are reached must be consistent with the national development goals.

Since the goals of development support communication are dependent on the specific development plans they are supporting, it is easier to discuss such goals in a more specific context. At the international conference on Communication Policies for Rapidly Developing Societies held at Mashad, Iran, in June 1975, a group of Iranian development planners and a group of international communication experts discussed these issues in the context of Iranian development. The working group assigned to consider development support communication reached a rough consensus concerning the goals of development support communication, which were summarized in the following eight points:

1. Determine the needs of people and give political credibility to the expression of those needs. (In other words, provide sufficient citizen access to the communication system to serve as effective feedback to the government concerning its development goals and plans.)

2. Provide horizontal and vertical communication linkages at all levels of society. (In other words, much more than a one-way broadcast communication system with feedback channels is required. In addition, there must be communication channels through which people at all levels of society and in all regions and localities have the capability to communicate with each other.)

3. Provide local community support for cultural preservation. (In other words, preservation of culture through events and entertainment on national radio and television would not be sufficient to preserve culture, which inheres in the activities of local people in their local communities. Local media and

National Development Support Communication

local support mechanisms are required in addition to the encouragement implicit in national recognition).

4. Raise people's awareness of development projects and opportunities.
5. Help to foster attitudes and motivation that contribute to development.
6. Provide relevant information; for example, job and vocational information and consumer information.
7. Support economic development through industrial linkages; for example, electronics industry, computer industry, printing and performing arts.
8. Provide support for specific development projects and social services, including health care delivery, agricultural or vocational skills training, and public health, sanitation or family planning projects.

Other lists, or variations on these themes could be easily elaborated. Different lists may be appropriate for countries with different development goals. Communication strategies for meeting these or similar goals are discussed in the following three sections dealing with communication technology, institutional structure, and choice of messages.

Communication Technology Planning

Perhaps the most serious mistake that can be made in a development support communication plan would be to make a prior assumption about the technology that should be used based on what is commonly in use in other countries, especially developed industrial countries. The development goals of other nations may be different, the institutional structures may be different and inappropriate to the developing nation, and the capabilitites for production of messages to be transmitted through the technology may be quite different.

In writing about the transition from agricultural to industrial societies prior to the invention of much of the information and communication technology of today, Marx argued that the technology of society (the underlying means of production) at one point in time determines the institutional structure of the society at a later time (the social organization of production), and that the institutional structure at one time determines the laws, culture and ideas of the society (the superstructure) at a later time. If there is any truth at all in these insights about technology in general, they seem to apply with even greater force to the communication technology of a society. The communication technology of a society determines who can speak to whom, over what distances, with what time delays, and with what possibilities for feedback or return communication. This is the heart of what is meant by social organization. It makes less sense to say that the social organization is caused by the pattern of communication interactions in the society than it does to define the social structure in terms of the patterns of communication (including order-giving). The culture of a society can be defined by the messages that are transmitted in these social patterns. The messages of a society are obviously shaped by the media they are transmitted through as well as being creations of the institutional structure of the society. Therefore, careful attention should be paid to the form of the communication technology installed in support of development. For example, a one-way nation-wide transmission system emanating from a single central source would force a centralized institutional structure, potentially subverting development goals of a country attempting to create a decentralized structure. Also, a technology requiring more costly message production than can be supported within a country, e.g., colour television, may create pressures to import programmes from another society, leading to a cultural dependency on that other society rather than development of the national culture (Katz, 1973; Contreras *et al.*, 1975; McAnany, 1975).

One of the goals for national development support communication cited above was to support economic development through industrial linkages. One of the major goals for India's participation in the communication satellite experiment in 1975-6 was to stimulate development of India's electronics industry. Although primarily an educational television demonstration project, the national decision to develop and manufacture all ground stations within India had an additional

National Development Support Communication

beneficial effect in aiding development of India's embyryonic electronics industry. Other countries may also wish to plan their communication technology in ways that foster national economic development, rather than by simply importing foreign technology. Importing of technology, rather than importing the ideas that make the technology possible, may create unwanted technical dependencies (even when sufficient foreign exchange is available).

Importing the ideas rather than the technology (or maximizing the import of technical ideas while minimizing the import of hardware) may have another beneficial effect that is harder to achieve with imported technology alone. The further benefit results from designing the technology to meet the local or national goals within the local or national environmental conditions. In the western industrial world communication technology has developed over a period of years in which new developments had to be competitive with what came before and in which the technologies appropriate for adding small increments to what already exists are quite different from what would be utilized if entire systems were installed de novo. Many of the technical designs are appropriate to high-density communication routes rather than low-density routes. They may be designed for a different scale of production or for a different ratio of technology and labour than is appropriate for a different country. They may be designed to require a higher level of training among the maintenance staff than may be available in some countries. They may assume the availability of a reliable power supply that does not fluctuate outside narrow voltage limits, rather than be designed for stand-alone rechargeable batteries that could be used in communities without electricity or with unreliable supplies. They may be the products of an institutional structure that is calculating how to maximize the profits from the system (even though some social needs remain unmet or remote regions unserved), rather than to maximize the national development effects of the technology.

Communication technology is a rapidly cost-declining technology, thanks to the invention of computers, transistors, integrated circuits and other technical advances. Given adequate knowledge and a willingness to change the assumptions that underlie other people's technology, it is quite possible for a developing country to implement communication technology that is much better suited to its needs and also costs less than apparently comparable technology installed in the so-called developed nations. Those nations wishing to achieve rapid development of rural areas should be particularly wary of western technology designed primarily for urban environments (Hudson and Parker, 1975).

What kind of communication technology will best facilitate rapid development? The most significant communication technology for development, especially rural development, is the telephone, or possibly two-way radio. Two-way voice communication does not require literacy and can provide rapid co-ordination and feedback. It can be used in any language and does not require programme production expenditure. It can facilitate trade, supervision of teachers and other development workers and the delivery of health care (Hudson and Parker, 1973).

Traditionally, telephones have been installed only in response to strong demand as an enterprise that is expected to be highly profitable in the short run. In 1975 the World Bank, despite its policies supporting loans for development of services for the rural poor, was still following the traditional practice of granting loans for telephone development only to those that could return a sizeable profit in a short time—in other words, for expansion of urban telephone service. It is to be hoped that the World Bank will soon modify its actions in telecommunications to be consistent with its new development policies instead of maintaining conventional telecommunication policies. Traditionally, costs of extending telephone service to rural areas were very high. Recent advances in telecommunications technology, including mini-computers for reduced cost switching, satellites for long-distance circuits with costs independent of distance, and single channel per carrier equipment for low-density routes, have changed the cost considerations in telephone planning. Until the 1970s telephone planning in all countries had been based on serving or interconnecting the most

National Development Support Communication

populous areas and then extending service incrementally beyond those areas. Before the recent planning by Iran, no country had taken the policy decision that all areas of a country are to be served, requiring the cost analysis of system alternatives to be based on complete coverage rather than on costs of reaching either the largest communities or those most easily reached (Lusignan et al., 1975).

Nations planning rapid development should not assume that telephone technology need be restricted to two-party conversations. For many development purposes, it may be highly useful to have conference circuit capability such that a group of teachers in a region can have a conference with a regional supervisor, or a group of health workers can have a conference with a doctor. Conference circuits are rare in highly developed western countries for historical reasons that may not apply to developing countries. First, the old telephone technologies that are already in place make conference circuits difficult. This constraint need not apply to newly implemented systems. Second, given the manner in which they are implemented in European and North American telephone systems, conference calls are not as profitable for the telecommunications entity as a series of individual two-party calls would be. Much more attention is now being paid to the potential of teleconferencing techniques for reducing travel costs in developed countries. Developing countries can plan such capability at the outset of installation of new facilities without having the difficulty of attempting awkward modifications to provide the capability later.

In the United States, where most communities were already served by terrestrial telephone lines and microwave interconnection, it was found that the most economical way to reach the approximately 100 communities in Alaska that in 1975 did not have telephones was by satellite (Davis, 1975). Decisions concerning which technology to use (or which mix of technologies) are quite dependent on the assumptions made at the outset. A policy to serve primarily the urban areas and to extend service to those nearby rural areas that can be cheaply served will result in technical choices different from those that would follow from a policy decision to serve close to 100 per cent of the communities in a country. Similarly, a decision to provide telephones only to those areas that already have both roads and electricity will lead to different technical choices than a decision to use communication to lead rather than follow these other developments. Once a communication satellite for domestic telephone service is considered as an alternative under a policy goal of reaching the entire country, the conclusion for many countries is that satellite communication rather than terrestrial microwave is more economical for most locations within the country. This conclusion is based not on the million dollar Intelsat ground station technology, but on small satellite ground stations costing $20,000 or less (Lusignan et al., 1975).

As indicated above, however, these decisions ought not to be based on cost comparisons alone, but also on questions of potential international dependencies (for example, satellite launch capability, importation of technology, or regional sharing of satellite capacity), foreign exchange considerations, and plans for development of local electronics industry. Technical choices that are correct for one country may be quite wrong for another country with a different set of policies and development goals.

The second most important technology to consider is radio broadcasting. Because it is cheaper to implement the one-way broadcast voice communication of radio than two-way telephone (or two-way radio) technology, radio may be the first communication technology to achieve 100 per cent coverage in developing countries. On the other hand, the cost of adding radio technology to a telecommunications plan for two-way voice communication to all communities is minimal. Radio has many technical advantages when compared to print media or to television. It can be programmed in local languages, it does not require literacy, it is highly portable (for example, farmers can take small transistor radios into their fields), and for a wide variety of subject matters has been demonstrated to be as effective a teaching medium as television at much lower cost (Schramm, 1973; McAnany, Jamison and Spain, 1975).

Planning for radio technology in support of national

National Development Support Communication

development goals should also include the technical capability for regional and local radio origination. Local radio capability, even at the most basic level of being able to plug a locally produced audio cassette into the local relay transmitter for a few minutes a day (as in the case of a local emergency) is technically easy, very economical and potentially a significant factor in meeting local development goals.

The third communication technology necessary to support national development is printing. Printing of national and regional information and provision of textbooks and other printed materials in support of education should be high priority development goals. Literacy programmes require print materials not only for their training classes, but for new literates to practise and maintain their reading skills after they become literate, whether through elementary school training or adult literacy programmes. Planning effective implementation of print technology requires more than provision of printing and publishing capabilities. Distribution networks and libraries must also be established to make print materials accessible to those who need them. In developed countries distribution depends on existing road, rail and airline networks and established postal services. Developing countries need to plan their print distribution networks in concert with the development of these other facilities. In cases where electronic communication networks are being established for telephone and radio, careful consideration should be given to electronic distribution of print materials (e.g., through facsimile or telecopier techniques), especially for locations without rapid and reliable transportation networks. Library and distribution services established for print media could also be used for storage and distribution of audio recordings, films, and other audio, video or electronic information.

The glamorous and prestigious communication technology for a developing country is television, especially colour television. The potential of television for bringing a shared culture to all of the people of a nation is considerable. The potential of television for augmenting and extending education services is great. The costs are also great, especially for production of programmes for television. The availability of television technology without adequate budgets for programme production may lead to a higher rate of importing television programmes from outside the nation than is desirable to further the cause of national development. Providing television, especially entertainment television, to only the urban population might be considered more in the nature of an urban luxury consumption item than part of development support communication. On the other hand, television can be used effectively in support of development goals, especially if used for vocational skills training, literacy training, or other educational services to the least well educated segments of the population in rural as well as urban areas. If television is already available in urban areas of the country, technical planning to make that service available to the entire country may be an important development goal. The costs of such extension may be relatively small if they are part of a technical plan for extension of telephone and radio services, even though the costs may be quite high if the technical system is designed as a special purpose facility solely for television.

The role of communication technology in development is not restricted to those countries often described as developing countries. The so-called developed countries are themselves continuing to develop, sometimes with rates of development that widen the gap between developed and less developed countries. The primary communication technology that is now playing a major role in the further economic development of advanced countries is computer technology. The place of computer technology in stimulating the development of technologically advanced countries was discussed extensively at a meeting of the Organization for Economic Co-operation and Development (OECD) in Paris in February 1975 (Parker, 1975). Nations attempting rapid development to close the gap between themselves and more advanced countries should also examine the potential of computer systems for their societies, at least to the extent of planning their telecommunications development in ways that will facilitate the later addition of computer networks and computer services.

National Development Support Communication

Institutional Structure

In the case of development support communication, the problem of devising appropriate organizational structure is not easily solved. Since the intent, by definition, is to provide communication in support of development goals, a strong case can be made for including development support communication as a functional task within the organizations assigned the major responsibilities for development, such as departments of health, agriculture, industry, etc. Because of the central role of communication in development, it will be important for each agency involved in development to have at least a small communication support group directly under its own control. Such a group or groups should perform or arrange for the performance of four tasks:

(1) the production of messages in whatever media are appropriate;

(2) arranging for the transmission of those messages to the locations where they are needed (or arranging that those in need of the information have adequate access to it);

(3) arranging the necessary utilization support or co-ordination with the ultimate receivers of the information so that the development task is effectively carried out; and

(4) bringing feedback and evaluation information from the recipients and intermediaries back to the attention of the managers of the development activity so that not only the communication support activities but the development programme itself can be modified to ensure that it effectively meets the development goals.

Not all of these activities should be necessarily wholly carried out within the development agency. There are certain to be economies of scale and shortages of trained personnel that will require the sharing of physical communication facilities and experienced people among several development agencies. In addition, in countries committed to rapid development, there is need for a national communication organization or organizations, such as a national broadcasting entity, independent of all other agencies. Without that independent communication entity that can report to the people of the nation on the activities of all the other agencies, there would be insufficient checks and balances to ensure that the other agencies are effectively carrying out their missions. Whether or not the national broadcasting entity owns and operates its own transmission channels, there is also need for a telecommunications entity to provide common carrier communication channels that can be used for communication between any individuals and organizations within the society. That telecommunications entity should have the responsibility for facilitating the flow of communication within the society and therefore should have no structural incentives to censor or inhibit the flow of messages.

The organizational problem for the development agencies is to provide appropriate liaison with the communication agencies that can provide communication channels linking the nation together, with the agencies that have the necessary message production skills and facilities (e.g., television production capability), with the local organizations in the locations the development programme is intended to serve, and with organizations that can provide feedback and evaluation information that is not distorted by the natural desire of the agency to make its programmes appear to be effective, whatever the reality. In some cases it will be necessary for the development agency to have the capability to perform these functions within its own organization. In other cases it will be appropriate to perform the necessary functions through procurement of services from other organizations.

From the perspective of an agency or agencies assigned to provide development support communication, these same four tasks need to be considered. The organizational problem is two-fold. One, is how to organize internally to carry out each of the four tasks. The other is how to provide the appropriate liaison mechanisms with the several development programmes they are supporting. For programmes to be effective there must be communication linkages within and between the organizations involved at all levels. Good vertical command and feedback linkages within each organization plus co-ordination at the

National Development Support Communication

top of the two organizational hierarchies will not be sufficient. There must be horizontal linkages between programme production staff in the communication organization and subject experts in the development agency. There must be horizontal linkages between regional and local field staffs of both organizations.

There is no simple prescription that can be given for devising workable organizational structures. It is seldom possible to implement an ideal structure de novo. Almost always it is necessary to work within a pre-existing institutional structure, making whatever adaptations, innovations, and reorganizations are possible. Previously existing institutions usually have a good deal of inertia, making change difficult. The specific national goals, the national geography, the existing technology, and the talents of the people involved all need to be taken into account.

Four general principles that should be considered in organizational planning are flexibility, decentralization, redundancy, and accountability. Flexibility is important, because rapid development means rapid change. With changing conditions, including changes in the underlying technology (for example, a shift to increased dependency on communication satellites with reduced dependency on microwaves), different organizational structures will be appropriate. An organizational structure that is appropriate for one set of conditions may be quite inappropriate for another. Ability to modify the institutional structure itself in response to changed conditions should be a prime consideration.

Decentralization and the delegation of responsibility and authority that goes with effective decentralization is particularly important in a rapidly developing country. The more decisions have to be made centrally, the slower the pace of development will progress, provided the local initiative can be channelled into activities that support national development rather than into destructive competition that threatens national cohesion or merely attempts to redistribute resources without increasing the total to be distributed. The organization responsible for development communications must take the lead in such decentralization, because it is highly visible and can be a model for other organizations.

Redundancy in the institutional structure may be the least understood principle. In attempting to create flexible, decentralized institutions that provide reliable, efficient services, it should be remembered that the components of organizations (the humans and groups of humans) are unreliable. It is quite possible, in theory and in practice, to devise reliable systems out of unreliable components provided there is sufficient redundancy in the structure. If one sub-unit of an organization suffers from bureaucratic inertia and fails to adapt rapidly, there must be another unit that can be assigned the task at hand. The existence of an alternative unit that could perform similar functions is the best way to insure that the first unit doesn't develop the complacency and inertia that is often associated with monopoly power. Redundancy may seem a remote goal for developing countries that are striving hard to create the first organizational unit to accomplish some task. Redundancy may also seem counter-intuitive as a way to enhance efficiency because it appears inefficient to have duplicate facilities or organizations. But redundancy in organizations should be neither a remote goal or a current inefficiency. Organizing the available production staff into two or more independent production teams should lead to more initiative and a higher level of total output than a single production team (Niskanen, 1971).

It may be more important to have redundant organizational components at lower and middle levels of an organization than to have completely parallel large organizations. For example, two independent national broadcasting organizations may each become somewhat inflexible and unresponsive to change if their internal structures are insufficiently flexible and redundant. It may prove more effective to have a single organization with flexibility and redundancy within its structure. With redundancy and decentralization at lower levels it is possible to restructure large organizations by reorganizing components. For example, an educational television unit could belong in a broadcasting organization or an educational organization (or both organizations could have educational television units) depending on which organization has the necessary flexibility and vitality at any given time.

It may appear obvious to say that institutions should be held accountable for the performance of their assigned tasks. Such accountability requires that the goals assigned to the organizations be well specified, that there be appropriate measurement criteria by which success can be judged, and that the rewards coming to the organization and its members be related to how well the goals are met. In order for the organization as a whole to accomplish its task, the component organizations should be held accountable for their sub-tasks. This requires devising performance indicators and delegation of authority and responsibility so that the unit and its members can in fact be held accountable for their performance. A development organization, especially one as visible as a communication organization, needs to follow development principles in its process so that it can serve as a model for development in other areas. Therefore, the goal of widespread stimulation of initiative and acceptance of responsibility should be demonstrated within the development organizations themselves, as well as being a social goal for the effect of their activities on the larger society.

The application of these four principles to institutional structures established for development support communication may have different results in different environments. The particular development support communication function that may present the greatest organizational difficulties is the programme of utilization and co-ordination in the field. The ultimate success or failure of a development programme depends on what happens at the farms, villages, towns, and industrial locations where development is desired. Communication campaigns without local coordination and feedback are virtually certain to fail. Local on-site fieldwork is needed to ensure that the messages get to the right people in an appropriate context at the right time. Local on-site fieldwork is also needed to provide to the message producers and development planners the feedback without which the development programme can not be sufficiently responsive to local needs and conditions to have much hope of success.

Edwin B. Parker and Ali Mohammadi

Field-workers, especially in remote locations, may have development tasks that cut across more than one development organization. Provision for adequate sanitary water supplies, irrigation for agriculture and disposal of wastes that might be health hazards for humans and needed fertilizer for plants are all interconnected, even though different branches of government may be involved. The education and communication requirements to permit a local community to carry out such a project on a local basis will need inter-agency co-ordination at the local level.

One possible organizational solution would be to have a development communication centre within each district. (In Iran, this might be one in each of the proposed 1,200 rural development area centres.) That centre could be given the responsibility of procuring and providing all of the printed, audio or video information needed for that district in support of local development activities. There would be considerable merit in having such a unit be directly responsible to the district government rather than to a national agency so that local co-ordination is facilitated without inter-agency jealousies at a national level getting in the way. To be effective, the local utilization unit must have reliable communication links with regional and national communication support offices so that they can procure (or arrange to have produced) the materials they need. They could be local distribution centres for print materials (combining a library, bookstore and news-stand function) as well as local audio and video centres making television, radio, video tapes, films, audio recordings and other materials available in support of education, literacy training, health, agriculture and development related activities.

Whatever organizational form is adopted, it will be important to stay flexible, keeping open options for change based on the performance experience. It is usually wise to start with pilot projects and experimental programmes in some regions or topic areas before committing national programmes. The experience obtained in smaller programmes may be essential to modify plans for larger programmes to increase their probability of success.

National Development Support Communication

In development activities, the most important point of institutional structure is not the internal structure of the development organizations and their relationships. The part of the institutional structure to be most concerned about is the relationship with the people who are to be developed. The goal should be to maximize the participation by the intended beneficiaries of the development activity. Doing things for people or to people may leave them passive and dependent (or, worse, resistant), with development proceeding slowly because it is wholly dependent on the activities of the development agencies. Doing things with people should be preferred to doing things to or for them. In that way, the people contribute their own energy and initiative, and learn that they can, through their own efforts, improve the quality of their lives. That learning process, which can only happen through participation, may be more important than the specific benefits of the specific project because it can start a 'chain reaction' without which rapid development is unlikely to occur.

The main point of contact between a communication organization and the people it is attempting to serve may be through field utilization centres or units, as discussed above. Acceptance of direction from a local advisory board or community government may be necessary to generate sufficient local participation. In order for such an organization to be effective, the regional and national offices of the development support communication organization must be in a position to accept, respond to, and generally assist local initiatives. It would be preferable if the local workers were hired and directed by the local governmental unit (although possibly with funds provided by the communication agency) so that they can effectively communicate the needs and wishes of their communities and districts to more senior people in the communication agency. If they were direct employees of the communication agency, their incentives are likely to be for career advancement in the agency (which implies pleasing supervisors), rather than for development of the community, which may mean that supervisors in the communication agency may need to be told things they would rather not hear. The arrangements for obtaining community participation will obviously have to depend on the specific circumstances, so it is difficult to make detailed statements. Nevertheless, the importance of such participation, particularly in communication activities that provide visible models, cannot be overemphasized.

Choice of Messages

As the preceding sections have indicated, much of the content of communication will be determined by the technology and by the institutional structure that is implemented. The significant contribution of communication to development may be in linking the society together so that the entire nation is bound in a shared interconnected system of communication. If the appropriate linkages are there so that people come to feel that they are part of a larger whole in which they participate, then the content of the messages becomes less important. The structure of who can communicate with whom is more important than the message content (which is produced in accordance with that structure). In general, the greater the level of participation in the communication system, the faster the pace of development is likely to be.

We can divide concerns about the content of communication for development in three general categories. One is the content of the national mass media—the culture, entertainment and news programming. The second is the content of media used for formal education. The third is other communication in support of development. Since each of the first two categories is considered elsewhere in this volume, this section will be restricted to a few remarks about the residual category of development support communication other than the national mass media and educational media.

Development support communication is sometimes thought of as non-formal education, or as information and persuasion in support of a development campaign, for example a family planning campaign, a campaign to change agricultural practices or a campaign to improve sanitation and public health. This

National Development Support Communication

view of development support communication has the disadvantage of looking at the communication process primarily from the perspective of the sender or producer of the messages. It is implicitly, if not explicitly, manipulative and control-oriented in its focus on how the communication process can be used to manipulate the receivers of communication to behave the way the senders want them to behave. It may not be conducive to the dialogue and collective decision-making processes that are likely to be required to mobilize the people of an entire nation to develop rapidly. This is not to say that non-formal education and information and persuasion campaigns are not extremely important. Rather, it suggests, as has been argued by Nordenstreng (1974), that to provide the information, context and perspective within which people can make decisions and choices may be an even greater contribution to development. In Goulet's terms, it contributes to freedom and dignity, but it is also likely to speed the process of economic development because of more effective mobilization of people to improve their own lives and their own communities.

It might be more helpful to think of the ultimate goal of development support communication as providing the means for people to have on demand access to the information they need to develop themselves. This implies that the messages are produced in ways that fit and are understandable within the context and viewpoints of the receivers. It means that receivers have a choice of information content so that they can receive family planning information when they are interested in that and agricultural information when that is their focus of attention. Stimulating information-seeking and providing opportunities through which people can obtain the information they seek is consistent with the development philosophy of fostering participation and local initiative. Local or district development support communication offices or facilities (or communication components of district development offices) should have the task of responding to the expressed and felt needs of the people of their district and obtaining from regional and national offices the kinds of information materials required to meet those needs. In some cases they may be able to participate in the local production of materials, such as local radio broadcasts or local bulletin boards (wall newspapers, as they are sometimes called).

To accomplish the communication support function of being an agent for local people in helping them obtain the information they need and facilitating their own expression there must be good technical channels of communication, so that requests can be passed on to information sources, and answers or appropriate materials received quickly. There must also be an organizational structure that encourages local offices to initiate communication instead of passively waiting for messages from central authority. This support function is different from a national broadcast media function, even though it could be conducted by an organization that also had broadcast responsibility, because it depends on the local distribution of stored media (books, newspapers, audio records, or cassettes, pictures, video casettes or films, etc.). That local distribution of materials selected for local appropriateness and made available at times most convenient locally may include access to local broadcasting facilities—for example, occasionally substituting local audio cassette input for the national radio broadcast fed to a local radio repeater station. Even when a wide variety of materials is unavailable, the result of providing local choice among even a small number of alternatives may be greater active commitment to development by those who learn to make those choices and perceive that they have some measure of power to develop themselves.

Policy and Planning Issues

By way of summary it might be helpful to outline the major policy issues to be faced in planning development support communication.

1. The first issue is the emphasis to be placed on information and communication relative to other development strategies. A commitment to human development, either as the major development strategy or as a way of providing the skilled labour force needed to implement other development strategies.

National Development Support Communication

will require significant allocation of whatever development resources are available to communication services.

2. The second issue concerns the geographic distribution of the technical communications infrastructure. Are information services to be made available only to urban areas or only to those areas that have previously developed transportation facilities and electricity? Or are information services to be extended to all areas, in advance of transportation and electrification if they cannot be supplied concurrently? It was argued that a commitment to complete coverage of the nation with communication facilities was desirable both on grounds of social equity and as an efficient strategy of development.

3. The third issue is the kind of technology to be adopted. The choices depend in part on policy decisions relating to geographic distribution. They also can influence that policy decision because new technologies, including communication satellites, now make widespread distribution economically feasible in a way not previously possible. Technology decisions should also take into account trends in technological development, the costs of various technologies, the relationships with indigenous industrial development, international dependencies and balance of trade considerations, and maintaining a balance between technological possibilities and message production capabilities.

4. The fourth issue concerns the kind of institutional structure that should be established to carry out development support communication activities. Planning is required for message production, message distribution, utilization support, and for feedback and evaluation. Such organizational planning should take into account requirements for flexibility, decentralization, redundancy and accountability. It was also argued that institutions should arrange for maximum participation by the people whom the development activities are intended to serve.

5. The fifth issue concerns the choice of messages. National broadcasting policies and education media policies are the subject of other chapters and were not discussed here. For other development support communication activities, it was argued that responsiveness to expressed audience needs and provision

of access to a choice of materials should be given a central place in message planning.

Note

1 Paper prepared for National Iranian Radio and television (NIRT) following the June 1975 Mashad conference on Communication Policy for Rapidly Developing Societies. The support of NIRT for preparation of this paper is gratefully acknowledged.

References

Contreras, Edouardo *et al.* (1975), 'The effects of cross-cultural broadcasting', Stanford University, Institute for Communication Research.
Davis, Richard T. (1975), 'Dissatisfied with phone service, Alaska buys its own satellite earth terminals', *Microwaves,* September, pp. 12-14.
Friedman, Milton (1962), *Capitalism and Freedom,* University of Chicago Press.
Fuller, Buckminster (1970), *Operating Manual for Spaceship Earth,* New York: Simon & Schuster.
Goulet, Denis (1971), *The Cruel Choice,* New York: Atheneum.
Hudson, Heather and Parker, Edwin (1973), 'Medical communication in Alaska by satellite', *New England Journal of Medicine,* 289, 1351-6, 20 December.
Hudson, Heather and Parker, Edwin (1975), 'Telecommunications planning for rural development', *IEEE Transactions on Communication,* 23 (10), 1177-85.
Innes, Harold (1950), *Empire and Communication: the Bias of Communication,* Oxford University Press.
Katz, Elihu (1973), 'Television as a horseless carriage', in George Gerbner (Ed.), *Communications Technology and Social Policy,* New York: Interscience Publication.
Lusignan, Bruce B. *et al.* (1975), *A Baseline System Configuration for Video Distribution and Telephony,* vol. III, First Year Report on Contract NIRT I, Assistance in Telecommunications Planning, Communication Satellite Planning Center, Stanford University.
McAnany, Emile (1975), 'Television: mass communication and elite controls', *Society,* September/October, 41-6.
McAnany, Emile, Jamison, D. and Spain, P. (eds) (1975), 'Radio's role in nonformal education: an overview' (paper prepared for a volume on *Radio's Educational Role in Development* for the World Bank, November.

Niskanen, William A. (1971), *Bureaucracy and Representative Government,* Chicago: Aldine-Atherton.

Nordenstreng, Kaarle (1974), *Informational Mass Communication,* Helsinki: Tammi Publishers.

Parker, Edwin B., with the assistance of Marc U. Porat (1975), *Social Implications of Computer Telecommunications Systems,* Stanford University: Centre for Interdisciplinary Research, Programme in Information Technology and Telecommunications, Report no. 16, February.

Schramm, Wilbur (1964), *Mass Media and National Development,* Stanford University Press.

Schramm, Wilbur (1973), 'Big media, little media' (report to Agency for International Development, Institute for Communication Research, Stanford University).

Schumacher, E. F. (1973), *Small is Beautiful,* New York: Harper & Row.

Vakil, Firouz (1975), 'A macro-econometric projection for Iran' (prepared for the NIRT Symposium, Tehran, June).

World Bank (1974), *Education Sector Working Paper,* Washington, D.C.: World Bank Headquarters, December.

III
National Experiences in Communications Policy

9
Integrated Development Support Communication in Dahomey[1]

Armand Defever

A Word of Caution

Less than ten years ago the title of this paper would have meant little, even to media specialists. But recent times have seen an unprecedented proliferation of phraseology. The game has become even more puzzling now that words covering vaguely defined concepts are strung together, multiplying possible confusion and misinterpretations. I am afraid that the object of this brief contribution is a case in point. The key-word in the title—'development'—is still a subject of controversy. The least one can say is that no completely satisfactory definition of it has yet been given. Economists, who also play their part in enriching our vocabulary, distinguish about a dozen stages of economic development varying from conditions prevailing in the least privileged countries to those in the 'rapidly developing countries', a class to which Iran undoubtedly belongs. It is obvious, to take another example, that Brazil has far more in common with France than with Lesotho or Zambia. Yet this huge and potentially rich country and the two little African states are considered 'developing', whereas France is labelled 'developed' once and for all. Since, however, my purpose is not to indulge in arguments, I shall adopt the most conservative and cautious definition of the word development, a definition which might apply to the whole world without distinction: 'a carefully planned process of change'—for better or for worse!

During the thorough and sometimes passionate discussions of the Mashhad Symposium, participants had ample opportunities to express their views as to what they meant by 'communication' in the context of development. No real consensus emerged but I was enlightened by the remarks of Professor Seyyed Hossein Nasr, not a communication specialist, who reminded the participants that 'communication' as we approached it in our debates was a western concept basically extraneous to the 'communication' notions of other cultures. In his rigorous analysis of the problem, he had the wisdom to refer to the etymology of the word: common, community. Here is a notion which is really universal and on which I have based my personal views on 'support communication': the use of modern communication media to create a *common* understanding of economic and social objectives to be reached by a *commonly agreed* plan of action.

Now consider the word 'integration'. Of all neologisms, 'integration' may be the hardest to define. In the development sector the notion of integration has taken shape mainly because sectorial approaches appear to have failed, or at least have not paid returns proportional to the financial and human investment. Innumerable definitions of the 'integrated approach in development' have been, and continue to be given. Herbert R. Kotter qualifies 'integrated development as a *package programme* which must take into account interrelationships of socio-political-economic and technical factors in a system approach', but he immediately adds: 'While there is a general awareness of this need, much research still has to be done to make the concept operational, i.e., to develop the general principles and to apply them in a given situation.' However big the grey areas may be, 'integrated' is opposed to 'sectorial'. It involves the idea of consolidation, co-ordination, unification, complementarity; in the field of communication, integration of the media for the pursuit of a common goal: a marriage of the media, a linkage of the topics to be dealt with.

Background to the Dahomey Project

In July 1968 FAO launched a rural broadcasting project in Dahomey. It was the first 'Development Support Communications' field project launched by the Organization, and the challenge was enormous. Dahomey is among the twenty-five poorest countries of the world and among the six least privileged in terms of natural resources. In fact, all it has is land and three million people to cultivate it. Dahomey is a strip 500 miles long, squeezed between Togo and Nigeria, with a coastal belt of only 40 miles. It cuts across different climates, ecologies, social, tribal and political structures. No less than ten major vernacular languages[2] and some two hundred dialects are spoken from north to south.

Problems resulting from the highly diversified agriculture are, in certain areas, complicated by conflicting interests between settled farmers and roaming nomadic livestock breeders. The capital city, Cotonou, is on the coast isolated from the interior. The road network is poor—only a few hundred asphalted miles—and dirt roads can be used only during the dry seasons, i.e., about six months a year. Agriculture is the only major resource. The farming population is scattered, isolated, and hard to reach. Illiteracy, on a national basis, is 85 per cent, which means 95 per cent in rural areas. Under such conditions, the government realized that the only hope was to mobilize in support of its development efforts the modest radio transmitter of Cotonou. Radio might break the farmers' isolation, inform and motivate rural communities, contribute to their education and seek their participation in the national economic plan. And, above all, radio might be the starting point for establishing a continuous dialogue with and between the various committees composing the national mosaic. Help from abroad was needed to plan and operate such a project. Dahomey called on FAO.

The Programming Strategy

A consultant, Mrs Beaurain-Pihkala (from Finland), went to Dahomey for seven weeks in 1967 to study existing activities and future possibilities for improving the use of radio and other media in support of the rural and overall economic and social development of the country. At the time the National Broadcasting Station was producing only a few 'farm' broadcasts, far too technical to be understood by farmers or to evoke their interest. The programmes lacked co-ordination and were strictly limited to agricultural issues. The texts of these programmes were usually written by civil servants of the Ministry of Agriculture totally unfamiliar with broadcasting techniques and often quite ignorant of the realities of the rural milieu. Other ministries, such as Health, Education and Labour, also provided the national transmitter with various kind of useless literature. A small audio-visual centre (Centre Audio-Visuel et d'Initiation pour l'Éducation Populaire—CAVIEP), turned out the most heterogeneous and unsuitable audio-visual aids on request from various ministries. The Centre maintained no working relationship with radio. On the receiving end, i.e., in the villages, the situation was equally bad, or worse. Radio receivers were very rare and film or slide projectors unheard of—and would have been useless in any case since most of the villages lacked electricity. Mrs Beaurain-Pihala made a series of recommendations to the government aiming essentially to:

— Co-ordinate all informative, motivational and educational broadcasts in one programme;
— establish a close co-operation between radio and the audio-visual centre so as to allow the latter to produce supporting materials;
— organize group-listening to induce discussion, understanding and active participation in the development process.

A strategy had to be found to implement these broad recommendations. The architect of the project was Mr Paul Daniel. His first step was to convince the government

— to change the title of the programme from 'farm broadcasting' to 'rural broadcasting'. The new programme would encompass information and news not only on technical aspects of agriculture but on all aspects of life in the village, including health, hygiene, law, civics, etc, and, last but not least, entertainment;
— to attach the FAO expert to the radio station, i.e., to the *medium* and not to the Ministry of Agriculture, which was only one of the suppliers of raw materials for the programme.

The second problem was to ensure a regular flow of broadcast materials from the technical services of a dozen ministries and

national institutions, and from the international and bilateral agencies operating development projects in the country. In a highly hierarchical country jealous of its newly acquired political independence, this was a serious administrative and political problem. It was solved by establishing a National Rural Broadcasting Council composed of high-level representatives from all State Departments and Development Agencies concerned with the preparation and/or implementation of the National Plan. The role of this Council which met and still meets at regular intervals (every three months on the average) is to establish the list of topics to be dealt with on the radio in the following months, and to see that the technical services concerned supply *in time* the basic materials for the preparation of broadcasts and the supporting audio-visual aids. In establishing this body the organisers had several other ideas in mind: to create competition between the various entities concerned; to develop their eagerness to be 'publicized' on the air, and to ensure easy access by radio workers to data and documents which might otherwise have been released only after long formalities if the broadcasters had to follow the intricate administrative channels of tightly compartmentalized ministries. Ready and quick access to facts and figures is particularly essential in agriculture where news and information is closely linked to seasonal factors. In brief, the major function of the Council was to establish a broadcasting calendar. The preparatory work was done by seven Provincial Councils, one per Province. Each Provincial Council consisted of regional representatives of the same institutions that made up the National Council: the provincial agronomist, medical doctor, veterinarian, public works engineer, social worker, teacher, etc. Each Provincial Council was:
— responsible for proposing topical items to be dealt with on the radio in the forthcoming months;
— entrusted with preparation of the basic papers which were to be used for drafting radio scripts;
— requested to comment on the quality and impact of previous broadcasts.

With the capital city located on the coast, it would have been

impossible to rely on centralized programming. Furthermore, field-level technicians have a much better knowledge and awareness of local problems and of the human environment. The regional approach proved to be correct. For the first time Dahomeans from north to south received programmes dealing with their specific problems, in addition to information of national concern. The project started with one weekly half-hour programme, divided into four sections linked by local music:
— an item on an agricultural technique;
— an item of a more economic nature;
— an item on any rural subject other than agriculture;
— a questions-and-answers period.
For at least 50 per cent of the content, this meant preparing ten programmes for the different regional needs, in their respective languages. These ten programmes were put on the air, two every working day of the week, between 1830 and 1930.

The Language Nightmare

The original radio scripts were prepared in French, the lingua franca of Dahomey. To the layman, to translate such texts may seem a simple mechanical operation. But our scripts had to be translated into languages which miss one word out of four or five, compared with French. Not only are the words missing, but the corresponding notions do not exist. How can one convey the idea of a letter, an envelope, a stamp or a mail-box to illiterates in isolated villages who have never even seen a letter? It was not a matter of translation but of *adaptation*. The search for talented and imaginative workers was a difficult task, for not only did the adapters have to render the sense of a western language into African dialects, but they had to give the scripts a 'radio flavour', a style. Most members of the existing radio staff proved to be unsuited, not because they had forgotten their native tongue but because they had lost their rural ties and could no longer speak to peasants. They were not very keen for this kind of work anyway: rural and educational broadcasting is considered a 'minor art' compared to newsreaders, theatre and cinema critics, sports commentators and so on. We had to search elsewhere. Ultimately, rural teachers, social workers, extension workers, nurses, etc., proved to be better suited: they spoke the local languages, lived with the people, knew their behaviour and could do the necessary paraphrasing to convey new concepts and words.

Group Listening

Group listening was and still is a 'must' in Dahomey. Few radio sets are to be found in rural areas and in 1968 many villages did not even have one set. This, however, was not the main reason for establishing radio forums. The aim was to break the traditional resistance to suggested changes proposed by government agents and supported by radio. In most traditional societies one can find progressive individuals, but they rarely try out innovations either because of fear or because the social pattern does not allow them to go against the consensus of the community. By grouping people around a radio and having them listen to motivational, informational or educational programmes and thoroughly discussing them under the guidance of a trained leader, the chance of getting some of them to decide jointly to try an innovation increases considerably. By the same token the work of the field extension workers is facilitated. Radio prepares the ground and gives the necessary motivation to the community to 'buy' the ideas of government agents whose 'credentials' are authenticated on the air. Just as when I was a child my grandfather used to say: 'It is true, I read it in the papers', I have heard many Africans say: 'It is true, I heard it on the radio.'

The idea of group listening is simple, but its implementation raises enormous problems of organization and management. It is also a relatively costly and time-consuming operation which is necessary under certain circumstances, but should be abandoned as soon as physical and social conditions no longer require it. The first question to be asked is how many radio clubs should be established and where. The number depends on the financial and manpower resources of the country concerned. In Dahomey we started with a hundred clubs scattered over the whole territory, on the basis of the following criteria:

- the villages should be representative of the average ecological, economical and social conditions of the province or region, neither too small nor too large; neither too rich nor too poor. The best advisers for the choice of villages are the local government and political authorities, whose approval is needed in any case.
- The number of members per radio club should not exceed thirty, the largest group for a co-ordinated discussion. Larger groups would, during a debate, split into smaller groups and it would be impossible to reach a consensus or to come to conclusions.
- The club should represent a 'slice' of the village community in terms of age, wealth, intelligence, progressiveness, traditionalism and, possibly, sex.
- The radio-club leader should be middle-aged, have no official functions in the community, but still be recognized as a man of 'natural authority'. He should be from the village, well liked, kind, gentle, helpful and prepared to set an example. He should have a certain talent for speaking, and ability to lead and conduct an orderly debate. And, of course, he should be literate, since he is expected to prepare the listening reports which provide feedback for the system.
- The leader should be assisted by a technical adviser. Usually the village agricultural extension agent, who can answer the questions raised by farmers during discussions.

In trying to implement these principles, we struggled with a whole range of problems which differ from province to province. Near the city of Abomey, for instance, where the tribal structure is still in full force, the chief of the village is 'the chief of everything', and is by right the chief of any new activity undertaken in the village. He is usually an old man and disinclined to support or adopt new ways. To overcome their conservatism, these chiefs were nominated 'Chairmen' of the radio clubs, while others were chosen as 'leaders' and 'technical advisers'. The prestige of the old chiefs was thus honoured and respected. They attended a few sessions but soon got bored and 'delegated' their power to the chosen leaders. Forty per cent of

Integrated Development Support Communication

Dahomeans are Muslims: mixed listening sesssions of men and women are therefore impossible. This problem was solved by creating separate clubs for men and women and by broadcasting on a regular basis programmes alternatively for each sex. The Peuhls in the northern part of the country are nomads, roaming for six to eight months over large grazing areas. They can be reached only during the sedentary period. At that ime, more programmes in Peuhl are broadcast to compensate for the months of isolation. Only in certain areas could we convince the authorities, both traditional and governmental, to let a village *elect* the members of the radio club rather than have them *designated*. The fact that radio-club members would speak of the listening session to their family and neighbours in the compound compensated partly for the lack of democratic procedures in the creation of the club.

The place where the club would meet was carefully checked. We encouraged the village to build a new mud-house to hold their sessions, but a leaf-roof on stilts was quite sufficient. A classroom, wherever there was a school, provided an excellent meeting-place, but never a private house, since members would immediately see their freedom of speech hampered by constraints of courtesy towards their host.

Once the village had been designated, the radio-club members nominated, and the leaders and advisers elected or selected, the training began. Six-day workshops were held in each of the provincial capitals for leader/technical adviser teams in the following techniques:
— checking the radio set, the batteries, the kerosene lamp: notebooks, pencils, listening report forms, etc;
— roll-call of members;
— announcing the major items of the broadcast to come;
— summarizing the programme after listening;
— opening and conducting the discussion;
— summarizing the conclusions;
— drafting the listening report.

Creating a Dialogue

The listening report represented the first attempt to provide feedback, to establish a dialogue between the *deaf* who talk into the microphone but cannot hear the reactions of the audience, and the *dumb* who listen to the speaker but never have a chance to voice their opinions, their reactions, their disagreements and, more than anything else, their suggestions. All the radio clubs were supplied with listening report forms to be filled out by the leader after each weekly session. These forms requested a great deal of information, such as name of the village, number of the session, number of members present, name of the club leader, name of the technical adviser, whether the radio functioned, whether the programme was understood, what were the points that lacked clarity, major points discussed, why was the debate restricted to these aspects, conclusions of the discussion, and remarks, comments and suggestions. At the end of each month radio-club leaders would send the four-weekly report to the Rural Broadcasting Service in pre-printed and pre-stamped envelopes.

At the end of the second year of the project, thanks to contributions by the governments of Switzerland, France and the Federal Republic of Germany, a second phase of the feedback technique was launched with the preparation of live recordings made by a team visiting the radio clubs throughout the country. These programmes had an enormous psychological impact on the rural communities: for the first time villagers heard their own voices on the air, and the voices of their fellow-farmers. The system was expanded gradually, ensuring vertical and horizontal communication. The visual support was modest but efficient: a series of simple wall charts prepared by the audio-visual centre of Cotonou, illustrating the major topics dealt with on the radio. These charts were distributed to all the radio clubs and hung on the walls of their meeting-places: they represented the visual summary of the oral message. They remained with the club for regular use by the leader and his adviser to refresh memories, reopen discussions and arguments.

In 1969 the number of clubs rose from 100 to 280. The government organized a first national seminar on rural broadcasting to assess the early results of the project and to make the necessary recommendations for its strengthening and

Integrated Development Support Communication

improvement. The Rural Broadcasting Service was officially and administratively established and given a budget. In 1970, the number of clubs reached 450.

Operation 'Radio Progress'

While this rapid progress was quite rewarding, the organizers still had no clear idea of the impact of the project. Listening reports gave an indication of the quality of the broadcasts, of the interest shown by listeners, of the pleasure taken in debating individual topics, etc. But nothing, or very little, was known on follow-up, on actual action taken by the community, on achievement, on self-help. No funds were available to carry out a systematic evaluation of the project. Mr Paul Daniel, the expert in charge, had the idea of organizing a national contest between radio clubs under the motto 'Radio Progress—We participate': we, the members of the Dahomean radio clubs, participate in the development of our country.

The principle of the contest was simple: the clubs were informed by radio of the launching of the competition in which they could freely take part by describing in their report the improvement or development actions taken in their villages as a result of advice given on radio. The promise of prizes to be awarded to the winning villages induced enthusiasm. Contributions in cash and kind were obtained through fund-raising compaigns conducted in Dahomey, as well as in Switzerland which had already assisted the project. More than 50 per cent of the radio-club villages participated in the contest. The jury was amazed to hear of the achievements: new land had been opened, rural roads were being constructed, wells dug, new crops introduced, villagers started raising chickens, ducks and rabbits, schools and dispensaries were being built by the farmers themselves and without external help.

Most of these actions had been taken collectively: the cooperative spirit was growing. Adadouhoue, the village which won first prize, has a population of 200 men, women and children. In two years the people have built a 1 mile long dirt road to connect their village with the national asphalted road; two concrete silos have been erected to store the maize crop; a new dryer, built collectively, reduces the losses in grain stored; a new well, almost 40 metres deep, ensures ample supplies of drinking water for all; twenty head of cattle have been bought collectively; a barn and water-troughs have been constructed; the newly built chicken-pen holds 200 birds, also collectively owned; Adadouhoue has built its new school and a radio club of bricks; 4,000 pineapples have been planted and 2 hectares of cotton; the children grow enough vegetables in the school garden to satisfy the needs of the entire population. When the Ministers of Information and Agriculture, followed by a great number of government and provincial authorities, reached the small village square on the day of the prizegiving ceremony, they discovered to their amazement that the whitewashed little building of the radio club carried a sign which read 'Cultural Centre'.

At the end of 1970 the Dahomean Rural Broadcasting Service registered another success. Organizers and programmers participated in the annual international contest set up by Japanese Radio and Television (NHK). In the category reserved for educational programmes, Radio Dahomey was awarded a Special Japan Prize for a broadcast entitled 'Our Crops, Wealth of the Country', described in the award's document as 'admirable in terms of its educational and motivational value'.

In 1971-2 the number of radio clubs increased to 700[3] and operation 'Radio Progress' was repeated with even greater success. In 1973 the project took a new turn and was renamed 'Rural Educational Radio'. In addition to the normal programmes for the villagers, special broadcasts were regularly transmitted for youth audiences and for extension workers in the field. By the end of 1975 the number of radio clubs will approach 1,000. The project has now reached its limits as a purely broadcasting operation. The response given by the farmers, and the ever-increasing number of requests for programmes by government services and experts, and from both international and bilateral aid projects, have created a situation for which only two options are open: either to limit the activities of the programme and, by the same token, its

Integrated Development Support Communication

possibilities of supporting rural development, or to evolve a new and more ambitious programme which will integrate rural broadcasting, production of audio-visual aids and extension services. The second option was chosen. Since the beginning of 1975 there has been a moratorium on the creation of listening clubs as isolated entities. The project is now oriented towards anchoring the clubs more firmly in the socio-economic realities of the country. The clubs will be gradually integrated with the 'groupements villageois'[4] and the co-operative structures. Radio programmes will also be changed to provide an even broader rural development perspective. The Rural Educational Radio now broadcasts 8.45 hours a day; it would be difficult to do more. The future is all geared to quality rather than quantity.

Shortcomings

An independent group of specialists will evaluate the project systematically before the end of this year (1975). But even now sufficient data are available to identify the major unsolved problems as well as the failures and shortcomings of the operation.

In terms of programming, the organizers still have trouble in obtaining in time what they need for the broadcasts. About 20 per cent of the information promised by the technical services arrives late, forcing producers to 'fill the gaps' with pre-prepared items, less topical or of minor importance and interest. Any programming deficiencies are clearly and immediately perceived by the listeners, who have acquired the *habit* of listening and have become much more demanding. The audience has started to complain about repetitiveness. This, by itself, is an encouraging indication, since it tends to suggest that the messages are understood. As a result, greater diversification of programmes is required, and this is hard to achieve with the small staff and budget available.[5] Very little can be done about internal conflicts in some radio clubs which may result in the decay and dissolution of the club. Innumerable reasons can cause such clashes: guarding the club's radio set, divergence of opinion between younger and older members, disagreement over paying for batteries, personal conflicts or simply lack of interest. These are some of the drawbacks of group listening. They have been experienced by all countries which have experimented with the system. In Dahomey about one-third of the clubs are not functioning well. This does not mean, however, that their situation is hopeless. The generation conflict, for instance, is in the process of being overcome by creating more and more radio clubs for young people.

Maintenance, repair and replacement of broken sets remain a big problem and a source of frustration and discouragement for listeners. In a country of the size and shape of Dahomey it is difficult to service radio sets. A mobile workshop might be the answer but the country has a very poor road network, much of which becomes impossible during the six months of the rainy season. Repairs, therefore, take place in the workshop of the radio station in the capital city.

Radio clubs do not always report breakdowns immediately, and group listening may be interrupted for several months. By the time the new or repaired set gets back to the village, club members have lost interest. Recommendations have been made to decentralize maintenance and repair, at least to one town in the centre of the country and one in the north. The increase in purchasing power over the past seven years has resulted in many more privately-owned radio receivers, and this does affect attendance in certain radio clubs. Indeed, why should the owner of a radio walk a couple of miles at night to go and listen to a programme at the club when he can tune in to the same broadcast at home? This phenomenon is not alarming; on the contrary, it is an indication that Dahomeans are gradually shifting from organized, difficult and costly group listening to spontaneous individual or group listening. It is still a tradition in most parts of Dahomey to invite neighbours to come and listen and chat. The only important element missing in this kind of radio reception is the guidance which the leader normally gives to discussions at the clubs.

Listening reports are, on the whole, disappointing. Conceived as the most important feedback element, they serve this purpose only in part. Only 10 per cent of the existing clubs send them in regularly. The way in which they are prepared is also unsatisfactory. It is obvious that the authors of the report 'fill in their own form' as an obligation, but without any real attempt to establish a dialogue with the rural broadcasting service. To increase the number of live recordings in the villages should ensure a much more interesting and reliable feedback.

The technical advisers of the clubs, i.e., the local extension workers, do not play their role effectively. It was probably a mistake on the part of the organizers to expect that low-paid agents would happily accept to do 'overtime' work without reward. Some of them have gone on strike, refusing to forward the listening reports.

Achievements

After mentioning the difficulties and failures, it is fair to point out the positive results as well. Before doing so, I would like to give some indication of the approximate cost of the project, since it may help to formulate a relative appreciation of the results of the operation.

FAO contribution	*US$*
Expertise (1968-75)	
(1 expert + 1 associate expert)	310,000
Equipment (radio receivers, tape recorders etc., vehicles)	80,000
Supplies and materials (tapes, paper, stationery, etc.)	60,000
	Total: 450,000
Government contribution	*US$*
Staff: 5 technicians and radio journalists, 10 vernacular adapters (part-time), 2 secretaries, 2 drivers	
Office and studio facilities	
Air-time	
Running costs	
	Estimate: 500,000
	Grand total: 950,000

Armand Defever

For less than one million dollars, about 5,000 broadcasts were produced over a period of seven years in ten different languages. Close to 1,000 radio clubs were established. All radio listeners in Dahomey, i.e., 50 per cent of the total population, *know* about rural programmes; 80 per cent out of this 50 per cent *listen* to the programmes; 60 per cent of all listeners *prefer* the rural broadcasts; 38 per cent of those who listen to the rural broadcasts listen regularly and 62 per cent occasionally. Enquiries have shown that a radio club member or a former club member 'listens better', i.e., distinguishes and understands the message better.

The Future

Seven years of experience have proved that a radio club, by itself, does not have a sufficiently strong, coherent and integrated structure in the rural economic production process to survive and thrive by itself. But the club can have a stimulating effect in preparing individuals not only to accept change but also to desire progress. The original equation 'information-discussion-action' has proved to be grossly oversimplified and unrealistic. The process of diffusion and adoption of innovations is far more complex. Besides, there are several other channels through which the messages reach the villagers. Too many hopes can be built on the cliché of Africa's oral tradition, and thus on the enormous role which radio could play in the development support process. Farmers tend to tire rapidly of the voice that comes out of the radio because they have not learned how to learn from it.

Radio and even television are not the magic solution to all communication problems in the bush. They will never replace school or face to face communication. Because of a pedagogical misunderstanding, which Paulo Freire calls 'the banking concept' of education, 'information instalments' were made with the hope of 'profits' in the form of concrete action. Innovations cannot be transmitted and adopted in this sketchy and unrealistic way.

The time has come to reorientate the rural broadcasting activities in Dahomey. In the next two years, radio clubs will be

Integrated Development Support Communications

integrated into existing socio-economic structures of the 'groupement villageois' type, with the dual purpose of:
— strengthening the existing cell with a group of active new members already engaged in the development process through co-operative structures; and
— giving the radio club the economic possibilities of maintaining, repairing and if necessary replacing the set of the group.

No new listening activity will be started in a village unless some socio-economic structure already exists on which 'support communication' can be grafted.

It is fairly easy to come to such conclusions in 1975; but in 1968, when the project started, there were no 'groupements villageois' or any other community development co-operative structures. Today, wherever FAO's assistance is sought in the field of development support communication, our first recommendation is to try and anchor such activities onto existing community development activities. This is the case, for instance, of our Rural Broadcasting project in Laos, which started a little more than a year ago, and where group listening activities are being added to already existing activities of village co-operatives.

In considering the case of Dahomey there is an aspect of communication which should be emphasized: talent! The relative success of the Dahomey project and the growing interest of the government in development support communication can be attributed primarily to the talent of the specialists who conducted the operation. The most sophisticated communication instrument would be useless if operated by communicators without talent. The object of development support communication is to motivate, to stimulate, to mobilize, to convince, to teach, to inform and explain and, above all, to open a dialogue; and this requires talent in those who have the enormous responsibility of using communication in support of economic development.

Elsewhere in Africa

In a small and poor country like Dahomey, with only one daily paper with a total circulation of 1,500, six cinemas and no television, it is obvious that *the* communication system is radio. It is also obvious that it will take quite some time before any multi-media approach can be started in such a context. This is also true for:

Togo with its three dailies, three cinemas and no television. Educational broadcasting is organized along the same pattern as in Dahomey. Radio clubs exist, at least on paper, in all the 3,000 villages of the country, but attendance of club members and impact of the programmes have never been seriously evaluated.

Mali is as underprivileged as Dahomey and Togo. It has, however, adopted an entirely different approach to rural broadcasting and development support communication. More than 90 per cent of the Malians are agriculturalists. The educational programmes, therefore, deal with the most diversified subjects on a nation-wide basis, making no distinction between farmers, civil servants, cadres, men, women, young or adults. The people (which in most cases means farmers) participate in programming and production. Indeed, most of the programmes are live recordings, interviews, debates, discussions in villages all over the country. A well-equipped mobile recording studio is permanently in the field, maintaining a constant dialogue between and among the people, as well as with government officials responsible at all levels.

If a farmer uses draught animals for ploughing, it is he who explains over the radio to his fellow-farmers why and how. If a mother weans her child properly, it is she who gives the reasons for it. If a group of villagers have established a co-operative, they themselves explain its advantages, the problems, the difficulties and the achievements. Technicians or professionals contribute to the programmes only by offering comments during the discussions or while the tapes are being mounted. The major advantage of this technique is that the broadcasts are extremely lively: Malians are constantly speaking to other Malians. People do not have to be encouraged to listen. There is no need for organized radio forums in Mali; collective listening is a spontaneous phenomenon:

Integrated Development Support Communication

villagers gather around their receivers quite normally and naturally. No problems of maintenance and repairs burden the busy radio workers responsible for educational broadcasting.

Another interesting aspect of this system is the integration of the written press in the communication network. Two reporters from the monthly rural newspaper *Kibaru* answer on the radio the letters addressed to the editor. In addition, each week on Friday evening (the Muslim holiday) a page of the *Kibaru* is read in the studio—which of course considerably increases the 'distribution' of the paper. We believe that Mali is the only African country south of the Sahara that has achieved integration of its very limited communication system in the overall economic development of the country. It is one of the very few countries which has established a dialogue with its people.

Niger, another poor and underprivileged country, has devised an original system of educational broadcasting. In 1962, the semi-private 'Association des Radio-clubs du Niger' was established grouping a limited number of radio forums—about 100—distributed both in urban and rural areas. This Association has its own status, but it is attached to the Ministry for Rural Development. The clubs are 'listening centres', equipped with simple recording machines used for registering discussions, questions and answers which are sent to the central broadcasting station for cropping, mounting and re-transmission, thus creating the starting-point of a dialogue. The reactions to the re-transmissions are put into a final programme, with comments from government officials, summing up the salient points and drawing conclusions. These three different types of broadcasts, which are closely co-ordinated, are called: 'émissions éducatives' (educational broadcasts); 'Émissions réponses' (answers); and 'émissions carrefour' (crossroads).

Zaire has a government-owned broadcasting service, now one of the most powerfully equipped in Africa, which operates sixteen transmitters broadcasting a total power of some 1600 Kw. It has two television stations, broadcasting a total of fifty hours a week. This impressive display of hardware produces a one-hour programme a week for farmers called 'Salongo' ('Pull up your sleeves'), prepared and produced by city-dwellers, and practically of no interest to anyone except urban people—just to see that they do not forget that eggs are laid by hens! None of the educational programmes is shaped in such a way as to induce motivation, conscientization and participation. The media do not contribute to promoting a dialogue among the people. The communication system plays no role and has no impact on the socio-economic development of the country, except, of course, for the fact that Kinshasa has more than forty jazz bands, that the hit parade is one of the key programmes on the radio and that record-making has become a very flourishing business.

The case of Zaire clearly indicates that there is no relationship between the power and the sophistication of a communication network and its impact on development.

In Africa those officials who are responsible for the mobilization and use of the media in support of development, with the exception of Mali and perhaps Niger, have not succeeded in overcoming one of the weaknesses of mass communication, i.e., its anonymous and impersonal nature. Because of the one-way flow of information through the mass media, the impact of the communication system has been appallingly low and the feedback negligible. Motivation, training and education efforts are ineffectual because the link between the programme and the felt needs of the audience is missing.

Notes

1 Renamed the People's Republic of Benin in December 1975.
2 Fon, Adja, Yoruba, Mina, Wama, Dendi, Ditamari, Bariba, Pila-Pila, Peuhl.
3 Dahomey in all has 2,800 villages.
4 'Groupements villageois' are community developments of a co-operative nature.
5 The total staff of the Educational Rural Radio, drivers and secretaries included, consists of eighteen.

10
Communications Policy in Brazil

Dov Shinar and
Marco Antonio Rodrigues Dias

Introduction

An increased interest in national communications policies and in their relation to development planning has evolved in Latin America over the past decade. This is mainly due to studies and analyses, mostly stimulated and financed by UNESCO and UN agencies, which show a correlation between the general development of a country and the development of its communication media.

Neverless, Latin American analysts have found that it is not enough to include in their economic plans adequate provision for the development of national information media. Several studies show that even though radio and television may be well developed, their contribution to development—when one understands development as a process of deep social and political transformations—may be limited or even negative, possibly because most of the media are controlled by private enterprise and are financed by commercial advertising, largely through foreign agencies (Beltran, 1975).

In Latin America, there are many instances in which governments have attempted to direct the structure and function of communications through licensing, control of the press and of the content of theatre, cinema, radio and television, and through restrictions on the import of cultural material. However, continuous and integrated policies for communication have not existed. Until recently no Latin American country had developed a systematic set of norms and principles to direct the actions of the state according to given concepts of the

Dov Shinar and Marco Antonio Rodrigues Dias

functions that communications should play within a determined scheme of socio-economic objectives and a specific political system (Fox and Beltran, 1975).

The first country which has seriously attempted to formulate a communications policy is Venezuela, in a paper called 'Proposition for a New Broadcasting Policy for Venezuela' (Proyecto Ratelve, Caracas—Antonio Paquali). The Ley del Consejo Nacional de la Cultura defines, in article 4, a set of priorities on matters of production, promotion, research, preservation, diffusion and use of the plastic arts, music, theatre and dance; also, on architectural, archeological, historical and anthropological subjects that can be expressed through printed, radioelectric and cinematographic cultural messages. 'The state will create and maintain services which will guarantee access to the use of these cultural facilities by all the inhabitants of the country'.

Brazil is the second country in Latin America where the issue of an integrated communications policy has been taken seriously. It has found expression in a new telecommunications code and in other documents. Nevertheless, up to the present time Brazil has been no exception to the general existing lack of policy. Despite ample legislation enacted since the early 1930s in the form of laws, decrees and decisions by administrative bodies in almost all fields of communication, a systematic approach has not developed and has not found expression in the structure, operations and output of Brazilian communications. It is the purpose of this paper to examine the reasons for this situation, to identify problems in communications policy and to make some recommendations. We shall be dealing primarily with one dimension of the world of communications: the broadcast media. Following the definition of communications policy, we shall try to analyse to what extent the goals of broadcasting have been compatible and integrated into a systematic frame of reference, to what extent these goals have been achieved, what the problems connected with the implementation of these goals are and what could be recommended to help solve them.

Special emphasis will be put on the three fundamental aspects of communications policy posed by the Brazilian Minister of Communications, Euclides Quandt de Oliveira in a meeting held in Brasilia in August 1975 (Quandt de Oliveira, 1975).

1. Do we have enough mass communication media to cover our necessities?
2. How are the mass communication media distributed? Is this distribution homogeneous in the whole country or does it show imbalances that must be corrected?
3. What is the nature of the contents of the communication media? Is it relevant to the development of the country or is it composed of trivial and banal subjects?

The Brazilian Broadcasting System: An Overview

At the end of 1974 the Brazilian broadcasting system comprised 1,006 radio stations and 64 television stations. The vast majority were private while a minority (7 TV and 4 radio stations) were operated by the Federal government, by States, universities and foundations for instructional and cultural purposes. The number of homes with television is estimated at more than ten million with an audience of more than fifty million. Brazil is the country with the highest number of TV sets in Latin America and the ninth country in the world, surpassed only by the USA, USSR, England, France, Japan, Canada, Italy and Germany. The total number of colour television sets in Brazil at the end of 1975 will be over one million. The number of radio receivers is estimated at more than thirty million.

The history of broadcasting in Brazil features a similar pattern of development for commercial radio (from 1922), commercial television (from 1950) and educational broadcasting (from 1967). By and large, this pattern is characterized by the adoption of the American broadcasting model and a process of wild and uncontrolled expansion followed by (usually tardy) efforts at control and regulation. Thus the number of radio stations increased from about 20 in the 1920s to 80–100 in the early 1930s and to about 800 in the early 1960s. A similar growth is characteristic of television and educational broadcasting.

The institutionalization of broadcasting has led to (a) a mixed system of government control and private ownership of the media, developing from small, closed broadcasting societies to a centralized structure of large commercial networks; (b) professionalization and industrialization of broadcasting and the appearance and predominance of corporate, rather than individual entrepreneurship; and (c) the development of trade organizations and other pressure groups.

The institutionalization of control has resulted in the gradual reversal of roles between industry and government with the government emerging in the role of active regulator responsible for the formulation of policies with a national rather than private-commercial orientation.

Characteristics and Needs of the Brazilian Audience

Brazil is the fifth largest country in the world. It occupies an area of 3.3 million square miles (8.5 million km^2) or half of the South American continent and more than the area of the forty-eight contiguous states of the US.

The population of Brazil in the mid-1970s was estimated at 110 million, as compared to 52 million in 1950 and 70 million in 1960. This increase in population is one of the world's highest, having reached an annual rate of 3 per cent in the decade of the 1960s.

The distribution of the population is very uneven. According to the 1970 census, 71 per cent of the population is concentrated in the southern and eastern regions, with the heaviest density along the coastal strip. There has been a huge growth in the urban sector which has risen from 31.2 per cent of the total population in 1945 to 56 per cent in 1970. This urban concentration is obviously connected with economic development. Brazil is one of the fastest growing economies in the world. Between 1969 and 1974 the GNP increased by more than 63 per cent, and exports quadrupled. In 1973, the balance of payments surplus reached $2,300 million and foreign reserves, the sixth largest in the world, exceeded $6,400 million. A similar increase has characterized foreign investment, with European and Japanese capital gaining steadily over the American.

This economic growth has been accompanied by many problems such as inflation and socio-economic polarization. For example, although the average annual *per capita* income in 1973 was $480, in the north-east it averaged only $250. The rate of inflation, which reached 80 per cent in 1963, has been declining but in 1973 was still over 20 per cent. But despite impressive GNP growth, Brazil retains many of the characteristics of underdevelopment such as a wide gap between the top and the bottom of the social ladder; dependence on foreign markets, bankers and investors; low levels of services in housing, employment, nutrition, health and education, and uneven distribution of income. The Development Plan for 1975-9 introduced by the Geisel administration emphasizes the building of a stronger domestic market, the eradication of illiteracy and the improvement of health and sanitary conditions.

Education seems crucial to the achievement of national goals. The increase from 2.4 per cent of the total GNP allocated to education in 1960 to 3.8 per cent in 1970 (about US 1 billion dollars) illustrates the importance ascribed to this area. However, given the magnitude of the problems, even the new sum seems small. In 1970 the official figures for adult illiteracy (over fifteen years of age) were 68 per cent in rural and 32 per cent in urban areas. The MOBRAL Foundation (Brazilian Literacy Movement), government ministries (Army, Navy) and church institutions have been involved in literacy campaigns but with only limited success. Between 1970 and 1972, for example, 7 million illiterates attended MOBRAL programmes, but less than half of them learned to read and write. In view of the rate of population growth and the deficiencies of the regular school system, a gain of 1.1 million literates per year is not enough. Of every 100 students attending first grade in 1960, only 23.2 reached the fourth grade, 8.6 the eighth, 6.3 graduated from high school and 4.8 entered a university. Not surprisingly, the highest enrolment figures were registered in the coastal southern States and the lowest in the central, north-eastern and north-western States. In 1970, 33 per cent of the 7-14 age-group and 56 per cent of the 5-24 age-group were not enrolled in any school.

A lack of traditional indigenous national symbols and values characterizes Brazilian culture, as illustrated by the fact that Portuguese, an imported language, has become the lingua franca of the country, replacing tens of Indian dialects. The Brazilian culture is a result of the interaction of European, Negro and Indian influences and of active efforts to promote a common culture and a national identity. Colonel Otavio Costs, chief public relations officer to former President Medici, commented to a newspaperman in 1973: 'We are a big country with big problems. The main one is the integration of our people and the infusion of their ideas and energy into a kind of nationalism. We need to inspire confidence, which is why we have many slogans and symbols' (Frenchman, 1973). In line with these objectives, the government has encouraged the development of national symbols featuring actions and ideas favoured by the regime, such as economic growth, the victory of the Brazilian team in the 1970 Soccer World Cup, development projects and parades and periodic disputes with the USA and other countries.

The political changes of 1964, whereby the armed forces have become the leading power, seem to have been the result of a political vacuum in the 1960s which resulted from (a) the decay of the agrarian aristocracy during the 1930s and 1940s, coupled with the failure of a strong bourgeoisie to emerge as a leading power (primarily because industrialization was in large measure promoted by foreign enterprises), and (b) the failure of the government in the 1950s and early 1960s to enlist the political support of urban and rural masses (mainly because of their incomplete integration into the social system).

Thus, the correction of socio-economic imbalances, the creation of shared cultural symbols and the achievement of national identity seem to be the main needs of the Brazilian society. They define the goals of communications media.

The Goals of Broadcasting in Brazil

The legal expression of the role of broadcasting in Brazil is that 'broadcasting systems are of national interest and have national aims' (Decree 20047 of 1931). Article 38 of the Brazilian Code of Telecommunications (Law 4117, August 1963) asserts that 'information, entertainment and advertising services provided by broadcasting companies' should be subordinated to the educational and cultural goals inherent in broadcasting. Article 3 of Decree 52795 (October 1963) states: 'Broadcasting serves educational and cultural purposes even in aspects of information and entertainment and is considered of national interest, allowing commercial exploitation only to the degree that it does not interfere with this interest and these purposes.' Law Decree 236 of 1967 confirms these goals and emphasizes the means to achieve them. Ministerial Decree (Portaria) 333 of 1973 stresses the priority of integrative goals and the need to promote broadcasting according to 'the imperatives of national integration and development'. These roles are also emphasized by Portaria 408 of 1970 which requires commercial stations to reserve air-time for cultural and educational programmes. A new Telecommunications Code now under study reinforces these principles. The 1965 Statutes and Code of Ethics of ABERT (the Brazilian Association of Radio and Television Stations), besides pledging to defend democracy and freedom of expression, defends private enterprises as a legitimate constitutional right.

Thus, national integration, socio-economic development and promotion of cultural and educational values on the one hand, and financial profit on the other, emerge as the main goals of the Brazilian broadcasting system. The legal texts are supported by pronouncements of representatives of government and industry. Addressing the participants of the IVth Gaucho (Southern States of Brazil) Congress of Broadcasting in October 1974, the Minister of Communications Euclides Quandt de Oliveira declared that, while the government has no intention of changing the present mixed structure of broadcasting, 'it expects the concessionaires to join efforts with the government in achieving the important task of forming our new man, so as to enable him to become a positive element and efficient participant in the development of the country' and that 'The Ministry of Communications expects that radio and television stations will fulfill their contractual and legal obligations, their Code of Ethics, so as to reach increased co-operation for the achievement of goals compatible with the efforts of a country ready for take-off from underdevelopment to its deserved position in the world picture.'

The Chart of Principles, approved by the participants of this Congress, includes a declaration that broadcasting is a new and strong force in Brazil, under the aegis of private enterprise and freedom.

Top executives of commercial broadcasting organizations view broadcasting as a combination of commercial enterprise and public service. They argue that since broadcasting (particularly television) is commercially oriented, programmes should be responsive to consumers' tastes and that production costs should be held low in order to allow for an adequate return on investments.

In general, broadcasting performance in the area of integration and related political goals has been more successful than the fulfilment of cultural and development roles. Commercial objectives have been largely met even though profits have been unequally distributed.

Integrative and political goals

The development of a transmission network through the expansion of line-of-sight and troposcatter microwave systems by EMBRATEL (the public telecommunications enterprise of Brazil) and the planned satellite system clearly demonstrate the priority given by the Brazilian government to the problem of coverage for purposes of control, creation and promotion of symbols of national identity and socio-economic development.

Brazilian efforts to become a regional leader vis-a-vis its neighbours, especially Argentina, and to counter external interference from Left-oriented countries have also been considerable. A propaganda war has been fought on the air since the 1960s. In the past, foreign stations had a certain advantage, but recent technical advances and legislative action designed to correct this situation should enable Brazil to 'defend itself' in the future.

But not all problems have been resolved. Commercial radio and television coverage has been directed at consumer centres rather than at sensitive socio-political regions of the country. Thus, despite the accelerated development of the transmission system, poor and underpopulated areas remain neglected by the broadcasting services. Radio covered 90 per cent of the urban but only 50 per cent of the rural population in 1974. Most of the ten million television sets and 30 million radios are in urban areas. 77 per cent of the total television broadcasting power is located in state capitals with 45 per cent concentrated in the prosperous States of Rio de Janeiro and Sao Paulo. 76 per cent of the total radio broadcasting power is located in State capitals with 40 per cent concentrated in Rio de Janeiro and Sao Paulo. There is a definite imbalance between set ownership in the rich south and south-east (76 per cent of all radio owners and 88 per cent of all television owners) and the poorly served north-eastern, central and western parts of the country, or in the rural areas of the better covered regions.

The only policy employed until some time ago to achieve the integrative goals was negative or preventive control. Censorship outlaws contents offensive to 'national interests' or not consonant with officially sanctioned concepts of authority, family morals and other conservative values. But otherwise there is no positive attempt to alter the prevailing criteria of broadcasts.

A few integrative side-effects of broadcasting in Brazil can be observed. Because of radio and television, a standardized Brazilian Portuguese language is replacing the different accents and regional expressions which predominated until the 1940s and 1950s. The 'carioca' (Rio de Janeiro) way of speaking has been adopted in all corners of Brazil, probably thanks to the electronic media and to the fact that Rio has been traditionally considered the cultural centre of the country.

Integrative and political goals have also found their expression in the organization of broadcasting. The regulatory policy adopted by the government since the mid-1960s and the resulting administrative performance of the Ministry of Communications and its operative agencies aim at fostering national rather than particular interests. The most conspicuous expression of this policy is the *Time-Life*/Globo case of the mid-1960s in which the government, at the instigation of broadcasting organizations and political elements, brought to an end the partnership between Globo-TV and *Time-Life* and prevented Globo from becoming a monopoly (Globo none the less captured the major share of the market at the expense of other organizations).

The centralization and industrialization trends of the electronic media seem to have promoted a one-way process of integration whereby the style and values of a few centres such as Rio and Sao Paulo are adopted by the peripheral areas. While this trend seems to be commercially profitable and politically advantageous, it does not augur well for the survival of regional diversity. The poor performance of local programming tends to confirm this view. At present, only four among the sixty-four existing Brazilian television stations produce more than 10 per cent of their programming—and all four of these stations are either in Rio or Sao Paulo.

Cultural goals

The emphasis on cultural goals which constantly appears in Brazilian legislation and official declarations has its roots in the history of broadcasting in Brazil. Stations like Globo, TV-Cultura and others take pride in introducing to their audience world famous personalities and their works as well as Brazilian art and culture. But serious shortcomings remain. First, in spite of the alleged Brazilian character of television, only a small fraction of the programmes are locally produced—an average of 31 hours out of a total of 109 hours of broadcasting per week by commercial television stations. According to the Minister of Communications this means that 'commercial television is imposing on the youngsters and children of our country a culture that has nothing to do with Brazilian culture'. Thus, instead of being a creative element for the diffusion of Brazilian

Communications Policy in Brazil

culture, television appears as a privileged vehicle of cultural import, a basic factor in the 'de-characterization' of our creativity' (Minister of Communications, 1974).

It is difficult to foresee when this situation will change in view of the precarious financial condition of television stations which with the exception of Globo, cannot afford to meet the high cost of local production, lack qualified personnel (and cannot compete with Globo for such personnel) and are not organized for local quality programming.

Since Globo and, to some extent, the Tupi network dominate the market, to what extent do they contribute to local culture? This has been a controversial issue since the early seventies, when Globo started to operate according to a programming formula based on the *telenovela*/variety/news triad.

It is true that Globo's television programmes are essentially Brazilian, featuring contemporary issues in the expansive, baroque style so characteristic of the country. This applies not only to the *novela*, but to the presentational mode of other programmes as well. Furthermore, the Globo has been able to recruit the best-known Brazilian talent.

On the other hand there is dissatisfaction with the stereotypic character of most *novelas*, with the emphasis placed on the importance of money and consumption and with the anti-modernization trend and romanticization of tradition. Moreover, the *novela* has been criticized for giving prominence to the life of modern, urban, middle-class Brazil and also for lacking authenticity.

The absence of Brazilian music has also been emphasized in order to illustrate how television and radio are not making the cultural contribution expected of them. The news, it is claimed, is poorly interpreted and overly concerned with events in the developed world. Entertainment is frequently of mediocre taste.

As for radio, a study conducted in 1974 by the University of Brasilia underlines the lack of programming policies. It mentions that radio news is often outdated, inaccurate and repetitive of press news and that most music is of foreign origin. Because of the structure of the record industry, it is cheaper to import foreign music than to produce Brazilian records.

Dov Shinar and Marco Antonio Rodrigues Dias

The developmental role

This is the weakest point of Brazilian broadcasting whether commercial or non-commercial. In a country where only about 30 per cent of the adult population are economically active, where 38 per cent of the income is in the hands of 5 per cent of the population, where infant mortality rose from 60 per 1,000 in the early 1960s to 80 per 1,000 in the 1970s, and where ambitious development projects are taking place, the contribution of broadcasting is almost insignificant.

In commercial television, the adult education programmes are ineffective as are the five weekly hours of cultural and educational broadcasting imposed by Ministerial decree 408 of 1970 on the commercial stations, both due to the quality of the programmes and to inappropriate scheduling.

With regard to non-commercial broadcasting, lack of planning, absence of clear objectives and unco-ordinated growth seem to have prevented the enormous financial, technical and human investment from achieving even modest results.

TABLE 1 Estimates of operational income and share of audience of commercial TV stations in Brazil, 1972-3[a]

Station	Year	Average annual income ($1,000)	Profit (%)	Share of audience (%)
Gazeta	1972	600	40	1.2
Bandeirantes	1972	2,000	12	8.7
Tupi	1972	6,000	6	21.5
Recored	1972	6,300	3	6.7
Globo (network)	1973	58,000	72	60.3

[a] The data for Globo are nationwide, while the others apply to the Sao Paulo area only.

Sources: Visao, 10 April, 1972, p. 71: 'Industria da Communicacao', Rede Globo, 1972/3: 'IBOPE' reports: personal interviews.

Commercial goals

The financial situation of Brazilian broadcasting presented in Table 1 indicates a generous measure of success in the achievement of commercial goals. The broadcasting business has been profitable since its inception in the 1930s.

Advertising has flourished in Brazil during the last decade. In 1974 it was worth $900 million, or 1.2 per cent of the GNP. More than half of this sum was invested in the broadcasting media.

The achievement of commercial goals has not been equally distributed throughout the system. The consensus in Brazil is that Globo has been the main beneficiary of the boom in commercial broadcasting in terms of profitability, dominance of the advertising market and leadership in audience ratings.

Problem Areas in Broadcasting Policy

The shortcomings of Brazilian broadcasting noted above pointed out the basic problems of broadcasting policy in Brazil.

Ownership, funding and control

The trend is toward increased concentration of ownership in the hands of a few private groups, who control 'media clusters'. This is a characteristic pattern of media ownership in many Latin American countries such as Mexico, Colombia and pre-revolutionary Peru and has been a matter of increasing concern. Although concentration of ownership seems to facilitate government control, it hampers integrative, developmental and cultural goals by tending to cater to urban centres and commercially profitable audiences.

Resource management

The commercial orientation of the system, which operates on the low-investment, high profit principle, is reflected in the relatively low professional standards of most broadcasting organizations. This criticism applies to educational broadcasting as well which, since the late 1960s, has expanded widely following the pattern set by commercial radio and television.

Local and foreign experts (Bretz and Shinar, 1972) have often noted the lack of planning and co-ordination, the separatist tendencies related to personal and political prestige, the waste of money and equipment and the shortage of qualified staff.

Distribution and reception

Despite the progress made in expanding coverage, there are still vast areas not reached by radio and television such as the central and north-western parts of Brazil. In addition, the commercial organizations install production and transmission facilities selectively, guided by commercial considerations alone. While, nationwide, the average number of receivers seems to be adequate (in 1974, 330 radios and 100 television sets per 1,000 inhabitants), there exists a definite imbalance between the prosperous parts of Brazil and the poor urban and rural areas.

Constraints on the System

In order to cope effectively with these problems, Brazilian policy-makers have to contend with a variety of structural, historical, political, economic and professional constraints. With the exception of Globo-TV, strong entrepreneurship, wild expansion and lack of policies have always preceded any attempt at rationalization, planning, co-ordination and control, thus permitting broadcasting organizations to acquire power and bargaining positions in the economic as well as in the political sphere.

Other constraints derive from the conflicting goals of government and private owners and from the lack of a well-defined set of government goals. Different administrations have pursued policies ranging from no involvement in broadcasting to amorphous and ambiguous participation, and to the more aggressive attitude of the post-1964 period. The earlier phase of non-involvement permitted private owners to expand and pursue their goals freely. If the government tried to interfere, situations of confrontation developed in which the industry usually won.

Communications Policy in Brazil

Since 1964, the stronger character of the government, whose attitudes towards broadcasting were better defined, made confrontation impossible. A reversal of roles has characterized the relations between government and owners with the former taking the initiative and the latter assuming a defensive stance. The relatively timid response of the industry to Law 236 of 1967 which severely increased government control, is one of the many instances of this new situation.

Supplementary Action and Recommendations

In order to pursue cultural and developmental goals and to improve its position vis-a-vis commercially owned media, the government has opted for 'supplementary action'. This includes considerable efforts to encourage non-commercial and public broadcasting. The following are among the steps taken.

(a) Establishment of PRONTEL (Programa Nacional de Teleducacao) in 1972. PRONTEL is a body connected with the Ministry of Education and Culture whose objective is the integration of broadcasting educational activities within the national education policy. It was established to provide co-ordination and rationalize action in the areas of programme production, educational television, transmission centres, programme evaluation, etc. Its plan of action, known as PLANATE (Plano Nacional de Technologies Educacionais), presented in 1973 has been regarded as the Brazilian policy for educational broadcasting. Its goals are now being reviewed following the compilation of a new 'National Communications Policy in the Educational Area' submitted in February 1975 by experts from the University of Brasilia.

(b) Announcement of the establishment of Radiobras, a governmental radio and television network, using existing equipment and uniting all federal government stations. Radiobras is to supplement the commercial system rather than to compete with it. Radiobras also seeks to correct structural anomalies in the government orbit, such as the proliferation of agency-operated broadcasting stations. These include the Ministries of Education, Finance (which manages confiscated stations which have run into financial or other difficulties) and Agriculture. Since the biggest problem of Brazilian broadcasting is the production of software, Radiobras will include a new production centre which will supply programmes to regional and local stations. It is hoped that this activity of Radiobras will influence the much criticized production of commercial stations and that in the future Radiobras will motivate the private sector to improve the quality of its offerings.

(c) **Reformulation of basic legislation.** This step reflects some of the current and future issues at stake in the definition of control policies in areas such as concentration of ownership, apportionment and distribution of programming (Rio and Sao Paulo's domination of programming versus the official intention to foster regional expression and creativity and reduce imported material on television), Brazilian versus foreign ownership, and financial structure for government-operated stations and the Radiobras network.

In order to reinforce the cultural and developmental goals as well as to weaken the negative effects of predominantly commercial systems, several pragmatic steps have been suggested:

(a) establishment of norms stipulating priorities and goals for the communications media, mainly in the cultural and developmental field;

(b) development of human resources for communications media;

(c) development of a truly national cinema (production and contents) emphasizing documentary films;

(d) development of recording firms for genuine popular Brazilian music;

(e) promotion of a policy of co-production in the areas of cinema and television, in which production will feature national interests;

(f) decrease of television air time (some stations broadcast sixteen hours per day) so that national production may be sufficient to fill the programming schedule;

(g) enforcement of a more serious policy of programme acquisition by broadcasting stations in order to select the best from the international production and not to submit to the commercial interest of international distributors:

(h) encouragement of research to achieve better integration between the mass communication programmes prepared and used in the big cities and older forms of oral communications still prevalent in rural areas.

The effective implementation of these supplementary steps will be, admittedly, difficult. Much remains to be done in policy formulation, facilities planning and human resources development. There are problems in the enforcement of existing legislation and in increasing the effectiveness of regulatory agencies.

The Second National Development Plan (1975-9) has as one of its basic goals the achievement of a more equitable distribution of wealth. The promotion of this goal might well be one of the major tasks and challenges of the communication media.

References

Beltran, Luis R. (1975), in *The Global Context for the Formation of Domestic Communication Policy*, London: International Broadcast Institute.

Bretz, Rudi and Shinar, Dov (1972), 'Brazil-Educational Television', UNESCO, Paris, Serial no. 2775/RMO. RD/MC.

Bretz, Rudi and Shinar, Dov (1974), 'TV-Educativa Distante de Objective', O Estado de Sao Paulo, p. 43.

Fox, Elizabeth and Beltran, Luis R. (1975), 'Towards the development of a methodology to diagnose public communications institutions', in *The Global Context for the Formation of Domestic Communication Policy*, London: International Broadcast Institute.

Frenchman, M. (1973), 'Development in Brazil', *The Times*, London, Special Report, 18 October, p. 1.

Minister of Communications (1974), 'Television as a medium of mass communication', Sao Paulo, pp. 18-19.

UNESCO, 'La télévision circule-t-elle à sens unique?', *Etudes et Documents d'Information*, no. 70.

11
Communications Developments in India
Robert T. Filep and Syed M. S. Haque

This paper examines the role of mass communications and educational technology in national development. The first section discusses the relationship between communication, technology and development in India and suggests some reasons why education through mass media can be important to national development. The second section reviews the past and present communication strategies of India aimed at resolving problems of illiteracy, low productivity in agriculture, health hazards, overpopulation, and focuses on the Satellite Instructional Television Experiment (SITE).

Relationship Between Communication Technology and Development

At the national level, developing nations are confronted with many major problems: scarcity of industries, lack of trained and qualified manpower, and weak organizational and institutional structures. At the grass-roots level there is ignorance, ill health and poverty, superstitions, limited means of transportation, and lack of institutionalized channels of communications.

If development and progress are to be achieved there must be first of all development of human resources. In a study of the manpower problems of seventy-five countries Frederick Harbison (1963) noted:

> The progress of a nation depends first and foremost on the progress of its people. Unless it develops their spirit and

human potentialities, it cannot develop much else ... materially, economically, politically or culturally. Hence, their first task must be to build up their human capital. To put it in more human terms, that means improving the education, skills, and hopefulness, and thus the mental and physical health of their men, women, and children.

To raise educational standards in developing countries requires the dissemination of knowledge on farming, industrial skills, health, nutrition and community development as well as provisions for mass education to overcome illiteracy. But in an attempt to accomplish in years what took centuries in developed countries, traditional educational methods appear inadequate. Mass media and scientific approaches seem to offer the greatest promise.

The Case of India

India is a vast country with people of widely different cultural, historical and sociological backgrounds. The population of India (1971 census) exceeds 550 million, about 80 per cent of whom live in rural areas scattered in 565,000 villages. India is a land of contrasts: modern buildings and ancient architectural ruins; primitive construction methods and reinforced concrete structures; lush green vegetation and parched deserts. Crowds of people everywhere—three times the population of the United States in one-third of the land area. Most villages have no brick houses, electricity or all-weather roads. They are ignored because they are not easily accessible, and because development agencies tend to concentrate on towns and cities.

Prosperity differs from State to State. At least 87 per cent of the rural population live at a subsistence level; 10 per cent of the households have an income of 1 or 2 rupees per day which allows for a limited diversification of consumption; the top 3 per cent have an income of 2 or 3 rupees per day and can afford to buy some manufactured items.

To implement any kind of development programme, whether

in agriculture, family planning or education, requires information about the attitudes, habits, social standards, local institutions, festivals and marriage customs—even about the significance of astrology. While the urban population in the different areas of the country tend toward some homogeneity, the rural population continue to cling to regional customs and taboos. As Mitra (1973) points out, 'rural living disperses services and industry and militates against large groups of people working in a common endeavour.'

In India, there are fifteen major official languages, sixteen major unofficial Indian languages and altogether a total of 800 recognized languages. The caste system is the main organizing principle of Hindu society. According to Dube and Rao (1969):

> to a very considerable degree, it governs the organization of kinship and territorial units. The segments are kept apart by complex observances emerging from an all pervading concept of ritual population ... Within a village, the caste system manifests itself as a vertical structure in which individual castes are hierarchically graded and kept permanently apart, and the same time linked and kept together by some well-defined expectations and obligations which integrate them into village social system.

The social strata are so rigid that even a discussion between leaders of different class groups in the community is governed by customs and regulations.

India consists of seventeen States and thirteen union territories, all very aware and proud of their individual differences. Although 84 per cent of the population is affiliated to the Hindu religion, the Muslim (11%), Sikhs (2%), and Christian (2%) groups are vigorous and active. There are approximately eighty-six agricultural regions in India. They are not coterminous with the language zones and each has its own particular information needs. These communities, physically cut off from mass media and transportation systems and socially isolated because of caste and class structures, cannot be directly reached by government information channels. Local leaders with high status in their community as a result of their caste position, as religious leaders, senior faculty or administrators, become the main link in the communication process between government and people. They also act as interpreters of new ideas and as legitimizers and rationalizers of social change.

Development strategies in the past

India pursued several sporadic development strategies in its post-independence era (1947-53). Then, as a result of the Grow More Food Enquiry Committee Report (1952) and the experiences gained through the Etawa Pilot Project (1948-52) and the Community Development Projects (1952), the Indian government in 1953 launched a Community Development and National Extension Service Programme on an experimental basis. This programme was subsequently extended to the entire country.

Aimed at the total socio-economic transformation of the masses, the programmes emphasize agriculture, small-scale and rural industries, *Panchayat Raj* (a three-tier system of democratic decentralization at the regional and village level), education, applied nutrition, health, co-operatives, youth services and other aspects of social education. This programme relies on a very simple social and economic infrastructure based on a common framework for each development unit (the block). The purpose of the programme is to raise the standard of living through education, to motivate the people to use modern knowledge and available services in their daily life and to provide services and supplies required in the rural sector.

Literacy and media use

Despite the Herculean efforts of many national development programmes, the 1971 Census Report came as a shock. It revealed that only 29.3 per cent of the Indian population were literate (defined as being able to read and write). Table 1 reveals the magnitude of the problem India faces in order to achieve the avowed goal of universal literacy (Article 45 of the Indian Constitution).

TABLE 1 Literacy rate in relation to population, 1951-71

Census year	Total population (million)	Literate (million)	Illiterate (million)	Percentage literate
1951	361	60	301.0	16.6
1961	439	105	333.5	24.0
1971	547	161	386.5	29.3

A national readership survey (*Indian Express*, 1972) which covered about 130 dailies and 170 weeklies and other periodicals and magazines showed that 43 million adults, representing 13.2 per cent of the total adult population, read newspapers and other periodicals. There are about 9.1 readers for each copy sold, or a higher average than is found in western countries—due perhaps to the scarcity and cost of newsprint and to lower purchasing power. The diversity of the Indian national audience is reflected by 821 daily and 4,102 non-daily newspapers. More newspapers are published in India than in any other country in Asia. As to the rest of the world, only the United States and the Federal Republic of Germany exceed India as to number of newspapers published and only the USSR in language diversity. (UNESCO, 1975).

The survey also covered information on exposure to cinema, 'Vividh Bharti' (a programme of All India Radio) and Radio Ceylon. India has one of the largest film industries in the world and produced over 433 feature films in 1971. Of a total of 326 million adults, 66 million (approximately 20.4%) attended the cinema, 43 million (13.2%) read newspapers, 39 million (12%) heard 'Vividh Bharti' and 32 million (9.9%) listened to Radio Ceylon.

Throughout its history, India has managed to survive and to develop socially and economically without most of its members being able to read and write. But with rapidly growing

Communications Developments in India

sophistication and complexity of modern life, illiteracy has become a major hindrance. The problem is further complicated by the great number of regional languages in current use. For the time being, in the planning of a communication and education system, the spoken word cannot yet be discarded.

Radio and television in India

The government-owned All India Radio (AIR) owns and operates 67 radio stations and a total of 137 transmitters. Medium-wave coverage is provided for 78 per cent of the population and short-wave for 100 per cent. There are 16.5 million licensed radio receivers throughout India with an estimated audience of 99 million. In addition there are probably a substantial but unknown number of unlicensed receivers (UNESCO, 1975).

In January 1967 Delhi acquired a fully-fledged television station which now serves as a nucleus for the gradually widening Indian television network (Srinagar, Amirtsar, West Bengal and Calcutta, Hyderabad, and Madras).

The range of Delhi TV was recently extended to 60 km to reach people living in parts of three surrounding States. Total television time is nearly 32 hours per week with an additional hour on Sunday. In addition to the thousands of privately owned licensed TV sets in the Delhi area, community receivers are provided by the Indian government to approximately 80 near-by villages on the basis of one set for each teleclub.

Apart from educational and agricultural programmes, the Delhi TV station offers a variety of features including news, light entertainment, folk music and dances, topical discussions, interviews with experts and eminent personalities, programmes for women and children, and films and documentaries. Programmes on agriculture, family planning and nutrition are usually presented by urban experts but occasionally opinion leaders from the rural community are invited to participate in discussion panels.

Shortly after the introduction of television in Delhi, its programmes were evaluated and the following conclusions were reached:

- Television, combined with group discussion, is an excellent means of imparting knowledge and stimulating plans for action (UNESCO, 1963).
- Radio forums and teleclubs can be catalysts for social and technological change.
- Agricultural and family planning television programmes increased measurably knowledge of innovations, willingness to try innovations and, in some cases, their actual adoption. Farmers who gained information from television broadcasts were found to be high in achievement and willingness to change their traditional methods. (National Council of Educational Research and Training, 1968; Kaur, 1970; Sharma and Mishra, 1967; Dube and Rao, 1969).

The efforts of mass media must be supplemented and enhanced by extension services and field agencies. The role of opinion-leaders must be co-ordinated with the work of extension workers whose task is to follow mass media appeals with a persuasive approach of personal contacts, group discussions and village meetings.

Television and radio programmes have been directed primarily at India's social and political elite. Consequently they have been of little interest to the masses. The needs and problems of the individuals who comprise the major public have not received adequate attention. As Rogers (1969) commented, 'The media feature messages about development plans and projects ... but there is little content about the specifics of new ideas in agriculture, health or family planning.'

To supply India's future television system with programmes tailored to the needs and interests of their audience, Indian communications officials realize that long-range planning is essential and that an immense co-ordinating effort is required.

The context for a communication satellite system

The problem of producing and delivering television broadcasts on a wide scale to meet multiple needs is of such scope that a nation is wise to exploit as fully as possible knowledge gained by others. In India, consideration was given to five major plans

Communications Developments in India

which would build upon the successes of other nations in using communications technology for development. These included (1) limited TV and extension of local radio, (2) ground-based TV, (3) direct broadcast from satellite, (4) rebroadcast of the satellite signal, and (5) a combination of ground stations with their own production facilities and direct broadcast from satellite. A number of studies concluded that to meet the diverse needs of the population, multiple channels for television would be required (Schramm and Nelson, 1969). After weighing the various options in relation to cost over a five-year period, a satellite system with low-cost antennas and rebroadcast capabilities was found to be particularly effective.

Attention was also given to the governance of such a communications system. Two distinguished committees, the Bhagavatam Committee in 1965 and the Chanda Committee in 1967, recommended that television be separated from AIR and the Ministry of Information and Broadcasting and made a public corporation, since they felt that television would thus gain both in terms of flexibility and impact. At the Film Institute in Poona, a television training institute was established by the Government of India with assistance from the United Nations and UNESCO to train staff to produce programmes for the proposed satellite project along with its overall mission of providing trained production and research personnel for India's expanding communications needs (Bashiruddin, 1975).

The Satellite Instructional Television Experiment (SITE)

Based on the valuable lessons in instructional television learned by other countries and after completing the essential preliminary look, the Indian government commenced a one-year experiment in August 1975 using an Applications Technology Satellite-F (ATS-6) launched by the National Aeronautics and Space Administration (NASA) on 30 May 1974. This pilot project, called the Satellite Instructional Television Experiment (SITE), is aimed at village-dwellers and is designed to test the assumption that instructional television can contribute to family planning, improve agricultural practices and promote national integration. With press and films unable to reach most of the rural areas where 80 per cent of the target audience live, SITE promises to be the most effective communication link currently available.

All Air India (AIR) and the Indian Space Research Organization (ISRO) are responsible for developing and producing the TV programmes; ISRO for co-ordination on the Indian side of the earth station and for the deployment and maintenance of the community TV sets; and NASA, of the United States, for the spacecraft. Programmes are transmitted in the 6 GHz band to the satellite from earth stations located at Ahmedabad or Delhi and downlinked from the satellite in the 860 MHz band.

The ATS-6 provides two audio channels and one video channel for this experiment, which involves broadcasting for four hours a day in six Indian languages to about 5,000 villages. The programmes are directly received by 2,200 villages from the satellite by means of an augmented community receiver without the need of terrestrial relay stations; the remaining 2,800 villages receive the programmes by rediffusion. Since most Indian villages lack electricity, the TV sets are solid-state, battery-operated models. Receivers for direct reception are located in clusters of about 400 villages in each of six States: Bihar, Madya Pradesh, Orissa, Pajasthan, Mysore and Andhra Pradesh. Community reception sets are also located in villages around Delhi, Amritsar and Nadiad (near Ahmedabad).

The main criteria for selecting cluster areas have been continuity of television service in the area after termination of SITE, similar agro-economic conditions and availability of suitable facilities and infrastructures to provide some assurance that the expectations created by the television programming will be satisfied. Other considerations included availablity of power and suitable location for installation of a TV set. Once the satellite experiment is over and until a domestic satellite system begins operation, every cluster can be provided with television service via a small and inexpensive terrestrial system (Mody, 1974a, 1974b, 1975; and Kulkarni, 1975).

The general objectives of the SITE include the following:
— To gain experience in the development, testing and

Communications Developments in India

management of a satellite based instructional television system, particularly in rural areas, and to determine optimal system parameters.
— To demonstrate the potential value of satellite technology for the rapid development of mass communications.
— To demonstrate the potential value of satellite television broadcasts for the practical instruction of village inhabitants.
— To stimulate national development.

The specific objectives of SITE are to contribute to family planning, to improve farming skills and promote the adoption of new farm technology, to foster national integration, to contribute to adult education, vocational skills and teacher-training, to increase literacy and to improve health and hygiene. From a technological standpoint, SITE provides a test of TV satellites for national development. It will serve to evaluate the design, manufacture, deployment, installation, operation and maintenance of the system; to determine optimum receiver density, distribution and scheduling, to test techniques of audience attraction and organization and to solve problems involved in developing, preparing, presenting and transmitting TV programmes materials.

The experiment's design and programme contents have been planned and prepared in collaboration with user agencies. The actual approach to adult education has been determined in the light of the known socio-economic, health and agricultural profile of the area and a whole and, whenever possible, of specific regional clusters. By and large, the programmes for adults will be of two types: those which are intended for general attitudinal change and those which are directly instructional (Chander, 1972).

On the basis of four hours of transmission daily, the total programme requirements for SITE will be 1,500 hours, including the 180 hours of common programmes to be shared with VHF stations. Before starting SITE, the government of India already had prepared and pretested 200 hours of programmes. Some programmes are scheduled for rebroadcast to reduce the need for new productions. ISRO will produce twice a week programmes on scientific subjects for primary school children. During the SITE year, morning programmes will be broadcast during school hours on 220 school days. The children's programmes will develop awareness of community living skills; provide instruction in mathematics, language and technical subjects; foster habits of hygienic and healthy living; promote aesthetic sensitivity, and will explore the modernization of life and resulting changes in attitudes (Mody, 1974). These programmes, rather than being curriculum oriented, will focus on enrichment of school lessons in terms of a broader cultural perspective. They will be broadcast in the morning for one hour and a half. Curriculum revision in science has been underway in India for some time with a number of senior scientists participating—much like the US Physical and Biological Science Study Groups. The work of these groups has been fed into the television productions with good results. One of the main objectives of these revised curricula is to make children and teachers realize that their immediate environment can be questioned, understood, explained and manipulated by them, using the scientific method (Pal, 1975). Since a large majority of science teachers in rural areas are high-school dropouts, science education materials are targeted primarily at them. The National Council of Education and Research has planned training courses for these teachers in cluster areas (Mulhay, 1975). By October, approximately 20,000 teachers will have participated in workshops linked to the television presentations (Pal, 1975).

Adults are the target audience for $2\frac{1}{2}$ hours of evening broadcast. The subjects covered include family planning, agriculture, health and hygiene, weather conditions and current events. Each day half an hour is devoted to a national programme which is received by all the direct reception sets and by TV receivers in the rediffusion areas. The remaining 2 hours are allocated so that each of the four clusters receives half an hour of the programme in the local language.

Regional theatre and travelling theatre groups are an important part of the Indian informal communication network. Actors and dancers are the vehicle whereby morality plays, news and cultural events are communicated across a region. They have great credibility and considerable standing among villagers. Their appearance on television helps to bridge the gap between the medium and villagers who have never seen television before.

Programmes for the experiment are produced in three production centres set up by AIR at Cuttack, Hyderabad and Delhi. Field units from these centres contribute local shots in the programmes. The two audio channels of each video channel will be fully used. For example, broadcasts to the Mysore and Andhra Pradesh clusters and the Madhya Pradesh and Orissa clusters are grouped together. But whereas Mysore and Andhra villages will share the same video, villagers in Mysore will listen to it in the Kannada language, while villagers in Andhra Pradesh will listen to in the Telugu language.

Viewing groups in each village will range from a minimum of 300 to a maximum of 3,000 including pre-school children and adults. Consequently, even a conservative estimate indicates a doubling in the number of people that will be exposed to television.

In direct-reception villages, the TV set is augmented by a 10-foot-diameter parabolic antenna developed by ISRO made of chicken-wire mesh and by a front-end converter to shift signals from UHF (860 MHz) to VHF and from FM to AM. Special roads have been built to reach isolated villages. In villages lacking telephone service procedures have been developed to handle equipment malfunctions so as to minimize down time.

Evaluation

Preliminary work for programme production, including audience-profile development and need-assessment studies, were performed jointly by ISRO and AIR. Several programmes have been evaluated to determine their effectiveness; parameters such as format, idiom, duration of the programme, and need for repetition of the message have been explored (Mody, 1975).

The experiment is being evaluated in terms of short—and

long-term results. Its design permits the measurement of influence of various environmental parameters on programme effectiveness. Programmes are pretested in the centres in Hyderabad, Delhi and Cuttack before final transmission. Responses from the field are being processed and sent to AIR for modification of future programmes.

The management group at Ahmedabad has developed a computer-based, cost-accounting system for every aspect of the experiment. In a country which has to be concerned about technological applications because of limited budgets, this should be a valuable tool.

The most difficult period for the experiment will be the first three months when heavy monsoon rains can create serious equipment and maintenance problems in the villages. Also, initial viewer acceptability will largely determine the success of the programmes. Considerable effort has gone into training the curriculum, agricultural and family-planning specialists and the village resource personnel who will link the telecast to each village.

Upon completion of SITE, ATS-6 will be repositioned to the Western hemisphere for additional US experiments. The Indian government plans to use ground links to continue broadcasting to some of the villages while other villages will be linked by microwave. Once budgetary problems are resolved, an Indian satellite will be launched.

The effects of introducing television to rural India are relatively unpredictable. Telecommunications enters an arena where a number of comparable approaches have been less than successful (Karamchandi, 1974; Eapen, 1974). The experiment seeks to provide answers to many questions about the feasibility of satellite-application projects in developing countries, particularly those with problems similar in magnitude, complexity and limited resources to India. The SITE project staff realized that telecommunications may be only part of a solution and only to some of the problems.

For effective use of new technology, a sensible integration of an older educational system is necessary. The people of India view SITE as a gigantic case study which may help to create a new and more viable system of mass instruction and enhance the current formal educational structures.

References

Bashiruddin, S. (1975), *Overview of TV Programme Research and Prototype Production Unit*, Poona: Film and Television Institute of India, December.

Chander, R. (1972), 'Problems of Programming for SITE', UN Panel Meeting on Satellite Instructional Television Systems. New Delhi, December.

Collins, L. and Lapierre, D. (1975), *Freedom at Midnight*, New York: Simon & Schuster.

Dube, S.C. and Rao, K.G. (1969), 'Family Planning Communication Research in India: Main Findings, Programme Implications and Future Research Needs (paper presented at the National Conference on Population Policy, New Delhi, December).

Eapen, K.E. (1974), 'Communication—Indonesian style', *Media Asia*, (2), pp. 35-44.

Harbison, Frederick (1963), 'Education for development', *Scientific American*, 209, September, p. 140.

Indian Express. 'Kerala tops in newspaper readership', 2 March 1972, p. 5.

Karamachandi, L. (1974), 'TV: a challenge and an opportunity', *Media Asia*, 1, (2), pp. 21-5.

Kaur, R. (1970), 'Impact of Television on Farm Women', Master's Thesis, IARI, New Delhi.

Kulkarni, V.G. (1975), 'Science education through ETV', in *SAC Courier*, vol. 2, Ahmedabad: Space Applications Centre, Indian Space Research Organization, April.

Mitra, A. (1973), Mass Communication: 25th Anniversary of Independence Series. New Delhi: Government of India, Ministry of Information and Broadcasting, July.

Mody, B. (1974a), 'Social Research and Evaluation of the Satellite Instructional Experiment', Ahmedabad: Indian Space Research Organization.

Mody, B. (1974b), *Rajasthan Cluster Needs Assessment Study*, SITE/SSG/REC/017, Satellite Instructional TV Experiment, Research and Evaluation Cell Ahmedabad: Indian Space Research Organization.

Mody, B. (1975), 'Television and Development: or What TV Cannot Do Alone', Satellite Instructional TV Experiment, Ahmedabad, February.

Mulhay, V. (1975), 'Designing an appropriate communication system for meeting certain problems' (paper presented at Seminar on Communication and Change, Poona).

National Council of Education Research and Training (1968), *A Quantitation Evaluation Study of Agricultural Television* (summary report to the Indian National committee for Space Research, New Delhi: Department of Atomic Energy).

Pal, Yash (1975), 'Evolution of Plan for Science Programmes for Children During SITE' in *SAC Courier*, vol. 2.

Rogers, E. M. (1969), 'Actualities and Potentials of Communication in Modernization and Development' (paper presented at the 11th World Conference, Society for International Development, New Delhi).

Schramm, Wilbur and Nelson, Lyle (1969), *Communication Satellites for Education and Development: the Case for India* (prepared for US Agency for International Development, vol. 2, SRI Project 7150).

Sharma, S. K. and Mishra, A. N. (1967), 'Impact of television on farmers', *Indian Journal of Extension Education*, 3, 248-54.

UNESCO (1963), *Social Education through Television: an All India Radio-UNESCO Pilot Project*, Paris: UNESCO, pp. 14-24.

UNESCO (1975), *World Communications*, Gower Press/Unipub/Unesco Press.

12
The Role of Broadcasting in Iran
Report of a National Survey

Majid Teheranian

The purpose of this paper is to review the role of broadcasting in Iranian national development as well as to report some of the findings of a national survey concerning that role. Iran, like other rapidly developing societies, has been going through a fourfold revolutionary process that involves economic, political, communication and cultural transformations. The evolution from a quasi-feudal to a modern industrial economy, from an absolutist monarchy (before the Constitutional Revolution) to political participation, from oral traditions to multi-media communications systems, and from a closed belief-system to an open and regenerative one is taking place simultaneously.

The rate of social and economic change has been extremely rapid during the last two decades. So has been the spread of radio and television. To explore their future role the Prospective Planning Project of National Iranian Radio and Television (NIRT) has conducted a national survey of the possible contributions of broadcasting to Iran's national development during the closing decades of the century.

Following a brief survey of broadcasting in Iran, this essay reviews the study's purposes and methodology, then turns to a presentation of its findings, suggesting some possible implications for Iran's communication policy.

Broadcasting in Iran: Past and Present

Radio

The first radio station in Iran was inaugurated on 24 April, 1940 by the Crown Prince who, following the exile of his father Reza Shah, the founder of the Pahlavi dynasty, ascended the throne less than a year later on 25 August, 1941 and addressed the nation by radio as the new Shahanshah.

During World War II Allied troops occupied Iran to establish a bridge for the transport of war materials to a besieged Soviet Union. The war and its aftermath brought to an end a twenty-year period of highly centralized control and unleashed internal centrifugal forces. With famine raging in the cities, the economic and political future of Iran looked extremely dim.

Under such circumstances, in a country as vast and heterogeneous as Iran, radio was clearly the most effective means for reaching the people and soon became an indispensable instrument for political struggles for power. Control of broadcasting shifted hands with the changing fortunes of dominant political groups. In its first two years Radio Iran was under the supervision of the Ministry of Post, Telegraph and Telephone. In 1942 it became an independent organization. After undergoing a period of administrative shifts and uncertainty it came under the Directorate General of Publications and Propaganda, attached to the Prime Minister's Office. During the political turmoils of the 1950s radio was often used for political mobilization both by Prime Minister Mosaddaeq and later by the succeeding governments. Indeed, the radio station was one of the first targets of attempts for political control. The practical as well as the symbolic importance of broadcasting could not be overlooked by politicians of the period (Lerner, 1958; Teheranian, 1972).

In an attempt to rationalize the government's communications policy, a new Ministry of Information was established in 1964 which incorporated the old Department General of Publications and Propaganda, and Radio Iran was placed under its supervision.

When television came on the scene and broadcasting activities increased in size and importance, radio broadcasting was transferred in 1971 to the National Iranian Television Organization in order to achieve greater co-ordination between the two media.

Television

In contrast to radio, which started because of government initiative, television was introduced into Iran in 1958 by a private entrepreneur. From its very inception television took on a commercial American style with Westerns and quiz-shows predominating. The government granted the proprietor a five-year monopoly to operate television transmitters and to import television receivers. Television of Iran (TVI) established transmitters in Tehran (1958) and Abadan (1960). At the expiration of the first five-year term and following some inconclusive negotiations aimed at the government takeover of TVI's operations, the concession was extended, but a separate public television network was established (Banani, 1971). On 20 March, 1966 the first transmission station of National Iranian Television (NITV) was inaugurated in Tehran. The new station set a style different from the commercial station appealing primarily to the more educated segments of the population. In June 1969 political considerations finally led to the nationalization of TVI after eleven years of commercial activity. With the incorporation of radio in 1971 and the takeover in 1974 of an educational television channel run by the Ministry of Education, NIRT has become a public broadcasting monopoly run as an independent government corporation.

National Iranian Radio and Television (NIRT)

Since its establishment in 1966 NIRT has grown rapidly in size and range of activities. It currently employs 7,000 people, of whom over 3,500 are stationed in Tehran; this number is expected to double by the early 1980s. Its radio broadcasting facilities include sixty-four AM medium-wave radio transmitters (active and reserve) in thirty-one cities with a total power output of 7,710 kw. The AM radio network covers almost all of the urban population. The Fifth Development Plan 1973-8 provides for a total coverage of the population by the First AM Radio Programme and more than 70 per cent coverage by the Second AM Programme. The number of radio sets in the country is about 8 million.

Majid Teheranian

NIRT operates a total of fourteen television production and transmission regional centres with 153 transmitters of total power in excess of 144 kw, covering eighty-eight cities and towns and 60 per cent of the country's population. Television transmission already includes occasional broadcasting of world events via satellite. The Fifth Plan provides for 70 per cent coverage by the First Programme devoted to light programming and 50 per cent coverage by the Second Programme committed to cultural programming. While television transmission covers about 4 million households, only about 1 million own their own sets.

Colour television in education programmes started in October 1975, and in all programmes of one channel will commence by 1978. While the technical resources for introducing colour television earlier unquestionably exist (the Asian Olympic games of 1974 were broadcast in colour) full colour programming has been delayed until 1978 in view of the domestic manufacturers' projected ability to fulfil the anticipated demand for colour television sets. The purchase of a satellite for use in educational as well as general broadcasting is under negotiation. An English channel for foreign residents in Iran (whose number has increased considerably in recent years) started operation in autumn 1975. Radio broadcasting in major foreign languages as well as in local dialects has been a regular feature of broadcasting almost from the beginning.

The educational television station established in October 1973 covers about 75 per cent of the school population at the intermediate level. It transmits more than 2,480 hours of educational programmes on Persian history and literature, foreign languages for primary and secondary schools, science, programmes for new literates, etc.

In addition to broadcasting, NIRT has engaged in an increasing number of auxiliary activities including a two-year undergraduate programme in communications arts and techniques, established in March 1970, two master-level programmes in communications technology and communications arts established in 1975, a Centre for the Preservation and Propagation of Traditional Iranian Music, a Childrens' Music

Workshop, a Theatre Workshop, the City Theatre of Tehran, the Shiraz Festival of Arts, the Asian Broadcasting Union (ABU)-Shiraz Young Film-Makers' Festival, the NIRT Chamber Orchestra, a growing number of rural television clubs, an expanding publishing house (Soroush) and the publication of a weekly periodical (*Tamasha*). Research and development activities in such fields as audience research, electronics technology and socio-cultural studies are rapidly expanding.

In 1975-6, at a time when most government agencies have had to reduce expenditures, NIRT's total budget has risen about 20 per cent. As shown in Table 1, commercial sources of revenue represent a declining share of total income. Capital investment in new facilities remains high but accounts for a smaller fraction of the budget. These facts suggest that NIRT is entering a new phase which calls for a shift of emphasis from hardware to software, from technological advances to programme production.

TABLE 1. NIRT budget, 1975-7 (in $US)

	2534[a] (1975-6)	2535[a] (1976-7)
Government contribution		
Operational budget	83,606,857	114,967,142
Capital investment	93,910,742	103,471,429
Commercial income	17,774,286	20,085,714
Total	199,291,885	238,524,285

[a] The newly instituted Iranian Shahanshahi calendar dates back to the beginnings of the Persian kingship under the Achaemenids. It runs on a solar year commencing with the vernal equinox (about 21 March).

NIRT Prospective Planning Project

To chart its future development, NIRT undertook in 1974-5 a national survey of the role of media in Iranian national development.[1] Its stated objectives were to define the problem in broad theoretical terms in order to set long-range research goals and assess the role of the media in Iran's economic, political, educational and socio-cultural development.

Phase I — Interviews

The first phase of the study consisted of interviews structured so as to elicit the interviewee's definition of the problem: what are his perceptions of national needs, which constraints impede progress toward the achievement of national goals, which policies and strategies might overcome existing constraints, what is the role of broadcasting in reaching the national goals and overcoming the constraints.

Two hundred individuals belonging to the socio-cultural elite of Iran representing the broadest possible range of opinions were invited to participate. They included communication policy-makers, communication policy-planners, communication professionals and several critical segments of the audience. These latter categories consisted of journalists, publishers, university professors, Islamic Ulama and performing artists; some youth, women, industrial managers and factory workers were also interviewed in order to provide some perspectives on the prevailing attitudes of the audience.

Table 2 shows by category the number of individuals invited to be interviewed. Of this total (223), 40 per cent were interviewed. The others could not be reached because of travel, illness or other reasons; because they responded negatively to the request; or because they could not be contacted in time due to repeated postponements.

The open and unstructured interview technique involves certain problems in the Iranian socio-culture context. Because of historical factors which can be traced to a difficult and often turbulent past fraught with uncertainties and perils for both governors and governed, officials and civil servants are not inclined to verbalize their attitudes. Those who accepted to be interviewed, however, tended to open up once a measure of trust and of mutual rapport was established.

TABLE 2. Professional distribution of members of the Iranian communications elite interviewed in Phase I.

	Invited	Interviewed
Communication policy-makers	24	10
Communication policy-planners	33	11
Communication professionals		
Broadcasters	14	7
Journalists	16	10
Publishers	6	4
University Professors	36	9
Islamic Ulama	19	7
Performing Artists	16	2
*Critical segments of the audience		
University students	25	17
Women leaders	7	3
Industrial managers	23	5
Industrial workers	4	4
*Total	223	89

The interviewees included people with a vast spectrum of ideological orientations ranging from the Ulama of the holy city of Qom to secular politicians and intellectuals and politicized university students. Thus, the effort assumed the nature of an ideational exploration.

In the following sections responses will be analysed along professional group orientations.

Communication policy-makers

Government officials interviewed included the Prime Minister, the Minister of Information and Tourism (who is *ex officio* Chairman of the General Assembly of NIRT), the Minister of Roads and Transport, the Minister of State for Development

Affairs, the Minister of Co-operatives and Rural Affairs, the Minister of Arts and Culture, the Minister of Commerce, a security official, the secretaries-general of the two major political parties at the time, Iran Novin and Mardom,[2] and the Director General of NIRT. Each interview lasted between two and three hours and ranged in topics from Iran's development prospects to the role of broadcasting in the shaping of Iran's future.

Apart from nuances which reflect differences in their respective responsibilities, the general outlook of these high officials is strongly optimistic. They have great confidence in the power of mass media to transform society even if they are not totally satisfied with the performance of the media at the present time.

The elder statesmen in this group see an urgent need to revitalize patriotism (*mihanparasati*), particularly among the youth. They believe that the occupation of the country during the wartime period, the subsequent political turmoils and the influence of Marxist ideologies have undermined national values. They feel that broadcasting ought to promote traditional Iranian institutions such as the family, along with its accompanying social virtues. There is a yearning for a reassertion of Iranian national and cultural identity. NIRT is viewed by some as liberal in its outlook and programming.

Several interviewees would favour greater regionalization of broadcasting activities but with inter-institutional co-operation at the regional level to assure that broadcasting remains responsive to government needs. Broadcasting ought to play a vital role in teaching new and desirable social habits such as courtesy in driving, respect for the law, electoral participation, etc.

Iranian programmes are preferred to foreign ones. But most interviewees in this group admit that they have little time for radio or television and listen regularly only to news broadcasts.

Credibility is of utmost importance and, to achieve it, broadcasting should enjoy some measure of autonomy. It was recognized, however, that it may be difficult and perhaps undesirable to provide such autonomy in the near future. Advertising should be limited and controlled. Broadcasting is considered too important to national welfare and security to be left in private hands (with the possible exception of some programmes production). Broadcasting should provide development support although, admittedly, few specific ideas were proffered.

Communication policy-planners

The professional concerns of the eleven senior planners in government ministries and planning organizations interviewed range from economic, social and cultural planning to youth and children's affairs.

On cultural matters this group feels that broadcasting should respond to people's real needs and demands, bearing in mind its official responsibilities. In this they differ from policy-makers, whose emphasis is on an educative-directive policy. Because of their technocratic orientation, they are less concerned with cultural and national identity and more with the issue of credibility.

They show great awareness of radio and TV programme content and are critical of some of the banality of news programmes and of the low quality of Iranian serials. Recognizing the human resources constraints, they emphasize the need for training producers. Regionalization is felt to be as strong a need as national programmes which aim at forging national unity and cultural integration. They note, however, that excessive audience segmentation may not be desirable. A function of broadcasting should be the safeguarding and diffusion of good Persian and they criticize the language used by broadcasters as affected and sometimes unintelligible to the ordinary public.

Members of the panel who have functions which interact with the broadcasting organization complain of lack of co-ordination and co-operation and would like to see more research on how broadcasting can better contribute to the process of national development. Except for those associated with the Free University of Iran (a multi-media institution of higher education), educational planners are not very familiar with multi-media education but are eager to acquire the hardware (radio,

TV sets, video-cassettes, teaching machines, etc.) for schools. They are committed to formal programmes being broadcast into the classroom. They do not conceive of a multi-media educational system as an integrated whole achieved through the co-operative efforts of educators and broadcasters. They are not interested in getting directly involved in NIRT and consider NIRT's role as primarily that of publicizing and legitimizing the activities of the formal educational system. By contrast, Free University planners are keenly aware of the potential of multi-media education and emphasize the need for close co-operation between educators and broadcasters.

Communication professionals

Broadcasters. This group included nine senior managers of NIRT, engineers, scientists and other professionals with extensive experience in journalism and radio broadcasting. Their attitude on the future of broadcasting fluctuates between extremes of hope and despair, between professional commitment to progress and intimate awareness of environmental constraints.

Their comments may be summarized as follows:
— Broadcasting should guide the public by responding to its needs and demands but should move only gradually toward a policy more closely mirroring what goes on in the society at large. It may be too early to deal openly with every social tension and conflict. Society must first develop adequate shock-absorbers.
— Education and entertainment ought to be blended. But this calls for expanding training programmes in all fields related to broadcasting, since currently human resources pose severe constraints (script-writers, directors, producers, technical crews, etc.)
— Rather than segmenting audiences along professional lines (workers, farmers, etc.) it might be preferable to consider regional-ethnic groupings. Increased regionalization of programmes, however, presents both political and human resources constraints. Of NIRT's eleven regional centres,

only a few have adequate programming capability.
— Broadcasting in Iran has steadily moved toward a monopoly position. In view of the dangers inherent in monopolies an attempt should be made to introduce more elements of competition. While organizationally programme production and transmission are separated within NIRT and different channels are theoretically in competition with each other, the fact remains that most programmes which are produced are also put on the air. For the time being one might foster competition within NIRT by reorganizing into competing networks as well as transferring certain production activities to the private sector.
— The relative autonomy of NIRT vis-a-vis the government is very much a consequence of the special concern of the Shahanshah for broadcasting. Broadcasting remains, however, vulnerable and its freedom of action depends on a keen sensitivity to changing parameters and on NIRT's own sense of responsibility.
— Broadcasters must be responsive to individual pressure groups but the mechanisms to ensure this are inadequate. Consultative programme committees (*shoraye barnameh*) have been set up to supervise programming in some fields but while a few have proved effective, those of a more controversial nature (such as those on language or religion) have not been established or fail to function satisfactorily.
— The rapid expansion of NIRT has created organizational contradictions and bottlenecks, high centralization in decision-making as well as disorganization, shortage of human resources as well as overstaffing, dynamism as well as lethargy. One observes, however, considerable sense of pride, of achievement and of loyalty toward the organization at the high levels of management. Attempts at decentralizing responsibility and authority have been only partially successful, perhaps because of the political sensitivity of broadcasting activities and a persistent tradition of centralized authority.
— Organizational policy should aim for centralization of

support services and modularity of operational functions. Greater regional autonomy would be desirable but can only be achieved in conjunction with political and administrative regionalization of the country as a whole.
— For the foreseeable future, broadcasting will have to rely on government financing because of the heavy investments required and the public nature of the enterprise. Ways should be found, however, to insulate public sources of support from severe fluctuations or from arbitrary or punitive cutbacks. A formula might be developed to relate budgetary allocations to some other sector of the budget, or endowment funds might be provided for certain of broadcasting's public activities. Commercial earnings ought to supplement government allocations.
— Capital-intensive technology is preferred for the following reasons: (a) foreign exchange availability, (b) relatively high rate of obsolescence of less capital-intensive technologies and (c) economies of scale in terms of population coverage of the latest technologies such as satellites.
— There is a sense of inexperience and uncertainty regarding development support communications policy, but also considerable enthusiasm. A pilot study in telemedicine is under way in southern Iran; experiments in regional development in a primitive region of Luristan will include the use of multi-media for agricultural extension services, literacy campaigns, public health services, etc.
— Educational broadcasting faces serious dilemmas: whether to intervene actively in the formal educational system, whether to respond only to requests for educational broadcasting services by the school system, or whether to set up multi-media schools to serve as educational models.

Journalists. This group included prominent publishers and editors of major newspapers and magazines: *Ettela'at, Kayhan, Ayandegan, Mardom* (the now defunct publication of the minority Mardom Party), *Zan-e-Ruz,* and *Javanan.* Their attitude toward broadcasting is, on the whole, unfriendly:
— the government, and particularly NIRT, attracts the best talent away from journalism by offering better salaries, a

The Role of Broadcasting in Iran

smaller work-load and greater employment security. Inflation has forced the press to raise prices, and readership has consequently dropped sharply.

— Government authorities are more lenient toward NIRT than toward the printed word. However, the new government policy of excluding 'undesirable elements' from the newspaper publishers' ranks is generally approved. Small-circulation newspapers exploited official advertising income and were known to demand bribes through the threat of blackmail.

Faced by a serious crisis (a worldwide phenomenon), some publishers and journalists are willing to be bought out by the government or to be incorporated into NIRT. Others, the oldest and economically most viable among them, ask for government non-interference. All agree that newspaper ownership should undergo radical structural changes. Some argue that only with newspapers becoming corporate entities and staff members participating in their ownership will journalism become a respectable and institutionalized profession not totally dependent on the whims and the political fortunes of a few publishers.

Newspapers should turn more toward investigative reporting and feature articles in order to gain in depth what they have lost in the speed race. The fact remains, however, that journalism as a profession is no longer as lucrative, influential or attractive as in the past when it provided one of the principal channels of social and political mobility and produced some of Iran's most illustrious personalities.

Publishers. This group consisted of the proprietors and senior editors of a few major publishing houses. It did not include the large number of small publishers of religious and a variety of other texts.

Until recently, book publishing in Iran was not a flourishing business. With the exception of textbooks and religious books, whose number of copies run into the tens of thousands and sometimes into the millions, few editions exceed 1,000 copies. But finally the economic boom has reached publishing as well. A new market of book-buyers has opened up, consisting primarily of university students and the middle class. Religious and literary works remain the most popular offerings, but socio-political subjects are gaining rapidly. Public libraries remain few in number and are not well attended.

Publishers do not consider broadcasting to be a rival, but a potential aid. Their criticism is that NIRT is attracting talent away from publishers particularly since a subsidiary publishing house has been established within the organization, and that it should do more to encourage reading of books. In their view, the increasing role of government into every aspect of cultural life (theatre, music, magazines, newspapers, books, radio, television, cinema) has its dangers. It may destroy private initiative and limit cultural diversity. More and more books and journals are published by government agencies. They are often very well printed without regard to cost and are distributed free of charge or at a nominal price. *Tamasha,* a lively and attractive weekly published by NIRT, is mentioned as an example of unfair competition.

The role of government in publishing, in their opinion, ought to be confined to providing better newspaper and book distribution facilities (something which the country badly needs) and to the construction of public and school libraries.

University professors. The ideological tendencies of the more establishment-oriented members of this group range from strongly Islamic to secular. They agree that broadcasting is a powerful medium for social and cultural change. Those with an Islamic orientation tend to be more critical of the programmes than those with secular views. While there is praise for the technological and organizational achievements of NIRT, there is criticism for what they consider the low quality of some programmes. The more nationalistic among them would like to see a revitalization of the Iranian and pre-Islamic past, purification of the Persian language with rejection of all foreign (including Arabic) words, and more cultural programmes to forge national unity and to attract people of Iranian origins from neighbouring countries. Those with an Islamic orientation would like to see Iran's Islamic culture and the country's ties with the Islamic world emphasized. They criticize broadcasting for lack of sensitivity to this heritage, excessive reliance on foreign programmes and cultural shallowness. Modern nationalists are happier with the programmes but feel that programme and levels of taste leave much to be desired.

Less establishment-oriented members of this group, while recognizing the political as well as resource constraints imposed on NIRT, would like to see NIRT move gradually toward a more responsive and pluralistic programming. Some condemn NIRT for being too subservient to government authority. While their discontent is primarily politically motivated, it frequently spills over into cultural issues.

Islamic Ulama. This group included a fair sampling of religious leaders: *ayatollahs* (learned men who have attained the position of *ijtihad* or the right to issue decrees or interpretations on Islamic laws), professors of divinity and religious writers, publicists and *Khateebs* (orators). Some were interviewed in Qom, the holy Shi'a city where many scholars and students of divinity reside.

On the whole, this group feels quite negatively toward broadcasting. Some state with pride that they seldom listen to radio and never watch television because of the frivolous nature of the programming. Their severest criticism is directed at religious programmes which are claimed to be devoid of authentic religious content. On the issue of whether and how broadcasting ought to treat religion three attitudes emerge: (a) the message does not suit the medium and broadcasting should shy away from expressedly religious programmes; (b) broadcasting of religious programmes should be under the strict supervision of a qualified *bona fide* group of Ulama; (c) religious programmes are out of place on radio or television, but the religious message ought to be infused into all programmes (such as children's programmes) effectively and with subtlety. All groups agree that days of religious mourning and holidays ought to be observed by radio and television in an appropriate manner.

With respect to the future of religion in Iran, a few foresee an inevitable decline in religiosity and express despair at the possibility of reconciling secular and religious cultures. Others note a rise in religious consciousness, particularly among women and university students. They offer as evidence the large and increasing circulation of religious publications such as *Maktab-e-Islam*, the fact that religious books and tracts outsell secular books, participation of women and youth in religious discussion groups and the volume of mail reaching the editors of religious journals.

Performing artists. This group was too small and its interests too diversified to permit many generalizations. NIRT's contribution to the development of traditional and new art forms is generally acknowledged, but it is argued that patronage of the arts in Iran tends to reflect the personal tastes and biases of those in charge of artistic and cultural affairs. Consequently, personal preferences are magnified into artistic policies. The formalist and decorative art forms favoured by the Ministry of Arts and Culture are partially counterbalanced by the avant-garde, popular and neo-traditionalist preferences of NIRT. But realistic forms have suffered and have sought refuge in university theatres and workshops.

Some critical segments of the audience. NIRT's concern and programming for children receives high praise, but with more imagination and inventiveness programmes could be made more relevant to the Iranian environment. Programming *by* children and youth under adult supervision and guidance rather than *for* children and youth might open up opportunities for creative self-expression and make for more interesting viewing. Education should be combined with fun, as has been successfully achieved in such programmes as 'Sesame Street'.

The position of women was clear and explicit: broadcasting has the special obligation to foster the emancipation of Iranian women. Some television serials unwittingly propagate traditional views of women as 'frail, conniving and boisterous'. They ask for programmes which bring the family together and in which the equality of the sexes as well as their mutual obligations are emphasized.

Industrial workers ask for programmes tailored to their special needs. Present programming lacks understanding of their problems and interests. They want programmes *by* workers and *for* workers rather than programmes by broadcasters for workers.

Managers of the private sector consider broadcasting a direct arm of the government which does not take their views and concerns sufficiently into account. They would like to see the private sector enter into the broadcasting field.

Phase II — Questionnaire

In the second phase of the study a questionnaire was forwarded to three groups whose views are considered critical to the future of Iran's communications policy: the communication elite (as previously defined), members of NIRT and university students. The questionnaire was designed to test the orientation of respondents with respect to (a) use of media, (b) values and ideological preferences and (c) perception of present official policies and preference with regard to future policies. In the present paper we will limit ourselves to a review of the results of item (b).

A few cautionary words are in order before we proceed to examine the findings of this survey. In the first place, the samples were selected as follows:

1. Communication elite: 500 prominent members of the communication elite were chosen from the 5,000 entries of Iran's *Who's Who*.

2. University students: questionnaires were distributed to all institutions of higher learning throughout the country. In addition, to ensure adequate returns, copies were also handed out by members of the project to their own students. This may, of course, have biased the sample.

3. Professional broadcasters: virtually every NIRT central and regional manager was contacted, as well as producers and some members of technical crews.

In the second place, the percentage of returns varied from group to group. Out of approximately 500 questionnaires distributed to members of the communication elite, to university students and to professional broadcasters the returns numbered respectively 186, 272 and 307.

The questions on the ideological orientation of the respondents attempt to capture the range of ideological positions prevalent in Iran: Islamic fundamentalism; Islamic mysticism; Islamic modernism; Pristine nationalism; moderate nationalism; liberal nationalism; technocratic orientation; nihilism; fatalism; cynicism; egalitarianism; opportunism. Definitions of these twelve ideological positions as presented in the questionnaire are included in the Appendix.

Respondents were asked to state which of these ideological positions reflect their current attitude. Their answers are summarized in Table 3. They show, in the first place, a consensus among all three groups (elite, broadcasters and students) on the desirability of social justice (82-85%), moderate nationalism (78-86%), Islamic modernism (77-82%), Islamic mysticism (67-79%), liberal nationalism (69-78%) and pristine (pre-Islamic) nationalism (64-74%). The combination of these positions may seem intellectually incompatible, but the respondents appear to accept them as emotionally valid and viable. With regard to these positions, there is little difference of opinion among the three groups even though they represent different generations, social backgrounds and political tendencies. This cluster of ideological positions may be said to represent the mosaic of affective orientations which have shaped the modern Persian mind.

Beyond this area of consensus one notes some significant differences. The youth group appears to be far more attracted toward a fundamentalist Islamic position (62%) than the communication elite (30%) or the professional broadcasters (30%). This may be accounted for by the fact that this generation of university students comes mainly from towns and villages and more traditional religious families.

Another striking difference between the youth and the other two groups appears on the issue of social opportunism. Their 46% agreement compares with 23% for the elite and 17% for the professional broadcasters. Either the youth are more intellectually honest or their perception of the adult world is unduly pessimistic.

All three groups score relatively high on technocratic orien-

TABLE 3 Ideological orientations (Percentage of individuals by category who *agree* with stated ideological position)

Ideological position	Communication elite	Professional broadcasters	University students
Islamic fundamentalism	30	30	62
Islamic mysticism	68	67	79
Islamic modernism	82	77	82
Pristine nationalism	64	72	74
Moderate nationalism	81	86	78
Liberal nationalism	78	77	69
Technocratic orientation	55	55	55
Nihilism	18	14	16
Fatalism	58	57	63
Cynicism	16	10	19
Egalitarianism	83	82	85
Opportunism	13	17	46

tation (55%) and fatalism (57-63%), but fortunately quite low on nihilism (14-18%) and cynicism (10-19%).

We shall not attempt to interpret these results in terms of broadcasting policy or development strategies. They do provide, however, valuable insights on the respondents preferences as to the kind of Iran they would like to see emerge in the years to come. NIRT's cultural and programme policy, has to respond to government objectives as well as to audience demands and attitudes. To the extent that the above ideological orientations reflect consensus or dissensus, broadcasting in Iran faces an important challenge to act as an agent of change as well as a channel of interactive communication.

Appendix   Classification of Ideological Orientations

Islamic fundamentalism: All individual and social problems can be resolved with the help of the Divine Law of Islam. If every one were to abide by it, human laws would become unnecessary.

Islamic mysticism: Islam's teachings enlighten us on the true goals of life. Piety alone cannot solve our problems. To be successful in the search for truth we should embrace the mystical insights of the Holy Koran and the traditions of the Prophet and of his rightful successors.

Islamic modernism: The mystical and legal traditions of Islam should be preserved. But it is the duty of all Muslims and particularly of the clergy to maintain harmony between religious precepts and modern spiritual and material needs. In this way Iran will play an ever-increasing role throughout the etire Islamic world.

Pristine nationalism: In order to promote the development of Iran we ought to be inspired by our culture and revive the greatness of Iran's pre-Islamic past. We ought to keep our culture free of foreign influences (including Arab) and rely primarily on our Aryan heritage.

Moderate Nationalism: We have at our disposal all the essential material and human resources required for rapid development, as the past few decades have amply demonstrated. But to join the ranks of the fully developed countries we ought to keep separate the religious and political spheres. We may have to do away with some of our old traditions and accept social and economic reforms.

Liberal nationalism: Western achievements depend on a free market economy and on a democratic political system. To reach

The Role of Broadcasting in Iran

the same level of development we should expand the role of the private sector and encourage the development of democratic political institutions (political parties, parliament, press, etc.) so as to increase the degree of participation.

Technocratic orientation: The west's success stems from scientific and technological innovations. In order to achieve the same level of development we should accelerate our scientific and technological progress. Only through science and technology and not through political ideologies are we going to solve our problems.

Nihilism: None of today's social and political orders meets man's basic needs. We will probably never come up with a satisfactory solution and all our attempts are doomed to fail.

Fatalism: Individual values are no longer relevant. Today's society imposes its own value system and we have no alternative but to accept it.

Cynicism: Life should not be taken too seriously. Those who do will be subjected to manipulation by others and ultimately disappointed. This life is only worthy of ridicule.

Egalitarianism: In order to become a developed society we should strive to achieve a fair distribution of wealth and of income and abolish present social and economic inequities.

Opportunism: A man is wise if he cannot be misled and knows how to snatch any opportunity that comes his way.

Notes

1 The Project consisted of four parallel studies on communications technology, international trends, national goals and objectives and NIRT reorganization plans. The present paper deals only with some aspects of the national survey. The international survey appears elsewhere in this volume. For reorganization plans, see the preface.
2 The interviews with the two secretaries-general assumes some historical significance by the fact that both officials were out of office soon thereafter. The multi-party system was abrogated with the Shahanshah's announcement of March 1975 which established a single party system under the banner of the Iranian Nation Resurgence Party.

Majid Teheranian

References

Banani, Amin (1971), 'The role of the mass media', in *Iran Faces the Seventies*, ed. E. Yarshater, New York: Praeger.

Lerner, Daniel (1958), *The Passing of Traditional Society*, Chicago: Free Press.

Teheranian, Majid (1972), 'Iran', in *The Middle East: its Governments and Politics*, ed. Abid-Marayati *et al.*, Belmont: Duxbury Press.

13
Towards a National Communications Policy for Iran[1]

Amin Banani

Any attempt at formulation of a national policy for the forthcoming twenty-five years should begin with the dynamic and emerging concept of nationhood. It is one that is moving rapidly away from the collective egotism of the last century into a pattern of interdependence and co-operation. Nowhere is this dynamic view more essential than in regard to a prospective communications policy, for if there is one factor which has contributed more than anything else to the obsolescence of the old world order and the emergence of a community of interdependent nations, it is the modern means of communication.

There is a hope and a danger in this prospect. The hope is for a more rational and humane approach to international relations. The danger lies in the erosion of all cultural distinctions and the emergence of a rootless homogeneity. It is particularly with regard to this danger that the role of mass media is crucial. On a global scale it seems that mass media have contributed more to the reality of this danger than to the realization of that hope. The principal function of any prospective communications policy ought to be the reversal of this trend.

Preservation, cultivation and propagation of a distinctive cultural tradition should not be confused with a sense of exclusiveness and superiority. It should promote, rather, a condition of unity and equality in diversity. For the main purpose of cultural awareness is a secure sense of identity, that is to say, knowledge of oneself which in itself is liberating and integrative. If, in the process of acquisition of modern technology and of the scientific outlook that goes with it, people of developing societies acquire and perpetuate a sense of inferiority and loss of confidence vis-a-vis the current sources of technology, the gap between developed and developing nations will continue to widen. To combat an endemic 'developing nation' psychology ought to be the central focus of an enlightened national communication policy in a rapidly developing society.

Just as a psychology of 'under-developed man' is injurious to people in developing societies, so *a priori* imposition of hierarchical values can have an alienating and stunting effect on emerging segments of these societies. It is crucial for agents of mass communications to project a sense of cultural identity that is varied and comprehensive enough to enable every segment of the nation to recognize and identify itself. This implies an ability to recognize and reflect an honest image of one's culture. If we begin with the premise that there are no ideal cultures in the world we have a greater opportunity of learning from both the positive and negative values of our culture. Denying the existence of any negative aspects would not help us to overcome them.

The unity and integration of a truly varied nation need not come through the imposition of a single set of cultural values and the suppression of that richness and variety that is so much an element of the vitality of Iranian culture. A cohesive ideological commitment should not be confused with a single cultural value system. Quite the contrary, only a profoundly humane, regenerative, ethical, dynamic and unifying set of beliefs can guarantee a plurality of cultural values.

Even within a highly homogeneous and uni-ethnic society one can recognize the existence of several strata of culture, if by culture we intend the total reservoir of acquired skills, knowledge and wisdom of a people. It enables the possessors of that culture to respond to the needs and stimuli they face. A fundamental point to recognize is that the process of acquisition, transmission and permutation of culture is continuous and dynamic. A tendency by any group to regard it in static terms results in the encrustation of traditions and in the isolation of that group from the rest of society. For the individual it has the paralysing consequence of alienation and the social diseases of snobbery and elitism.

For an Iranian, awareness of his true cultural identity will result in an integrative and balanced inner sense of wholeness, will breed a sense of dignity devoid of feelings of superiority and will enable him to relate to the rest of humanity with confidence and compassion. The survival of what may be called a unique Persian culture has been precisely due to this open and dynamic view of what is universal and essential for human existence. Measured by this basic criterion, all cultural influences and values borrowed from other societies are easily adapted and made an organic part of Persian culture.

The clash of cultures in the recent past bred by exploitation, imperialism and racism has shaken the natural balance and reciprocity of cultural diffusion and interaction. To restore that sense of dignity and self-confidence—not to assert one's superiority, but to take one's place in equality—is the demanding and delicate challenge we face. To become once more a creative receiver and a decisive contributor to the collective wisdom and well-being of the human race is the ultimate objective and inevitable goal of our time.

It should be clear from the foregoing that in identifying culture-bearing as the primary role of national mass communications media in Iran in the coming quarter of a century we are not advancing a limited and exclusive notion of culture. To translate these guidelines into rudiments of a national communications plan has ramified and complex but coherent implications that encompass every phase of the objectives, structure, programmes and activities of NIRT.

A primary objective of NIRT in the immediate future should be the closing of the gap that has traditionally existed between rulers and ruled in the Iranian society. The very structure of political organization is being transformed with unprecedented enlightenment and leadership. The final outcome depends upon the mobilization of ethical values and upon a genuine moral rejuvenation of society which stimulates a sense of commitment, participation and belonging among individuals. If NIRT is to play an effective role in bridging this gap between rulers and ruled, its corporate identity must be sharply focused as an independent public enterprise and not as a mere government mouthpiece. This means that the reciprocal channels of communication, consultation and decision-making must be open between NIRT and the government on the one hand, and between NIRT and the general public on the other.

Another crucial consideration, particularly during a period of dynamic transformation of society and mobilization of all its physical and spiritual resources, is to find the proper balance between individual interest and collective welfare. It would be politically futile and sociologically unwise to get caught in the artificial dichotomy between individualism and collectivism. This a volatile and potentially disruptive abstraction which does not correspond to functional models of human interaction. These models which, incidentally, are frequently found in the traditional structure of Iranian society are interrelated and reasonably small functional groups with a community of needs and interests. The individual versus group interests often assume a conflicting relationship within a 'nation' or a 'society'; but within smaller functional groups such as 'family', 'neighbourhood', 'community', 'guild', etc., they resolve themselves into a harmonious pattern of mutual support.

This has a profound implication for the prospective outlook of NIRT. Identifying, nurturing and gaining strength from constructive groups in furtherance of national objectives becomes a self-fulfilling process. It is a key to the structural and organizational health of NIRT. Thus, the whole issue of central versus regional organization can be seen in a different light. A pyramidal structure of smaller functional units generate and initiate activity, maintain communication with their public roots and make decisions within their domains—all in reference to a rational central authority.

The overall developmental support role of NIRT may be best fulfilled by stressing within a consistent and harmonious framework the development of the full potential of the individual within a meaningful and dignifying common goal. There can be no social and economic development of lasting value without developed and fulfilled potentials of the human beings that make up the society. The nature of these potentials differ but the element of personal fulfilment which provides happiness and gives meaning and equality to one's life is basic and universal. By encompassing the full spectrum of potentials and addressing itself to the widest variety of needs, the mass communications media can become part of the development process.

Those aspects of mass media development support role, that are common to all rapidly developing societies, are largely self-evident and a brief summary suffices to place them in perspective.

— A qualitative improvement of life which incorporates basic social needs and services.
— A more equitable distribution of resources and services that narrows disparities by increasing the share of the less privileged and points ultimately to an elimination of excesses of wealth and poverty.
— A rapid development of human resources.
— An effective development and utilization of natural resources.
— A rapid but rational industrial development.
— Strengthening of the basic infrastructure to facilitate continued rapid development.
— A genuine effort to motivate people to participate in public decision processes.
— Within the Iranian context two further considerations should be added:
— A strong commitment to the needs of the rural population and to the development of the agricultural sector.
— A genuine recognition of the regional variety and richness of Iran and a commitment to regional development which will prevent the emergence of a mono-metropolitan state with all of its social and psychological disadvantages.

It is hardly necessary to point out that the stresses of accelerated change are intimately linked to the impact of technological and social policy changes in the communication system. NIRT, as the key element in the mass communication system of Iran, has a decisive role to play in these areas.

Amin Banani

In what kind of communities will Iranians live in the coming quarter century? How will they be employed? What basic social services will be available to them? And most important of all, what sense of satisfaction will they derive from their role and how will they relate to the rest of society? These are questions of vital concern to the nation, and NIRT can make a significant contribution in fostering positive attitudes and solutions.

Fulfilment of this role will prove neither easy nor simple. The following may be expected of NIRT.

(1) To determine the needs of the people and to give political credibility to the expression of those needs. In communication terms this means effective feedback.

(2) To provide horizontal and vertical communication linkages at all levels of society.

(3) To provide local community support for cultural preservation. (The Tus Festival of 1975 is an excellent step in this direction, and an expanded programme of local folk festivals might be another logical step.)

(4) To heighten mass awareness and foster positive attitudes and motivations in regard to the development process with a minimum of overt propagandistic tone and a maximum of subtlety and variety.

(5) To make contribution to economic development through industrial and cultural linkages such as electronic, computer and printing industries and the performing arts. In the latter category, NIRT ought to give continuous and sensitive attention to its role as major patron of the arts.

(6) To support specific development projects and services such as health-care delivery, vocational skills, public health and sanitation, family planning, environmental protection, consumer information and protection, fostering social discipline (solution to Tehran traffic?), creative use of leisure, and the broadest and most innovative use of media for basic education not only adapted for the Iranian setting, but created specifically for it.

Any projection of the role of NIRT and formulation of communications policy must incorporate intensive, periodic reviews, perhaps at five-year intervals. Due consideration ought to be given to fostering attitudes within NIRT which encourage new patterns of growth as well as greater access to airways by the emerging segments of the nation. Equally important for future planning in a rapidly developing society is the maintenance of a long-range view. The desired motivational and behavioural attitudes require time to develop and may not take hold until the next generation. This is why planning and programming for children is so important.

With regard to programming, the traditional time-slots and categories such as drama, documentary, etc. are becoming inadequate and obsolete. A creative restructuring of formats can be a powerful catalyst for change. Such dynamic programming objectives and policies should, to a large extent, shape the internal structure of NIRT rather than the other way around. This implies a trend toward modularity and regionality in the internal structure of NIRT. No single programme area should be the exclusive preserve of a special unit or department.

To sum up, NIRT's role in the rapid development of Iranian society must be threefold. It must provide support for other agencies, it must act as a catalyst of development and it must be an active agent of development. The policy implications of this role encompass every phase of production and operation of mass media (including print) not only within NIRT, but for other institutions and agencies.

The two fundamental areas of experimentation and growth are regionalization (in the area of socio-structural development) and feedback and interaction (in the area of psychotechnological development). With regard to regionalization, it must be remembered that local initiative and autonomy are not incompatible with clear and rational central authority; with regard to feedback and interaction that there is no phase of communication media functions whose effectiveness cannot be enhanced by appropriate feedback.

The development of means for socio-structural development suited to the Iranian setting requires a blend of enlightened adaptation and perceptive innovation. NIRT should not be content with importing technology in order to accomplish its goals. Research organization and activity as well as advisory and consultative bodies must augment the developmental plans of NIRT in the coming quarter-century.

No projection can have a ring of the possible unless it is related to the reality of the present and rooted in the accomplishment of the past. In offering these suggestions toward the formulation of a rational communications policy for NIRT I am deeply convinced that it is within the grasp of NIRT to attain and surpass its most ambitious objectives. In 1968, only a few months after the birth of NTV (the original organizational nucleus of the present NIRT), when I was writing a brief history of the role of mass media in Iran (YarShater, 1971), it would have seemed sheer visionary optimism to envision what has been accomplished during the past eight years. It bodes well for the future that most of the ideas advanced in this paper for the years to come are already present in the thinking and in the organizational trends of NIRT.

Notes

1 At the outset it should be stated that this paper represents the authors's reflection—or refraction—of a complex of views and opinions expressed in the course of a five-day symposium by a number of eminent and valued colleagues. It owes much to their professional knowledge and experience, but it is filtered through the writer's perception. As such, it is not, and could not be, a comprehensive and balanced model for a national communications policy. It is, rather, a series of considerations which I deem essential for a policy model for Iran. If there is a thread of coherence in these considerations it is the attempt to relate certain universal problems to the particulars of Iran and to project the uniqueness of Iran into an emerging global community.

Reference

YarShater, E. (1971), *Iran Faces the Seventies*, Praeger.